TOUCH

for Maggie

Graham Mort

TOUCH

SEREN

Seren is the book imprint of
Poetry Wales Press Ltd
57 Nolton Street, Bridgend, Wales, CF31 3AE
www.seren-books.com

ISBN 9-781-85411-512-6

A CIP record for this title is available from the British Library.

This book is a work of fiction. Like most fiction it is taken from life; for this
reason names and details of characters have been altered to protect actual
persons.

Cover photograph: Stewart Dunwell

Inner design and typesetting by books@lloydrobson.com

Printed by The Cromwell Press Group, Trowbridge, Wilts

The publisher works with the financial assistance of
the Welsh Books Council.

Versions of these stories have appeared in:

Outlook, BBC Radio 3, *Krax*, BBC Radio Lancashire, *Critical Quarterly*,
Fisheye, *The North*, *Global Tapestry*, *Panurge*, *Northern Short Stories* 1989, 1996
(Arc Publications), *Metropolitan*, *Fish Short Story Anthology*, *London Magazine*,
Arabesques, *The Bridport International Writing Competition Anthology 2007*,
Riptide, *Dreamcatcher*.

Contents

'Our skin is what stands between us and the world.'
Diane Ackerman, *A Natural History of the Senses*

A Walk in the Snow

Snow fell again last night, blowing against the windows, tapping its fingers as we lay huddled up in bed. It fell in huge sweeps. Total. A white anaesthetic dulling the trees and hedgerows. Putting to sleep rabbits and weasels, the badger and the shrew as they hid in the curdled earth. I imagine ice crystals shaken from their fur, nocturnal prints as they snuffle in the snow under a nail clipping of moon. Foraging, surviving, killing. I imagine the deep drift of hibernation, sleep piling against their dimming minds like snow driven against autumn. These are days of hunger. This morning black and white cattle stand grouped in the meadows, heads inward, shoving up gouts of steam from the centre. They trample piss-coloured hay, bellow with sadness or slowly kindling rage. High up on the fells the sheep have almost disappeared. They try to melt the snow with faint identities.

Now you're at the window, burning peepholes in patterns of frost with your hands. White fronds have stiffened on the glass overnight. You shiver in your nightdress, exclaiming at a wilderness of cold. I call you back to bed, warm your body with mine. It is soft, infinitely caressible, smooth where my lips brush against it. Your hair is tousled like a boy's and your eyes are dark in this room of frost-filtered light. Our mouths close together with desire, the hunger of touch. Outside, the street holds the silence of the Sabbath. Inside, this other silence thickens under our quick breath.

Downstairs, the dishcloth has frozen to the sink. There is a chink of ice as I lift the teapot. The gas ring blooms, blue with heat; water is brittle in the cheap kettle. I scramble some eggs in the frying pan and we eat them with buttered toast. You've kindled a fire from last night's embers. Fresh flames hollow out the log that has smouldered through hours of darkness and falling snow. The coal sends up twists of yellow smoke. A bubble of tar bursts and plumes with flame. You're wearing your Herdwick jumper, your breasts sloping inside its coarse wool. For a moment I want to stop everything. To take you and kiss you behind the ears, on the nape of your neck where your hair curls, feathery and dark. Instead, I bend my mouth to the creamy yolks on my plate. Traffic begins to swish past on the road.

On the window seat lies yesterday's newspaper. On the front page, a photograph from the war in Iraq. No blood or soldiers or weapons. The picture shows a room with distempered walls. The barred windows are set high up. Light is falling through at a steep angle, so it is late morning or noon. The room is striped with shadows. There is a single bed and on the bed a woman sits in her black burka, face covered. Her hands are folded. Beside her, on the stained ticking of the mattress, without a sheet or pillow, lies her small son, a boy of seven years old. His hair stands out in dark tufts; his eyes are closed above black rings, his lips pursed in sleep. The boy's arms are drawn up above his head and his legs are splayed. Both end in bandaged stumps just below the knee. The bandages are crusty with discharge from his wounds. The light falls, the colour of clear acacia honey, and his mother waits. On her arm are three silver bangles. The boy is called Saddam. *Saddam.* This means he is a real boy in Mosul in a real war, not just a figure in a photograph. It's hard to look at him, even though the picture is beautiful: its artful composition of light and shadow, its timeless tableau of suffering, its pietà.

Eager to get out into the miracle that has fallen upon us, we drop our plates into the sink, pull on socks and boots against the cold. We struggle into our coats, catching our jumpers in the zips, then unbar the door to let ourselves out from the room's warmth. A patch of plaster has fallen from the wall and the horsehair shows through. It's odd to think of a horse that died so long ago embedded here in the wall. A little heap of snow has sifted against the doorjamb, leaving a clean edge when the timber pulls away. You place the first footprint on the step and blow out a gasp of white air. I lock the door with the iron key, drop it into my pocket, take your hand. It seems lost in its shapeless mitten. We step out together.

Down in the village the thaw has already begun. Pavements are inscribed with interlocking footprints. A big dog has walked along at the very edge of the kerbstones. Melting snow slips from the church roof. It lies curled at the edge then slides into the graveyard where headstones sprawl. Where the names of the dead congregate. The living are already inside, repelling the cold with prayer and hymns, shuffling their feet on the numbing flags.

Snow drops onto the pavement from the eaves of the Black Horse. It is sliding away from all the roofs in the village. Dark slate is pushing through and the centre of the road is already clear. Snow-water floods the gutters and gurgles into grids. In one solitary entry we find undisturbed snow. It peers back at us like a blank page, quiet as a swallowed cry. We walk on up the hill leading out of the village where snow still lies thick on the road. It clings to our boots and trouser bottoms. The school on our right gleams with pale lights. On our left, amongst bare trees, its chapel sticks up dark as a mediaeval tower gutted by fire.

We come across tyre marks that have slewed off the road and then half filled with snow. There are discarded cigarette butts, three crushed beer cans, a pink hair band. There is a mobile phone with its face smashed and frozen into the slush of snow. Here are footprints with their heavy tread. There, a yellow patch where someone pissed in the ditch. Faint light is glimmering on the stained-glass windows of the chapel. The air hums with prayer.

We walk on between crusted hawthorn hedges. The road undulates northwards beneath its immaculate shroud. We hardly talk now. As if words are being pressed back, as if these are the black covers of a bible we are shut between. No birds sing. The day is silent. In the night the earth has slowly crystallised under our dreams. And we are its twin pivots, its speechless megaliths. You take off your gloves and run a finger across a fencing stake. A brindled fur of frost stands up from it. The weather is a white beast. You shudder and smile, but the cold is already stiffening our lips. The thaw has turned back on itself, the temperature falls towards zero.

We'll sleep in each other's breath tonight. The overhang of snow on our roof will freeze into a wave and under it we'll make love again, our mouths moist, our hands amazed at desire, at touch itself. Icicles will bar the bedroom windows, frost fossilise the glass. The earth will turn toward dawn in its caul of ice. And your skin will flow under me like pale cambric, like warm cream tilted from a jug or the freckled petals of foxgloves. Sun will ghost the moon, a spectral eye. The real sun will rise elsewhere, relentless, proud in its tyrannical heat. It will stand molten at its zenith to scorch crops and dry up creeks and burn away sweet hope and future.

A flock of rooks rises from a copse across the fields. They turn in the air, a ragged choreography, scraps of soot blown up from a dead fire. The sky is a grey sheet, uniform, heavy with an imponderable weight of snow. Its thin light is amplified by reflection, surviving like the breath of that boy whose life flickers from heartbeat to heartbeat. *Saddam.* We trudge on through the drifts, feeling our knees slow under their seizure of cold. When we speak our breath vaporises, rises and is gone, air into thinning air.

A limestone boulder squats beside the road. It's a skull, a brainpan with its huge jaws buried in the earth. It is straining to utterance, holding the speech of centuries. All its thoughts inarticulate or lost. It cannot utter a single syllable for us. Nothing. It is blind to the light that falls around it, that bleaches it day after day, season upon season. It's deaf to the cry of that carrion crow turning on splayed wings above the fields. It's deaf to death, blind to life. Absolute.

Now we're walking downhill. The land is a white quilt stitched with hedgerows. Sheep huddle, yellow against the snow, chewing a bitter cud of grass. The land is smudged with woodland. Its horizons are vague. The river's meanders gleam in ligatures of light, making for the coast where the invisible sun will set in a few hours' time.

The air is raw with the scent of coming snow. Wind has begun to whip up flurries of white dust from the drifts. It is stripping the flesh from our faces, replacing it with a numb blubber-mask. Each gust drives a needle of ice through my temple. I see your hand go up to the same place. We are featureless. We daren't speak, daren't squander the last warmth in our lungs. In the pockets of our coats our hands are forming into snow. Our lips are dumb, our feet stupid, directionless. Ice crystals are shaping themselves in the bone of our knuckles. We are plumed with breath, struggling like beasts under tremendous loads. The cold is burning us to pillars of steam.

It begins to snow again, drifting at first in a few whirling flakes, then driving into our faces. We try to speak but speech has congealed. Snow smokes across the fields, obliterating them, white dust devils in a frozen desert. When we look up, the sky is a vertigo of black specks. They give the sensation of falling upwards into everything beyond. They whirl inside our eyes, particles of the cascading universe. We are fighting for breath in a vortex of choking flakes. A vacuum drags past our ears. It levers us against the hedgerows, twisting our steps. Twigs scratch our faces. Our hands are cut by thorns that pierce our gloves.

Halting, we try to speak, but words bale out into a slipstream of air. We were heading for the crossroads, but now we're meeting the snow head on. We gesture towards the village as if there is still a decision left to make that was not written out and erased by snow a thousand years ago. I take your arm and we turn for home. I think of that stifling hospital room in Mosul with its stink of septic flesh. I think of the Tigris flowing, of the ruins at Nineveh that yielded up an ancient poem scored onto baked tablets of clay. Gilgamesh. An epic poem forgotten for centuries, then found again. Like all epics it is a poem of lost life and love.

Now the boy, Saddam. His mother sitting with folded hands, her eyes hidden behind her veil. *Saddam, Saddam, Saddam.* Her suffering is almost unimaginable. Yet not quite, for anything can be imagined for a moment. Each night she will sit and wait in his ebbing whisper of breath, an electric bulb flickering outside. Sirens screaming. Dogs howling from walled yards across the town. The moon filling out its blister of pus. Each day the sun will rise and fall through those high, barred windows. She knows – against hope – that her son's life is slipping away in millimetres, in seconds, in creeping shadows and abandoned syllables and motes of slowly spinning dust.

Now light is fading from the sky's faint incandescence to enclose us in a void of grey. Wind drives us before it, packing snow against our backs, making us stumble into drifts that pile through hedgerows and barred gates. It's a sheep dog gone mad amongst its own flock; its howl rises and dies like high notes on a church organ. We struggle back up the hill. Numbness takes our limbs, one by one. These flakes are silting up our eyes, clinging to the lashes, closing up their slits. Our hearts will fail here. Breath will falter in the ice-hung caverns of our heads. Our lungs are slowly drifting full of snow. We stumble onwards but our brains are ice-locked. There will be stillness, into which we'll fall, then sleep. We'll glisten for a moment, white as sculpted angels of snow, the whole weight of sky pressing upon us, pressing us to the permanence of crystal.

Then we'll be gone. Snow-wraiths in winter. Meltwater in spring. A draining residue that will find the sump of our tribe and sink there. Except for this fragment. This faint trace of ourselves. These scattered moments set down for you in words of an ever-fragile language. You, who'll come after us in the wake of our lives, your hands touching the page where we are youthful still and still kiss with hot mouths under drifts of ice and suspended sleep and frozen time. Or lost, maybe, and never found. Our walk in the snow.

Annik and Serge

The smell of the cake frightened him. A smell like hot fried aubergines. He hung up his coat and dropped his briefcase. A smell he'd missed for so long it felt wrong. He'd imagined a restoration. One day. That things would come right. Full circle. Things being what they were. Out of true. After the electric shocks. After the hospital sheets folded like white platinum. After Annik's shaven head. But Serge had never imagined a cake, the smell of baking, or that it should pull a fine thread of fear from his belly like this.

Annik was sitting at the kitchen table. All the lights were off and a white candle burned in a blue pottery candleholder in front of her. There was the low hum of the fan oven, its lit glass door, the top of the cake crowning like a baby's head. The candle swayed in the draught of his entry. It threw a shadow up from Annik's chin onto her mouth. She was wearing a long black dress and twirling a wine glass in her fingers. In the glass was a single flower head: a red carnation.

Serge closed the door. The shadow over her mouth trembled. Silver studs gleamed in her ears as she turned her head.

'Annik?'

No reply. Just that dipping of her neck. The nothing game.

'Are you alright?'

Why ask when he knew she wasn't? Even he could follow

that logic. It was nonsense. But he'd learned to stop looking for sense. He was looking for her. She came and went. Pure mystery. Like a childhood scar that a cold day makes visible. Something that has stopped hurting and has become elusive. The reminder of a past hurt. A part of himself. He looked for her on days like that. Clear days branded with frost where everything seemed sharply etched, super real. Days like those in his childhood when icicles had dripped from under the eaves and there had been skaters writing on the pond with steel blades. Days that had probably never existed.

'Annik?'

She looked up dreamily. She would see him as a configuration of light and dark. Colour. Movement. She'd see him smiling, holding out the paper-wrapped box he'd taken from his coat pocket. He put it on the table in front of her. Annik turned her head away, showing her pale neck again above the dress.

'Go on. It's for you.'

She smiled like a child and the candlelight misted her frizzy hair that was the colour of brass wire.

Annik put a finger against her lips then turned to look at the oven. It was lit like a little shrine in the dark kitchen. She touched a hand to the stem of the candle.

'It's alright. I've made a cake for them.'

'For who?'

'For the children, of course!'

He tuned in to the steady hum of the oven, letting it calm him, then tuned out again. These days everything seemed to have to make a noise or to be lit by pilot lights. There was no stillness any more.

'Oh yes, the children. How are they?'

'They're well.'

She smiled again, touching the glass to her face.

'They're very well I think.'

He didn't reply. Didn't need to. Instead he stood next to her and pressed his face into her hair. It smelled of lemons. Then, faintly, of vinegar. She'd been cleaning the windows again with handfuls of brown paper. To let the light in, she always said. To let it fall.

Annik pushed the glass away and yawned, tilting her head back from the candle.

'Aren't you going to open it?'

She stared at the parcel.

'It's for me?'

'Of course.'

Her delighted smile clouded suddenly with doubt.

'For me, for me, for me, for me!'

She sang the words like rhyming couplets. Like a spell to ward off something. Which he knew it was. Serge went to the sink and ran the tap until the water was cold. He held a glass underneath then held the glass to his mouth and drank. He needed a proper drink.

'I'm going to the cellar.'

Silence. The gleam of her pale skin, her face downcast. Serge went out of the kitchen and unlatched the cellar door. The cold air soothed his face at once. He switched on the light and went down the steps. He took a bottle of red wine from the rack and ran his finger over the label. Médoc. A decent wine he'd got from Fabier's shop in the marketplace.

Back in the kitchen, the oven hummed. Annik had still not opened the parcel. Nor had she prepared any food. Some days she did; others she simply forgot. You could never tell. Serge broke a piece from a baguette and cut a wedge of cheese. He poured black olives into a bowl and sliced some tomatoes which he sprinkled with fresh basil and olive oil. He pulled the cork from the bottle and placed it on the table next to Annik's glass. He imagined racks full of bottles of red carnations, their petals pressed against dusty glass.

'Hungry?'

Annik shook her head and then her lower lip trembled.

'Oh I haven't...'

She trailed off and Serge was behind her touching her neck with his fingers.

'It's alright, I'm not hungry tonight. Anyway, you've made a cake. Remember?'

He poured some wine for himself and sat down at the table opposite his wife. The bread tasted dry and bland. When he was a child they'd still used the communal oven in the village every year on Bastille Day and the rye loaves had tasted of wood smoke. His mother used to bring them home in a long basket and he and his sisters had been allowed to break off bits of the hot crust. Delicious. Serge took an olive and bit into the flesh, leaving the stone carefully on the side of his plate. Annik was watching him with her head tilted to one side. She began to sob, her tears glinting in the candlelight.

Serge took a hasty gulp of the wine. He leant across the table and gathered Annik's hand.

'Don't cry, darling.'

'I can't help it, Serge, I can't.'

'I know, but they'll love it.'

'Love it?'

'The cake.'

She looked at him blankly, the tears suddenly stayed.

'The children, I mean.'

Annik's face cleared, she leaned back in the chair and sighed.

'They shan't have it if they've been naughty!'

'Have they been naughty?'

That old game again. Annik didn't answer. She giggled then frowned, then leaned forwards with her elbows on the table.

'Sometimes they are; they're so naughty!'

Serge drank, watching the wine cover Annik's face as it tilted in the glass. It burned in his belly, reminding him he was hungry. He took a slice of Cantal and balanced it on the bread. Cheese cost a fortune here, not like in the Auvergne. Things were still reasonable, there. That was city life for you.

He remembered his father shaking his head when the letter came saying that he, Serge Durand, had been accepted into the Civil Service. He'd blown a sigh through the gap in his front teeth, propping his hayfork against the barn.

'City life, boy! That's shit!'

That's all he'd said before spitting on the barn door and going in for his breakfast with the farm dog slinking after him. Serge had stood there as the valley emerged into the light. Mist thinned out above the trees and the sound of cowbells tinkled like a thousand churches calling them to mass. His mother had wept quietly, saying simply, 'You'll need a suit now.'

City life. His parents had come to their wedding like shrinking things. Cities were places they'd read about in books. They'd gone back home in the old black Citroën after one night in the hotel. Serge had been terrified that his father would embarrass him by belching at mealtimes or pissing in the street as was the habit of the men at home. He was thankful when they'd gone.

Two years later, when Annik was pregnant, they'd gone home for a visit. Sleeping in the huge mahogany bed his parents had abandoned for single beds. Nestling into the soft mattress and bolster. Even making love, though she was over three months gone. They'd slept like children until the milk wagon woke them at six o'clock, then dozed again until they'd heard his father calling the dogs.

The day before they were due to return he'd walked Annik up to the plateau to show her where the gentians and mountain violets grew. Two of the village dogs had followed them, a golden retriever and a black lurcher. The retriever bitch belonged to the squire's teenage son and the lurcher to the local postman. It had amused Serge to think of the litter of mongrels they'd produce. They'd been like a comic duo, plunging into horse troughs to cool off from the heat, bounding through the fields, startling the red Salers cattle. They'd stopped at the auberge for a glass of Avèze, a bitter-sweet liqueur made from gentian roots. Annik had screwed up her face at it and the men around the bar had laughed and slapped Serge on the back. He'd felt happy for some reason. The dogs had hung about outside the bar, then followed them all the way home. That night she'd woken with a temperature and there had been blood on the sheets. They'd had to telephone for the doctor.

Serge pushed his plate away. Funny how you could trace things back to one night. As if all sorrow went back to some point that might have been different, or avoided. Annik was watching him. The sound of their breathing was broken by the buzzer ringing on the oven. Annik smiled and rose from the chair. She was a tall woman. Half a head taller than him. Which had puzzled his father.

'It's ready. What a surprise!'

Serge watched her take up the oven gloves and put them on luxuriously like gorgeous fur mittens.

'Be careful!'

She laughed gaily.

'Careful! I've made a thousand cakes and never burnt myself once!'

Annik opened the oven and stood back to let the hot air gush into the kitchen. The light of the oven reddened her hair as she bent down to take out the cake and place it to cool. When she switched the oven off the kitchen fell silent.

Serge remembered how the wasps had swarmed in the Russian vine under their window on the morning of the walk. The wall had hummed like a tremendous electrical current circling them.

Annik stood uncertainly for a moment then shook off the oven mitts and sat back down. She took the carnation from her glass and wiped her finger inside the rim, making a faint squeak.

'Wine please!'

Serge poured an inch of wine into her glass. He'd spent the day answering emails and processing planning applications. He was dog-tired. And his father had been right, in his way. He'd been right about a few things. Annik put her hand on his wrist, covering the face of his wristwatch. Then she touched the wine to her lips, which parted for a second and closed again, merely breathing across the surface.

'What a surprise!'

She clapped her hands and shook back her hair.

'What a wonderful surprise!'

'But you haven't opened your present.'

'Haven't I? Haven't I?'

Her eyes were wide with happiness. Annik took the package and opened one end. A little jeweller's box slid out. She tilted her head.

'Is it something nice?'

'It might be.'

He tried to be jolly.

'Go on, open it!'

'Ok.'

She said it with a tinkling, silvery tone. Not a word, but a droplet of pure sound spilled from her throat. It made him afraid again, that little thread beginning to unravel and tug him into the unknown. He took another mouthful of wine and topped up his glass.

'Go on.'

Annik took the box and flipped it open. Serge toyed with the ring of olive stones on his plate. His present was a necklace of amber beads. Annik pulled them from the box and draped them on her neck. She was trying to fasten the clasp.

'Oh, I'm so clumsy, Serge. Come on, help me!'

He helped her to fasten the clasp, squinting without his glasses. Annik rose from her chair and kissed him softly on the cheek.

'It's lovely. I'm sure it's lovely. I'm going to look!'

She left the kitchen and Serge heard her running upstairs to the mirror. He poured more wine. The bottle was almost empty. Annik's glass was still untouched. He downed that too and sat back in the chair, rubbing at his eyes. Thank God tomorrow was Saturday. Footsteps scuffled in their bedroom upstairs, then silence.

Serge waited. He began to roam around the kitchen, touching things. The working surfaces, the steel sink, a Mexican plate hung on the wall. Annik had made a sponge cake with almonds arranged into a smiling face on top. He could smell cinnamon and lemon zest. Serge pushed the cake from its tin and peeled off the greaseproof paper. It had risen perfectly. How odd to find perfection here, in a cake. He sat down again and waited, sipping at the wine until the glass was empty and then the bottle was empty. He could hear Annik's footsteps on the stairs, then in the corridor.

When she stepped from the shadows into the candlelit room Serge felt the tug of fear again. Annik was still wearing the necklace. In front of the bathroom mirror she had slashed her face with lipstick, drawing it down over her cheeks like tribal scars.

'Serge?'

It was as if she couldn't see him, even though he was there. Even though he was sitting there. Her voice trembled as she said his name.

'Serge?'

He couldn't answer. He was crushed by tiredness.

'Serge, darling, am I beautiful?'

He said nothing. There was nothing to say...

'Am I?'

She began to sway in front of him unbuttoning the black dress.

'Stop it, Annik! For Christ's sake stop it.'

He was shouting. Annik stepped back, clutching her arms across her chest.

'Stop it! Stop it! Stop it!'

He crouched on the kitchen floor, pressing his head against the table leg. There was silence, Annik frantically buttoning her dress. She knelt down next to him and took his head in her arms, stroking his hair.

'It's alright, it's alright. I'm here.'

She sat down next to him and rocked him in her arms. Soothed him against her breast, pressing her hair against his face. The candle went out, leaving the kitchen dark except for faint lights from the neighbours' houses. Somewhere a dog barked and there was an answering yelp. Somebody went out of their house, spoke to the dog, coughed. A door slammed shut. Then a small motorcycle buzzed past. Like that day when the wasps had swarmed in the vine.

Annik stood up slowly and drew Serge into a chair. She brought another candle and set it into the candlestick, lighting it with a silver cigarette lighter. The amber necklace glowed against her skin. The top button of her dress was still undone and Serge could see where her breasts began and smoothly divided. The candlelight showed the lines around her mouth, the violet circles under her eyes. She still wore the scarlet slashes of lipstick on her face and neck. But she had forgotten them. They had happened long ago.

Annik brought two plates and put the cake on the table. She took a knife and stood it up in the middle of the almonds. The weight of her arms pushed the blade down through their smile. The cake still held a faint warmth, like body heat. Annik put a slice down in front of him. She tilted her head, whispering.

'Don't worry, Serge. We're going to eat it all up. All of it.'

Blood from a Stone

I fluffed a gear change taking the last bend into the village and had to brake pretty hard. There were star-shaped yellow flowers under the hedgerows and little stands of snowdrops. The kind my mother used to love. Earlier on we'd seen a rabbit or a hare crossing the road then leaping the ditch. It looked as if it was heading straight back to bed. Rabbit or hare? We couldn't decide. The tyres skidded a little but held. I heard Carol gasp as if she'd suddenly woken up. She reached for the handle above the passenger door and held it as I pulled into the car park. Milking it. You'd think I'd just missed a multiple pile-up. Anyway, I didn't say anything. I just got out and pushed some pound coins into the parking meter.

I opened the driver's door to stick the ticket to the window. Then I put my head back into the car. I could smell Carol's perfume. Jasmine. I kept meaning to tell her that I'd never really liked it. In fact it made me want to throw up. Especially after a few beers. Not an easy thing to say, that. Not to Carol.

'You can see the house from here. Look.'

'Where? Oh, ok.'

She stared up at the grey semi with its red tile roof. It squatted on the hillside where the road climbed out of the village on the other side of the river. Taking a look was all my idea, so she sounded less than delighted. Carol pushed the car door open, put a leg out and shuddered.

'It looks grim.'

'It's a grim day. Couldn't be worse, really.'

Carol clutched her coat tighter around her. She was five months pregnant and it was starting to show.

'I know it's a long shot.'

'Yeah, yeah, they're all long shots…'

I helped her out of the car. We'd driven out from the town and over the moors to get to the village. As a kid I'd been able to look out from my bedroom window to where the hills rose up beyond the rubber factory and weaving sheds and the new housing estate and the scrubland behind the house with its stinking brook. Some days they looked close enough to touch. Today they'd been hidden in mist and we'd driven down through skeins of cloud. Thirty-five minutes, so it was do-able. I could still get to work.

We'd met at the hospital. Carol was the ward clerk in orthopaedics and I was in radiography: secure, low-paid jobs, since illness never went out of style. Carol still had a few months to go before her maternity leave. We'd not planned much beyond that. Beyond that was still very hard to imagine.

The car park smelled of soot and the trees were bare. Some of them cradled the silhouettes of old birds' nests: crows or rooks. They broke from the branches, calling out with rasping cries. The days were starting to lengthen and the birds were taking notice. We had to step over puddles to reach the path. And it was cold, the kind of cold that's worst in April. The sort that grips your chest: wet and rich with consumption. Last week I'd X-rayed a Zimbabwean refugee with TB. His lungs had looked like rotten rags. A hundred years ago it would have been common in sodden little places like this, when they were still scraping peat from the hills to keep warm and working for a pittance on the estate. I looked at my watch.

'We're early. We've got almost an hour. What about some lunch?'

'Ok, let's. Where?'

Carol wasn't at her most talkative. We'd both taken some free time from work to look at the house. I guess she might have spent it at home looking through catalogues for baby clothes or maternity wear or something. But here she was dragging through the rain with me on a half-arsed quest for the perfect home.

There was a café next to the car park and a toilet block put there for tourists and weekend visitors. Escapees from tight little north Lancashire towns. It didn't look promising. Carol shrugged and took my arm. I pulled away.

'Hold on a sec, I need the gents....'

I stood in the smell of stale piss and disinfectant whilst Carol waited in the cold. My pee stung as it dribbled out, a baleful yellow. The taps were broken and I had to lift the lid from a cistern to wash my hands. They were raw with cold when I caught Carol up and led the way to the Jackdaw Café.

Four bikers sat at tables outside with bacon sandwiches and mugs of tea. Their machines were leaning on side-stands behind our car. A Kawasaki and three Hondas. I'd never fancied Jap bikes much, myself. I'd once had an ancient BMW twin that leaked oil for England. Or Bavaria, to be more accurate. Breaking my wrist playing football put paid to that. I'd never got back into it somehow. Sold it to a real arsehole who knocked me down seventy quid. But for a couple of years I was out every Sunday, up on the A65 to Devil's Bridge at Kirkby Lonsdale, standing with a mug of tea and a bacon bap, watching those crazy kids leaping off into the river for a dare. It was a kind of freedom, I guess. But with my scabby old Beemer I'd never fitted in.

The lads nodded to us as we came up to them. The café was tiny with a few tables, a chalked Specials board and a chipped Formica counter. Behind that, the kitchen was hazy with bacon smoke. The proprietor was a fat guy, middle aged with wavy grey hair, a silver earring and a striped apron. He waved at us across a couple of customers queuing for tea.

'There's room upstairs. Help yourselves.'

I nodded. His fingers were yellow with nicotine, two of them missing from one hand.

'Thanks. This way?'

He nodded and I guided Carol to the stairs, going up behind her, watching her knuckles whiten and relax as she gripped the rail. I imagined the fat guy losing his fingers in an industrial accident and then setting up the café with the compensation. Lucky bugger. Unless he'd played the violin, that is. It didn't seem likely, mind you; and all luck is relative.

The upstairs dining room was little more than a landing. But it was crammed with tables and a coal fire burned in an iron Victorian grate. There was a row of alcoves, each one stuffed with dried flowers. The walls were hung with photographs of ancient country folk, teams of shire horses hitched to ploughs, agricultural labourers lined up in front of a steam-driven threshing machine. Myths from the Golden Age of child mortality: diphtheria, measles, galloping consumption and pox. At the back were the toilets and a tiny kitchen with a dumb waiter. Then a real waitress squeezed her arse between the tables towards us. We ordered parsnip and coriander soup and a roll. There wouldn't be time for much else.

Two elderly couples hunched over their food at separate tables without speaking. I thought of my father after my mother died, riding round the town on his bus pass, eating alone in cafés and chippies and pubs, wondering why his children hardly visited. The way he'd phone up at dawn to ask which day of the week it was. Even now an early morning phone call could crack me from the sheets like a whip. We stared at the river through a square of window. There were black and white birds with long orange beaks whirling over the water. They looked quarrelsome, as if their hormones were raging. I knew a bit about that from Carol. She had two kinds of PMT – pre and post – with maybe a few days respite in the middle. I reached across and took her hand. It felt dry and thin. Her wedding ring was loose against her finger. I wanted to say something reassuring.

'It's ok. It's only a house. It's not such a big deal.'

'Only!'

'Come on, it's a day out. We could be at work.'

I gave her what I thought was a supportive smile, but she thought it was something else and frowned, looking past me. Then she jogged my arm.

'Look out!'

I felt something bump into my chair.

'I'm sorry, he's half asleep!'

The waitress was at my elbow with our home-made soup. It was greasy and thin, bland with a coil of cream like a white turd. It came with a granary roll that tasted of nothing. I bent my head to the spoon. If I complained, Carol would say I was a snob. She didn't have much time for fads. Her idea of cooking was parking a takeaway in the microwave. I did all the fancy stuff in the kitchen. It helped me unwind after work.

By the time we were eating the fire was scorching my back, so that I could smell the hot wool of my jumper. The heat made my scalp itch. It reminded me of having chilblains as a kid in a house with no central heating; the way we clung to the fire and took hot water bottles to bed and burned our feet on them.

Three female cyclists came in, piling their helmets on a chair, sniffing from the cold. They wore tight leotards against their flat bodies. When the waitress presented herself and they ordered their food, I noticed that one of them had an Italian accent overlain with Lancashire vowels. She sounded weirdly cosmopolitan. What was that word Terry used? *Other*. Which was bollocks, because everyone is. But even those hard cases fell silent in that grim little room. A few spots of rain speckled the window. The birds had disappeared downriver. I thought of them fucking in the wet grass, or whatever birds do when they do it. I thought of Carol stroking me to get me hard that last time, then gasping as I went in. Faking it, probably: I wasn't that good. But you wouldn't think it to look at her now. And the old couples must have been like that once, before their skin loosened and crinkled like tissue paper, before whatever it was that had been between them became something else. Companionship. Exasperation. Hatred, even.

One of the old ladies pushed past our table to the toilet, catching her dress on the back of my chair, unhooking it and moving on without a smile. I pushed back the cuff of my jumper and felt a little ball of sweat curl down from my armpit. It was almost time.

It was a five-minute walk to the house, if that. We'd down-loaded the details from the estate agent's website and I carried them rolled up into a peashooter. The vendor was showing us around, which, as Carol had already observed, is rarely a good idea. A half-timbered suburban semi – even though it was stone-built, even though it was in a desirable village location – wasn't quite our thing. We just needed a little more space in the house, a spare room for the baby, a garden where it could play out. Maybe space to grow some vegetables. We just needed a bit more of everything. Which you couldn't get.

Predictably my father had died without leaving a will. My brother and I had to go to probate and, eventually, after months of waiting, we'd been able to split the value of the house. The contents were worth nothing and we'd ended up paying for a house clearance. It didn't do to think about what my father would have said to see the furniture and knick-knacks he'd collected with my mother treated as junk. There wasn't much left after paying outstanding bills. Not much to show for his life. But it was something. It was a start. And maybe it could work for us. Terry had banked his and gone back to Kuwait where he taught English to the kids of ex-pats from the US and all over Europe. Cushy, as he often admitted. He was well out of it.

We were keen to move away from the town. Well, to be fair to Carol, I was keen. I'd lived there all my life. She was from Wolverhampton and it never seemed to bother her. She'd have been happy with a new house on one of the estates that made me want to scream.

Here I was, thirty-three, and still shopping in the supermarket where I'd had a holiday job as a teenager. Still seeing lads I'd gone to school with, looking years older than they really were, yelling at their kids in the town centre or trapped against the window in Burger King. Some of them had already got divorced from the teenage girls they'd married. Some had joined the army and came home on leave from wherever and whatever it was they'd learned to kill. You saw them drinking alone in pubs, pulling at a cigarette, staring at the one-armed bandits as they jerked down the lever. They were always glad to see you, glad to bribe you out of a few minutes of your life with a pint. Sometimes you met them jogging down the canal towpath at weekends with their Walkmans and iPods. Occasionally, they turned up in the local papers, injured in a car accident or blown to pieces in Iraq or up in court for kicking somebody's head in over a girl. Maybe all three, but not in that order.

I hated the feeling of belonging. Today offered a chance to put some distance between the past and me. For a house in the country, this one was suspiciously affordable. It wasn't the cottage with beams and a tiled kitchen that I'd hoped for, but on the website the rooms had looked spacious and it boasted long views of the valley. Even a wide-angle lens couldn't fake that. The house faced southwest where it would catch the sun for most of the day. The write-up was ambiguous about the garden and, now we were here, it was definitely close to the road.

We huddled in the little mock-Tudor porch, half turning to the view of slate roofs crouching on the opposite side of the valley. Carol was dabbing on lipstick. Smoke was curling over grey stone houses, crows calling from the copse on the hill behind. There were streaks of white shit down the clay tile roof and the drainpipes were crooked where the fixings were missing. Someone was clearing his throat.

'Mr and Mrs Peyton? Hi, I'm Martin. Come in, now.'

The 'now' was meant to be homely. But it sounded false. We shook hands and he brought us inside. He was a man in his thirties, like me. Medium height, thinning hair, a hollow-cheeked, long-nosed face with broken veins purpling his cheeks. His teeth were stained and when he smiled, his face twisted slightly out of true, as if he'd once had Bell's palsy. I knew about that because Carol's mother had suffered from it and it had left her with a drooping eyelid.

Martin walked with a dropped shoulder, a faint lopsided-ness. He was wearing a pale blue Reebok tracksuit and tartan bedroom slippers, broken down at the heel. There was a smell in the hallway that leaked through the house. It was the smell you find after a week's holiday when someone turned the freezer off by mistake – a mixture of forgotten fish and stale cat food. I'd done that once and Carol had gone berserk: coming back from a week's camping in France, which she'd hated (surprise, surprise) to that.

'Can I take your coats?'

Carol shook her head. Her tight coral lips told me that her first impressions hadn't been good. She flicked her hair from her forehead and pulled the coat closer.

'We're alright, thanks. This is a lovely space…' I didn't really mean that. But you have to try to say something positive, because you're about to trample through someone's life and maybe that's all they have. It doesn't matter that it isn't true. Not much is, after all.

Martin's face brightened up at once and he led us into the front room, where there was a white leather three-piece suite, a bright rag rug – red, orange and purple – and a fire licking at some damp logs in the grate. I noticed a copy of *Lancashire Life* left out on the coffee table. Martin's wife – presumably he had one – was nowhere to be seen. I wondered if she was waiting upstairs or if she'd gone out and just left him to it. More likely, she was simply at work. I pictured her as a receptionist at the medical practice in the village. Her blonde hair was pulled back and her fingernails painted with an efficient, pearly sheen.

What Martin did was hard to figure. Whatever he did, the house was their unfinished project. We'd seen a few of those, had almost got used to staring at half-built dreams. 'It's a nice property,' (never merely a house) the estate agent would say, but it was another empty nest, another gloomy mausoleum where another old couple had gradually slipped away from half-life to death.

This house had stripped floors and big bay windows. High ceilings with plaster mouldings. Lots of light. They'd even tried to retain or replace the original thirties features: panes of stained glass above the windows and heavy brass door handles. The kitchen still had the original green-painted cabinets and a solid fuel Rayburn. It looked like a lot of work to get hot water. Everything there was original from the pantry with its slate shelves to the downstairs toilet with its Royal Worcester hand basin and grubby roller towel.

Carol was looking pale and impatient by now. Martin led us upstairs, limping ahead. In the smallest bedroom was Disneyland wallpaper and a miniature chest of drawers. A giant purple tortoise made of stuffed fabric lay on the bed; the kind you keep your nightdress or pyjamas in. The other medium-sized bedroom was full of boxes of books. A computer was still switched on at the small desk where he'd been working before we knocked. There were a couple of badminton rackets and what looked like a wetsuit hanging out of a tea chest. In the main bedroom, the iron-framed bed was tightly made up under a pink tasselled coverlet. Apart from one pair of men's black shoes, an alarm clock and a box of tissues on the bedside cabinet, it was empty. There were a couple of freestanding, oak-veneered wardrobes, depressingly like the ones my parents had. We didn't pry inside. The beige carpet was shiny and felt too soft, oddly furtive beneath our feet. Martin moved us on quickly, muttering something about the light coming in each morning.

It was when he led us through the back door that my heart sank. We'd hoped for some garden space, but apart from the strip of rockery that wrapped round the front of the house, creating a barrier from the road, there was only a yard. The space to build the house had been hewn from the hillside and a fifteen-foot cliff of cement wept water a few feet from the back door. Lined up against the wall were a series of wire cages and some bags of sawdust. He must have seen us exchanging glances.

'Andorra rabbits… and guinea pigs. We used to breed them for shows.'

I smiled in what I hoped was a fascinated way. It would be good to get away without doing him too much damage. The look on Carol's face said RATS.

'Blimey, you must have had quite a few!'

'Yes, my daughter loved them…'

A little twist came to the corner of his mouth and an awkward silence dropped on us like a butterfly net on something rare and free. Rain still fell in a fine drizzle. Water rippled slantwise across the yard to the drain. It was bloody cold. I watched a slug gliding at the rim of the grate and remembered how they mated, hanging from a twisted rope of slime. The female bit off the male's penis after copulation. Or tried to. Which was nice. Martin turned to leave the yard. The slug's eyes extended warily on their stalks, and the rooks were at it again, calling out and flapping in the black sticks of the trees. The concrete wall was green with moss and algae. Damp seeped everywhere, glistening on every surface like sweat on fungal skin.

Carol gathered herself and asked if she could use the toilet. Martin directed her back upstairs. We heard her scrabble at the heavy lock.

'How far gone is she?'

If I was surprised at his directness, I tried not to show it. His voice was thick. It was odd to think he'd been looking at her.

'About four months. So we're looking for more room… a bit of space for the baby.'

He smiled wryly and his fingers went to his neck where a purple birthmark disappeared under his collar.

'Yes, I'm looking for a bit less, now…'

He picked at a fingernail with his thumb, dropped his voice to a whisper.

'She wanted blood from a stone. Then she came back for't fucking stone!'

His mouth twisted again, his lips chapped and bloodless. Just then, the sun charged through clouds across the valley and a rainbow arched above the village, fading just as quickly. He turned away into the kitchen, his footfalls silent in the tartan slippers, and I followed.

We spent the obligatory fifteen minutes looking around on our own as he hovered discreetly. The house reeked of other lives, living and dead. An old lady had eked out her last years there, he'd told us, before they'd moved in. That's why so much of the house was original. There'd been a lot to do and there it was: still to do, still unfinished. We left awkwardly, mumbling our thanks. The door clicked behind us and we saw a shadow at the window, watching us walk away. I put my arm around Carol so that he could see. See that I cared, that life hadn't yet driven its wedge of desolation between us.

We walked to the river bridge, staring into the water for a moment. It was dark brown with peat from the fells. Then we walked back towards the café and hopped through the puddles to the car. The lady cyclists were just pulling away, their calf muscles tight as hawsers. Carol shuddered into her seat and pulled her coat tight.

'Ugh!'

'Yes, poor guy.'

'Poor guy my foot! It was disgusting! You should have seen the hand basin and the stains in the toilet.'

'Yes but he was alone wasn't he? I wonder what happened to his wife and kid?'

I didn't want to tell her that I knew. That she'd come back for the stone after drinking the blood. I thought I'd test her.

'They could be dead I suppose... an accident or something...'

'Yes, but there's always bleach.'

Carol snapped on her seatbelt. I slipped my hand between the belt and her belly to feel our child there, but she pushed my hand away. There'd been a lot of that lately.

'No, Steve. Not ever. Not there. Not in any way, shape or form.'

'I wasn't suggesting we should make him an offer.'

'An offer? I'd rather die. Fuck, no!'

The windscreen wipers dragged a sycamore leaf across the windscreen, tormenting it until it blew away at last. I started the engine and reversed, bouncing backwards through the puddles. Rain began again, streaking the windows. Down at the river the black and white birds were back, tramping at the water's edge. I could see their bright beaks dipping to the mud and rising again as if they'd been dipped in molten fire.

We drove home in near silence, back to the dark clot of the town, to the terraced house we moved into after we got married. Tomorrow was Saturday so no work, not this week anyway. I opened a bottle of wine and watched the football for an hour. Leeds versus Arsenal and a crap game. Carol took herself off to bed early, saying she was tired. I snuggled in next to her just before midnight, feeling her pull away. But I couldn't sleep. I kept thinking about my dad, how I didn't want to end up like that: a sour old man with no friends. Riding around on the buses all day. Falling asleep, then waking up who knows where. He'd refused to have any help from social services and when a neighbour found him he'd been dead two days. I still felt guilty about that, but wild horses wouldn't drag Carol to the house. My dad's eyesight had been failing and he couldn't keep the place clean any more. I always went home stinking of disinfectant from scrubbing the sink and toilet, but I'm not sure he even noticed. If there was one thing Carol couldn't be nice about, it was him.

I lay awake, and I couldn't stop thinking about how we'd emptied the outhouse after the house clearance. We'd found a buyer who was planning to gut the place, but we'd forgotten to give the outhouse keys to the clearance firm. Our Terry was staying over with us and came with me. He'd gone for cigarettes, so I'd made a start without him.

The outhouse was just a brick lean-to, part coal shed, part glory hole. There was a set of stepladders in there, a load of smokeless fuel that my dad hadn't used but that the cat had pissed on, some stiffened paintbrushes, and dozens of cans of old paint that he'd hoarded, all of them useless. I piled the stuff into black bin liners and tied them off for the tip. The fuel would have to stay, but that wasn't such a problem. Then, right at the bottom of the shed, there in the filth and spilled oil, I'd found a little dark-skinned toad with a white speckled chest. Its eyes were bright amber specks. A huge ginger centipede crawled past it and disappeared into a gap in the wall. There was something otherworldly about them that made my flesh creep. When I reached for the toad it cringed away from me, trying to flatten itself against the wall. And for some reason its fear filled me with shame. I found a thin sheet of cardboard and slid it as carefully as I could under its haunches, carrying it down into the field behind the house.

When Terry arrived, I'd almost finished. We set to and had the stuff loaded in the boot of my car in half an hour. Then we checked the house for the last time, shut the front door and posted the keys. We'd both grown up there, even sharing a bedroom before my dad had made a room in the loft, which we'd fought over. Terry got it, of course, being the eldest. We ended up going for a pint in The Firwood, but even then, there didn't seem to be much to say. I didn't mention the toad, but I couldn't get it out of my mind. The way it had been so afraid there in the darkness and filth of the shed. It reminded me of the way my father had died. The way we all have to die.

Now I lay in bed next to Carol with my arm around her, feeling the child growing in her belly. I couldn't get Martin out of my mind either. That row of empty rabbit cages, the stuffed tortoise, the purple birthmark, the smell of loneliness that wafted through the house. His wife with her cold little voice answering the telephone down at the surgery. Martin's heart, the bloodless stone. A piece of the grey pumice my dad used to clean his hands. Then the toad with its speckled chest that looked as if it was streaked with paint. The way it had shrunk from me into the filth and junk of my dad's outhouse. I wondered if we'd ever move away or if we'd just stay there in the town where I'd always lived.

When I awoke the next morning I could hear Carol in the kitchen downstairs, the empty wine bottle clanking into the bin. The kettle coming to the boil sounded like the sea pulling at shingle. The bed was warm where she'd been lying and I slipped across so that my body lay in the heat of hers, in the heat of our child's life that was just beginning. There was the faint smell of jasmine on her pillow. I thought about the snow-drops and the hare leaping the ditch, about the golden stars of flowers whose names I didn't even know.

I must have dozed off, then, because the next thing I knew Carol was slipping in beside me, putting a cup of tea on the bedside cabinet, lips nuzzling into my neck, hair tickling my skin. She was warm against me and I turned to slip my hand under her pyjamas and across her belly, stroking it, circling lower and lower. The baby gave a little kick against my hand. Even without looking at her, I knew she was smiling.

Travellers

It was hot.

'So hot you could piss steam!'

If O'Donnell said that again he was going to scream. Or smash his bloody face in. They were standing at the edge of the track, looking down towards the town. Steel lines converged into an unsteady haze. Fireweed smouldered on either side of the track, making a purple smudge above wavering iron. A wood pigeon cooed softly and insistently in the ash trees behind the station. The air simmered. O'Donnell took out a blue handkerchief and dabbed at his forehead.

'Christ it's hot, so hot...'

He tailed off, seeing the frown go across Peterson's face. He stared for a moment at his angular features with their dark shadow of stubble already forming. The eyes were a pale grey, too pale, as if they'd acidified in that thin face. Ah, what the hell. He was a cussed bastard. Truth was they were both getting bad tempered in the heat, and no bloody train. It was already twenty minutes late.

Peterson spat onto the platform, hardly able to muster a globule of moisture from his parched mouth. The ball of froth rolled in the dust. He pulled his shirt away from his back. It was unpleasantly wet. Peterson thought of the luxury of taking a bath. Cool water, a long soak with a drink to hand. He cursed the late train and the platform from which all other passengers had evaporated except O'Donnell who sat like a plump, stupid seal on his suitcase. The thought of the stained enamel bath at their lodgings made him angry. That bitch of a landlady who was too mean to allow more than two baths a week. The thought of the black hairs he always found clogged with soap in the plughole. O'Donnell's hairs. He wanted to be sick. Everything made him want to puke.

O'Donnell mopped inside his shirt with his handkerchief. It disgusted Peterson. It put him on edge, as if O'Donnell might suddenly produce one of his overheated internal organs – the heart or a piece of liver – from its unbuttoned front. A sparrow hopped onto the arm of the signal and shat. O'Donnell put away the handkerchief. He glanced up at Peterson.

'Jesus...'

Peterson jerked his hand up.

'Don't tell me it's hot, that's all, just don't!'

O'Donnell shrugged. His mouth made a black O. Peterson walked down to the ticket office. The platform burned through the thin soles of his shoes. He couldn't afford to get them mended. That made him angry too. Fucking angry. He scowled in through the office window. The ticket clerk sat in twilight, filling in a yellow form. Impossible to tell whether it was a man or a woman. When they'd got their tickets that morning they still hadn't known, swapping glances as the clerk handed them their change and thanked them in a flat, neutral voice.

Peterson rapped on the window. The head jerked but didn't look up until the last movement of the pen was made. He opened his mouth to speak but the clerk cut in.

'Forty minutes late, sir.'

Peterson glowered, slapping his hand down on the dark

wood of the counter. He'd wanted to say something but she –
he was sure it was a woman – hadn't given him a chance.
They called this a railway! Bloody hell, he'd show them when
they got to Doncaster! He stayed in the narrow shade of the
station-house wall to avoid the sun. O'Donnell squatted on
his suitcase with Peterson's own case beside him. Both full of
samples. What was the good of being a traveller when you
couldn't travel? Peterson thought of other reps who had
motor cars, slick bastards, selling everything from wrist-
watches to cigars. They'd just sent a man into outer space, so
you'd fucking think they could get the trains to run. He spat
another impoverished ball onto the platform. It evaporated at
once, shrivelling in the heat. Yuri Gagarin. That was it. A
Russian, too.

The pigeon cooed on and on, reminding him of cool leaves,
of liquid. Then the moment emptied, like opening a book and
finding a blank page, not being able to read on. O'Donnell,
the station, the train that wouldn't come, that sexless creature
squatting in the ticket office, cunning as a spider.

He moved out of the shadow and walked down the platform towards O'Donnell. The parched air that he disturbed
brought no relief. He imagined the train stuck between
embankments of willow herb, slowly frying its passengers.
The bastards could burn in hell for all he cared. Then he
heard the sound of a train and felt a faint vibration under
his feet. He quickened his pace, trying to place the sound.
O'Donnell had stood up and was reaching for his jacket
where it lay over Peterson's case. Shit! O'Donnell's face was
abject with misery. The train was going the wrong way. Going
not coming. Peterson wanted to laugh hysterically. He wanted
to run down the platform and smash O'Donnell's dumb
bastard face in with all his might. The train passed through in

a faint veil of dust, without stopping. Faces at its windows hardly even looked their way. The clerk had come out onto the platform to watch it pass. She shrugged, as if talking to herself, and went back inside the office. O'Donnell sank back down onto the cases. Peterson watched him through narrowed eyes. If he wasn't careful his fat arse would burst it open. Peterson imagined him straining on the toilet. *There'd hardly be room to drop a turd from those cheeks.* He recited it quietly, as if it was a line of poetry, or a speech from a famous play. He gave a short yelp of laughter. O'Donnell looked up in surprise. He opened his mouth, frowning, but thought better of it and let it sag shut again.

Peterson turned round, walking back up the platform like a prisoner repeating his route around a courtyard. He put his hand on the iron handle of a luggage trolley and withdrew it with a gasp. It was as hot as the barrel of a gun. Now he was walking up the line. Up the line towards where he wanted to be. Away from here. He thought of taking the suitcase and setting off to walk to the next station. He thought of throwing it under the next train and fuck the company. Just walk off. Piss off and leave them forever. To wallow in their own shit. It was a good thought, satisfying for a moment. He glanced at his watch. If what the clerk said was true, then the train was due seven minutes from now, at the revised time. At the revised time. He turned the words over in his mouth, hating the feel of them. Bollocks to this. He needed a beer. A cold beer, the bottle beaded with condensation, straight from the fridge in Driscoll's bar. He needed a bath, clean socks, a clean shirt, clean underwear.

Overhead the wood pigeon cooed. It was insane. Such a calm, clear sound. It was filling him up with heat, with fury. He was near the ticket office and stepped forwards, rapping his knuckles on the window. The clerk looked up mildly. She had put on a green eyeshade that covered half her face in shadow. This time Peterson got in first.

'Where the hell's this train got to?'

'It's a signalling fault, sir, it shouldn't be much longer.'

Her voice was almost like a man's, but dry with age, arid with answering the same questions, year in year out. Peterson felt her weariness settling on his shoulders like dust. He wanted to snap some cutting remark back at her. But his tongue was numb. Impotent. He clenched his fist against the wooden counter then beat it softly against his thigh.

Peterson went back and sat down on his own case next to O'Donnell. The younger man shifted uneasily away from him. He was a fat bastard and not good for much. Not really. They sat for a time without speaking, feeling the sweat form on their foreheads then run down their faces. The pigeon cooed on and on. Peterson snapped upright.

'That fucking bird!'

O'Donnell looked up with calm blue eyes.

'I like it, it's soothing.'

'Soothing?'

Peterson stared at him in disbelief, his thin face utterly amazed.

'Soothing? You must be bloody mad!'

O'Donnell shrugged and scuffed his foot along the tarmac. He wasn't going to argue about it.

'Soothing? It's a fucking nightmare!'

Peterson would argue with himself if he was left alone for long enough. After all, it was only a pigeon.

'I'm sick of it all! Fucking sick!'

For a moment O'Donnell wanted to laugh. He felt the corners of his mouth creasing. But Peterson was turning away again to prowl down the platform.

He walked as far away from O'Donnell as he could. But wherever he stood the bird was there, just as loud, just as insistent. The sound was coming from inside his own head. His mouth had dried out. He couldn't swallow. An hour ago he'd wanted to piss, but the contents of his bladder had been absorbed back into his body. He stood looking at the green side door of the ticket office. There was a little window let into it, dusty and filmed over with cobwebs. Curious. Peterson walked up to it quietly and peered through. The ticket clerk was sitting at the table with a newspaper spread out before her. A newspaper! He was frying in the heat and she found time to read the fucking paper. Very quietly Peterson lifted the catch and pushed the door open. He was stepping into the room before the ticket clerk knew he was coming.

Peterson closed the door behind him with a little thud and stood there. It was very still in the room. It smelled musty. The smell of old timetables: the smell of lateness, dereliction of duty and decay. The stink of disorder. The clerk twisted round with a little gasp.

'You can't come in here…'

But she broke off, clutching at the table in front of her. Peterson said nothing. He stood there, silent. The sweat drooled down his body in icy balls. He had to snatch each breath hastily from the hot air. Even now he could hear the faint calling of the pigeon. He stood for a long time and the ticket clerk sat, immobile, breathing too quickly, watching his corrosive grey eyes. No other sound but the rasping of their breath and the soft cooing of the bird outside.

Peterson reached forward and snatched off the clerk's eye-shade, snapping the elastic fastener and ruffling her short grey hair. She winced to one side, her hands fluttering up to touch the side of her face. It was a woman alright.

'You!'

That was all. She shook her head slightly, denying it. Peterson leaned forward, pushing his starved face next to hers. She could smell his sour breath.

'You and the other bitches, eh?'

'No, no, please!'

The clerk began to rise from her chair, shaking her head all the time so that her dewlap chin wobbled. She started to cry softly. From the distance could be heard the far-off drumming of a train.

'You and all those other bitches, oh yes!'

Peterson lunged forward and grabbed a handful of her hair, twisting her head. He'd fucking snap it off, the bitch. She was frightened. Oh yes! Her fear delighted him. Never been fucked, he'd wager a tenner on that. With his other hand he ripped open the front of her uniform. Her body was soft. The train came nearer, louder, and the bird was still there, faintly calling.

Christ! It was hot! The sweat boiled out of him. He tore the blue shirt, still twisting the woman's head, ripping off the buttons, dragging at her breasts. They surprised him, full and smooth, like the breasts of another woman. Her skin was damp. She was whimpering now. He twisted her head, making her gasp.

'Please. Please leave me alone! Don't hurt me.'

The train was nearly on them, hammering on the track, drowning out the signalling bird. Peterson broke away, tearing out a handful of the woman's hair as he pulled his hand free. She staggered against him, losing her balance. He was suddenly terrified that she would try to detain him. To hold onto him.

'Away, you bitch, away!'

He kicked at her, pushing her backwards. She lurched

away from him into the table, her hands trying to pull her torn clothing together. Peterson turned his face away. Then he smacked his hand across her face, two stinging blows that brought the blood gushing from her nose, splashing down over the hands that still tried to make the halves of her blouse meet.

'Please go… please!'

But the train was drawing to a halt and he was already running out into the heat.

O'Donnell was looking around, bewildered. He grinned when he saw Peterson hurrying towards him.

'Thank Christ, I thought you'd got lost!'

'Get on, get on! Don't just stand there!'

Peterson shoved O'Donnell towards the step and the open doorway but his own suitcase caught against the edge and burst open. He made a grab at it. But everything was tangled up in O'Donnell's feet and the bibles were spilling out onto the platform and under the wheels of the train. Where they belonged, under the bastard wheels.

It was a joke. What a fucking joke. Laughter was building up, a huge bubble in his chest. From the corner of his eyes he saw the ticket clerk stagger out onto the platform, her face covered in blood. When she saw Peterson, she began a high, wild screaming which brought every face to the window of the train. She was pointing at a thin man who was kneeling on the platform stuffing red and black books into a suitcase. Over the commotion and the grumbling of the engine the soft cooing of a wood pigeon went on and on. Peterson began to giggle as he fumbled. O'Donnell put his own suitcase inside the train. He turned to watch the ticket clerk.

'My God, will you look at that!'

He saw Peterson crease up with laughter. He laughed until the tears came. Putting his hands over his ears. Rocking backwards and forwards in the shadow of the train that had come at last, laughing until he cried under the softly tolling notes of the wood pigeon.

Daniel

The light is pale. Sharp as newly sliced lemons. The cat sleeps in the dust under the sideboard. That smell of old apples, urine and mould; an earthy scent of geraniums. They've shed petals and brown leaves across the kitchen sink. There's a stain on the rag rug where he must have spilt something. He doesn't remember when or what that was. Daniel cups his chin, thinks about a shave. The bristles are white, sharp against his palms. His nails are broken, black at the rim. His fingers smell of bacon fat and diesel oil. He brushes crumbs from his lap. Light creeps in at the window. He stares at the ginger cat that never blinks.

Daniel rises from the chair. Its screech is brief across the tiled floor. The tiles glow in dawn light, rich and tawny as plums. The fire in the cast-iron grate has slumped again. He throws on another log, watching the bark curl from it as the flames begin. The black tissue of ash turns grey and then white. That tree came down in the bottom pasture. They'd played in it as children; now it's burning in his grate. He'd taken a chainsaw to the tree, dragging it in sections to the barn with the tractor before gapping up the wall. Then a day on the crosscut: sawing logs and stacking them. That way you get warm twice. It takes two years for pear or apple wood to season. Longer for hawthorn or elm. Now the chimney sucks at the ash. It flocks like ascending snow.

Last year the weather had been freezing after Christmas. A real cold snap. Sudden, but not startling here, where it was to be expected. Snow had harried them, coming down in dry flakes for days at a time. One afternoon, feeding his stock from the trailer up there on the fell he'd almost lost it. Let himself go. Things had seemed to sink away around him so that there were no passing moments, just a blur, a whiteout of time. He'd no idea how long he'd been up there, staring at the windscreen. It had filled with snow before he came to. He could have frozen to death. He wouldn't have been the first. It was said his father's great-grandfather had been lost that way. Up there was the place to forget yourself. To forget everything. Up there on the fell gathering sheep with the wind coming straight off the North Sea. A Russian wind, full of Siberian ice. Full of slaughtered stoicism. He'd always remember that winter.

Now another winter was about to pass, blowing away through the black buds on the ash trees, letting light and warmth in at last. He kicks the log into place with his stockinged foot and catches the smell of singed wool. Annie would have scolded him for that. For his daftness. Putting his feet in the fire. But he's burning the past, burning memories. And you had to be careful. Memories made memories – and some things were best left be.

He'd wept that day, alone on the moor. Dragging hay bales from the tailgate. Struggling with chains and pins clarted in frozen cow shit. It'd been sweet summer hay with grass and clover and buttercups all mixed in. Better than that stinking silage he wouldn't make. He'd wept then, crumpled up against the trailer, his shoulders shaking. Then crawling into the cab where no one could see him. Banging his head on the steering wheel, pumping the accelerator, making the wheels spin on the piss-stained crust of snow. Frightening the sheep in their draggled fleeces. And beyond the windscreen the wind had chased away the last flakes of winter towards a spring she'd never see.

That last night she'd asked for an oatmeal biscuit with warm milk. Whatever you fancy, love, he'd said, laying his hand beside her head on the pillow, noticing how broken it looked. How swollen and useless it had become. Then he'd lain down beside her, listening to her fluttered breaths. He'd fallen asleep. And so had she. When he woke, she was stiff beside him, her hands locked, her cheeks cold as a churn. She'd died easily in the end. She'd died at peace. In the morning the windows were covered in swirls of frost and the room was full of milky light. He'd pressed his thumb against the glass, melting a hole to look out to where sheep huddled against white fields. Then he'd got back in beside her for the last time.

Daniel rubs at his cheeks. The bristles prickle like iron filings against his fingers. Memories had to be watched. Watched in case they prised the lid off things. He takes his hand from the mantelpiece and sits down again. All that had started with a log burning there in the grate. Why should a log bring that back? It made no sense at the end of the day.

But it's the beginning of the day. He remembers that. Another day. The cat rises from its sleeping place. A show of static electricity flickers along its tail. The log settles in the grate. The cat hisses at the fire. The fire spits back, but the cat turns its back to lap at a saucer of milk, drinking the full moon that has turned blue in the night. Another month. Daniel reaches out a hand and the cat's spine arches, a purr rising in its throat. Like the crosscut buzzing against the grain of a beech bole, snowing dust over his boots. His hands guiding the timber through. Each season, each year's ring of grain bisected by steel. Today he saw the first celandines huddled in the hedgerow, their bright stamp of gold putting a seal on things.

Three more ewes to lamb and he'll be through. All that newness. The first time he's lambed alone. Last year the children had been home to help. Returning to their teenage roles. Now he makes up his own sandwich and thermos of coffee. Even with his hand inside the ewe, that hot tunnel of slime and blood, tugging at the lamb's tucked-in hooves, he wondered why he was still alive. What use was he to anyone? What use to the life that was in him? It ran on, obeying its own time; it couldn't be rushed. But there he was again, joining things up that weren't really joined. Though, in a way, everything was. Everything came together in the end. Everything meant something, though you couldn't often say what or why. That was the thing. You could hardly ever say why.

Daniel knuckles his eyes. He licks salt from his palm. Sunlight glitters on a flaw in the window glass. A spider is tying the clothes rack to the door. He has to squint to see its tightrope of silk. And now the kitchen clock is chiming, cracking open another hour, another day. *Whatever you fancy, love.* The pillow's drift of linen making her hair almost invisible. Like that spider web glistening and disappearing. Suddenly, everything is hard to see.

Daniel gets up to put his plate in the sink. He sweeps his hand across the crumbs on the table, sticks the cellophane cover back over the jam jar and fumbles the elastic band over it. When he replaces it in the pantry he sees her rows of preserves. *Damson, Plum, Strawberry, Greengage, Raspberry.* Then bitter orange marmalade and a line of pickles and conserves neatly labelled in her handwriting. He remembers what it was like to eat the last loaf she had made before she died. The last loaf from the freezer. Thawing it, knowing she'd never make another. It was as if he was eating *her*. Her body and blood. The bread had blessed and choked him.

The dogs are barking, yelping at the length of their chains. Maybe they've caught scent of the fox that's been creeping around since lambing started. He hadn't had the heart to take a gun to it. Not yet at any rate. Wasn't there room enough for every creature? Every creature in its place. People could make room. Let him do his job properly that was all. Let the fox take its chance. He didn't seem to have the heart for killing anymore. But that was wrong and he knew it. You couldn't go against nature for long without making a mess of things.

It's the postman's van the dogs have seen, toiling up the dips and curves of the track, which needs another load of quarry bottoms after last April's rain. It'd felt too much at the time. Too much like going on regardless. So he'd left it for another year. Annie had died in early December. And at home, not in the hospice. He was glad of that. He'd got her home and hadn't been too proud to ask for help like his own father would've been. Like his own father was when his mother had pressed a hand to her head and gone on working at the washtub, trying not to heed the pain. When she went raving that winter in '61 they'd tied her to an armchair with sheets and lashed it to the trailer. Then they'd towed her over snowdrifts to the doctor. She hadn't lasted long after that and neither had his father, dropping dead in the shippen with the feed pails in his hands. Annie and he had moved from their rented cottage to the farmhouse. Starting out for themselves.

That had been a time of hope. Hope mixed with the grey suds of fatigue. That few months before Peter was born seemed like the happiest of all now. But maybe that was just the way things were with hindsight. Looking back was easy like that. The kids had done well. They'd got out of farming. Peter was a teacher and Kate working part-time for the insurance people. The farm was no life for young folk any more. They'd never wanted their kids to go into the farm, unlike some. Like Daniel's father had, taking his belt to him that time when he'd wanted to stay on at school. *This'll be the only school tha'll ever need, and I'll school thee!* And so it had been. The farm had been his education. So he'd not been sorry when his father dropped face-down in the muck. He'd been hard, bitter through and through, the way sloes are.

When Annie fell ill, Peter had come home with his wife, Sheila, whenever he could. Though they didn't like bringing the children towards the end. That was understandable. That smell for one thing. And by then Annie hardly knew them. There had been things to understand and they'd got through together, as a family. Kate had been able to leave her own kids and stay for a few days at the end. She was the image of her mother. He'd noticed her grey hairs as she bent over Annie to pull the draw-sheet from under her. It seemed odd to have children who were growing old. Like a wheel turning, gripping, then turning some more. Oh, it wasn't wrong. It's the way things are. To grow old, to die. But not alone, dear God, not alone. He'd never expected that.

Daniel's hand slips the door catch. He stamps his feet into his Wellingtons and goes out to meet the postman.

'Morning Daniel. It's a cold un!'

'It is! Owt fresh?'

'My patch's still clear, touch wood! They've put disinfectant traps all along the main roads. Whether they'll do owt I don't know. It's a sad do.'

'That's about time. I've not been out, mind.'

'No.'

The postman is sorting mail on his lap. Daniel scratches his head, as if talking is a new thing.

'Will you come in for a brew?'

The postman hesitates. He's a slight chap with a thick head of red hair and a coppery beard.

'I'd best not. I'll have to disinfect. And there's still snow at Henby...'

'Still? That's a rum do! It's way lower than here...'

The postman hands him a bundle of letters from the van, all junk mail. Then a small packet wrapped in brown paper and sealed with string in the old-fashioned way. Daniel doesn't know the writing. Pale blue. Should he know it? Henry puts the van into gear, still talking over his shoulder.

'It dun't get much sun over that south slope. Yesterday't track were still all drifted up, like.'

'Have they lambed yet?'

'Reckon so. Reckon they're about done. How about you?'

'Just three more ewes, then I'm finished.'

'Champion!'

The postman is turning the van, the engine puttering out a fantail of smoke.

'See you tomorrow, Daniel.'

'See you, Henry! Go easy at Henby, then.'

'Aye, I will.'

And now he's just a vague face, a hand waving from behind the tinted glass of the post van which goes down the track crookedly, a bead of blood trickling across white skin.

Daniel glances again at the handful of junk mail and dumps everything but the packet into the bin. *Things.* Everyone seems obsessed with things these days. Loans, mobile phones, clothing, cars, furniture. But he needs nothing. He's well supplied. That's what he likes to say when those chattering sales folk ring him up. *Well supplied.* It has a kind of finality for him. He'd want for nothing, thank you. It was like a different language. A language from another world drifting into the headsets of the telesales centres. A few of them chat to him for the quaintness of his language, for the old-fashioned flavour of his voice, the taste of a world that lies somewhere beyond theirs. Above theirs, Daniel would say. Not just beyond. His world is up here where the Siberian wind comes to die in moorland grasses, between grouse butts and the harried fleeces of his sheep. He'll want for nothing.

At the kitchen table, Daniel takes up a knife. It's a thin, carbon-steel blade, sharpened a thousand times so that it curves inward. Annie's doing. Sharpening it with that flick of her wrist. The way she mixed a pudding or a cake. He cuts through the string and throws it into the fire, watching the sealing wax sweat, then melt and sputter into blue flames. That faint drift of incense. Now he tears away the paper and the Sellotape until he's holding a small envelope. There's something hard and round inside. It's wrapped in ridged cardboard, so it feels like he's rubbing his thumb across a kitten's ribs.

Inside is a letter from his sister in Filey. Effie. Effie who married a trawlerman when she was still only eighteen. She'd left home even before that, working in some nursing home on the east coast. Just a few words on a scrap of paper. *This is mother's ring. I want you to have it.* And more about her illness, about bearing up. His mother's ring. Why had she done that, now? What does he want with a ring? Daniel sees Effie swinging from the farm gate in her pigtails, climbing the rope in the pear tree, her knees grazed and dirty. He sees her in a cream marriage gown, holding her husband's hand. The husband who had even less to say than Daniel. They'd stood awkwardly at the wedding, cupping pints of bitter in their fists, munching sausage rolls. Annie had been pregnant with Peter then. He'd felt proud. Substantial in his gifts. Wanting for nothing.

But he'd hardly seen his sister since, and anyway, she was an old woman now, not the girl he'd chased across the shaven meadows at hay time. The plain gold ring had worn thin from his mother's work, then thinner from the years of his sister's life. It sits snug on his little finger, tight above the swollen knuckle that he's snagged on gates and walling stone and fencing wire. His little sister, grown old now. Poor Effie. The thought is like a gasp of pain, like the memory of Annie when she was young. A thought he couldn't bear now. The smell of her hair which he'd slept and breathed in. The taste of sun on her skin when they'd put the farm to rest for the night and made love in the bed his parents had shared.

Daniel places the ring on the table with the crumpled letter, staring out to the orchard. The sun is touching the branches of damson and apple trees. Making them glow, making them exist. It's the light of a new day.

Daniel leaves the house and walks to the shippen. He pours out feed for his cattle, checking their feet for sores, their mouths for blisters. He brings logs to the house, washes down the tractor and goes out into the fields to check the sheep. One of the ewes has lambed in the night. A single, sickly little tup that staggers awkwardly, trailing its thread of umbilical cord, bleating after its mother. Daniel steadies the wriggling little thing between his knees, rapping it sharply between the eyes with his fist. When it connects, he feels the lamb shrink back into his hand. Then something seems to clear and it finds its legs, scuttling under its mother to drag at her teats. His father had shown him that trick, though the vet might have something to say about it these days. The unlambed ewes are swollen and clumsy on the fell. All around him the fields are loud with new life. The sun is looming above the horizon, behind clouds tinged with orange and apricot.

By afternoon the wind is strengthening from the east. This is the wind of knives. The Russian wind that flays flesh from bone. He's already listened to the weather forecast over a corned-beef sandwich with pickles and a mug of tea at lunchtime. There'll be worse to come. And there'd been another foot-and-mouth cluster near Longtown. It's getting closer. Like in the sixties when they'd closed down the farm. The disease had spared them that time. You'd think this time the Ministry would stamp it out. But these days all sorts of rubbish went into the feed. Cattle and sheep were being carted from one end of the country to another to be sold or slaughtered. Mostly they were worth nothing, or next to it.

Now he's out again, wrapped up in a trench coat and balaclava, making sure that ice is broken on the water tubs, checking the sheep licks, watching the ewes. When he gets back to the Land Rover, it's almost dark. He doesn't know where the day has gone. But he's kept busy. Kept on top of things. He starts the engine and lets it grumble for a moment, staring at the dim fascia. Then he drives back to the farmhouse, silencing the dogs with a yell of mock anger at the gate. With a little grunt of surprise, he finds the house empty, the fire almost out.

Daniel rouses the embers, banking up the fire with coal. He throws on a log and presses it home. The smell of sulphur stings his nostrils. The chimney needs sweeping. He opens a tin of cat food and shakes it into a dish. The golden jelly is appetising and the cat nuzzles his hand. Stripping off his overalls, Daniel washes himself at the kitchen sink. Then he opens a tinned meat pie and puts it in the Aga, boiling a few potatoes and brewing a pot of tea to see it down. The wind rushes up to the windows and turns away in little shrieks and howls. The wind's company for a lonely man. That was the saying. Daniel picks up an old *Farmer's Weekly*, meaning to catch up on an article about feed supplements. But he's mislaid his reading glasses and can't be bothered to find them. What the farm will yield hardly concerns him now. It's like hay and silage: he'll do what serves *him* best, not the bank manager.

He sits, watching the fire rouse itself, gazing towards the blank television screen, waiting until it's time for the news. News of the world beyond this world. It's hardly real, all that, but it's there. And he's part of it, somewhere. This farm a tiny bleb on the turning world. Indiscernible in all the blackness of space. A needlepoint of light to be swallowed up in time. A part of everything and nothing. Daniel dozes off, then wakes with a jerk. Again that little grunt of astonishment. Opposite him is Annie's empty chair. Apart from the sleeping cat, apart from the wind, he's alone. The dogs are restless again, yapping at the night. He dozes, letting the bluster of wind fade.

What wakes him is the full-blooded baying of the dogs. Beyond that, the bleating of sheep. It's an agitated tumult, a sound beyond the usual call and answer of ewe to lamb. The cat is prowling at the windowsill, its tail flicking, fur brindled all the way down its spine. Daniel rubs his forehead. The skin of his hands is dry; his nails are chipped and roughly cut. He rises from the chair and struggles into his overcoat. The longer he sits these days the stiffer he gets. His knees are cold despite the fire. It's a draughty old place, the doors sagging on their hinges to let in the freezing air. He puts his feet into his Wellington boots and feels the cold gulp at them.

Unlocking the gun cabinet, he takes out the twelve-bore and a handful of cartridges. He buttons his coat, breaks the gun, loads both barrels then drapes it over his arm, just as his father taught him.

When he steps from the house, the wind has dropped. There's a brilliant crescent moon, as if the full moon was pressed against a horn-shaped slit in the sky. He passes the dogs straining at their chains. He doesn't speak or comfort them. The fox knows they are chained, that he is free and they are slaves. And the dogs know it too, savage in their servility.

Daniel clumps off down the path towards the field where he's been lambing. He tries to put his numbed feet down lightly. The air is searingly cold. Patches of wool are scattered on the grass. All around him, the clamour of lambs calling to their mothers, the peremptory *baa* of mothers calling back. Wind gusts towards the house from the field, taking his scent away from where he's sure the fox must be. If he was a fox, he'd work the bottom end of the field where it dips away down the fell. Here a stray lamb is easier to pick off, unsteady as it struggles up the slope. He'd found their bodies there in the past, their throats gored, intestines dragged out. It was a waste – and that's one thing he could never bear.

Daniel treads downhill, keeping the wall between him and the field. A footpath crosses his land a little lower down. When he reaches the stile, he climbs over into the field and sits on the bottom step, facing the commotion of bleating ghosts. Gently, he closes up the gun and lays it across his knees. The click of the catch is satisfying. He strains to see into the gloom, where he knows the fox must be moving. The merest rumour of a shadow. Rippling close to the wall. Slipping through the history of its race. Its purpose to kill, that's all. To kill and then to die. Maybe to find a vixen then leave her to rear his cubs. It could know nothing more. Lurking at the edge of human affairs, to take what it could find. Winning a life from the flock, then dissolving back into the dark, the taste and lust of blood in its jaws.

Daniel must have dozed off, despite the cold. What wakes him is a snowflake drifting into his face. He opens his eyes to find the moon gone, the temperature a few degrees higher, snow thickening the night around him. The sheep are quieter now, recognising the deeper, wholesale threat of snow. A fox is a fox, but snow is a wolf pack. They have that memory in them, behind their vacant, urine-coloured eyes. Now they stumble into a rough line against the far wall of the field, marshalling their lambs. The pregnant ewes stumble awkwardly, shaking their tails, falling to their knees.

Snow has made the fox bold. From the corner of his eye, Daniel sees it haunching across the middle of the field. It moves belly-low like a dog rounding up its flock. There is snow on the gun. Daniel wipes it away with his cuff and raises the twin barrels slowly. The fox is twenty yards away. It hasn't scented him yet. Fire, sweat, soap and gun oil: the stink of man. But the wind is taking the message away, shredding it over the fell. The stock nudges Daniel's shoulder. He lines up the bead. The fox turns. It has heard something. Perhaps the swish of the gun against his coat. It sweeps its brush beside its legs then points its face towards the man on the stile. Now that stare: frozen across the centuries, the fox's eyes hewn from ice.

Snow comes down between them in small, rapid flakes. Twenty yards of snow between man and fox. Daniel thinks of the dogs in the yard, easily quelled by his voice. This fox is beautiful and still free. A rebel, a refugee, a doomed renegade at winter's frontier with spring.

The fields are turning white. Snow falls like sifted flour, faintly reflecting the moonlight that is stifled now behind clouds. In that moment Daniel sees the uncut pear tree, the rope swing tossed aside. Effie laughing with her front teeth not yet grown back. Then white sheets. Annie's imprint on the bed when they took her away from a room with frosted windows.

The gun barks and snaps into his shoulder. The fox is leaping in the snow, lashing the whole length of its body as if pinned to the ground by its tail. The shot has torn open its shoulder to the bone. The flock sets up a tremendous bleating, scattering from the shelter of the wall. The second shot takes the fox full in the face and it lies down, its paws threshing snow.

Daniel walks to where it lies, almost slipping down the slope as he goes. Snow creaks under his rubber boots. He picks the creature up by its brush. It's a dog fox and its body is surprisingly heavy. Then that smell of fox, rank and sharp and feral. Bloody foam has already spread across its muzzle. Its eyes are dim, glaucous in death. Daniel climbs back over the stile awkwardly, the gun in one hand, the fox dangling from the other. He trails the corpse as he goes. Snow is driving strongly now. He can only just make out the farm-house lights. A trail of blood falls into his footprints. They'll freeze overnight and he'll find his own trail in the morning, strewn with smudged scarlet flowers.

At the yard gate, the dogs go wild at the scent of fox. Daniel ignores their row. He takes the corpse into the kitchen. The cat hisses under his feet and flees. Daniel stands the shotgun in a corner and, with one hand, spreads an old newspaper on the armchair opposite his. He lays the fox in it. Its ruined face, its rictus snarl looking towards the door as if expecting a visitor.

The fire has burned low. Daniel drops on another log and sparks shoot towards the hearth. He slips off his Wellingtons and stands them at the back door, in readiness. Two ewes have still to lamb. He puts his hands into his coat pocket to find the unfired cartridges, weighing them in his hand. They're dry and papery, their brass percussion caps cold to the touch. That touch of ice, numbing everything. There is something perfect about their weight and proportion. He empties the breech and throws the spent casings on the fire. Then he locks the gun and the spare cartridges away. They shan't tempt him again.

Only then does he ease himself into his own armchair opposite the fox. The room is warm after the fells. The fire is catching. Daniel takes his mother's ring from the table and slips it onto his swollen finger. His cheeks burn. He needs that shave. Tomorrow, maybe. He's tired now. His eyelids droop towards sleep.

The meadows are shorn of hay, burned to bronze stubble. A rope pulls taut on the pear tree under a girl's weight. Effie's hair is haloed in the sun of a summer fifty years gone by. The lightning bolt has not yet split the tree. Sap rises in its leaves each spring to make them green. To make the tree blossom and bear a few half-ripe pears. That's what Annie's breasts had reminded him of the first time he'd covered them with his hands. There'd been no honeymoon. Just an afternoon's work. Then entering the bedroom, tired and expectant. Pine boards creaking under his heels. His arms glowing from sun and a cold-water wash. Annie watching him from her pillow, smiling with dark eyes.

Now Annie turns the colour of smoke. Her white hair flows through his fingers. Snowflakes slide down the window. Darkness presses against the electric light inside. The dogs are silent, though sheep still bleat from the fells. The fox gazes towards the door.

When Daniel wakes, he holds up his hand to stare at Effie's ring. Wind is sucking at the chimney. It stirs up ash, kindling a glow from the hollowed log. The fox's blood has dried across his knuckles. He leans forward to touch its coat, stifling a yawn.

Ducklings

Lucy's mother was working at the kitchen table, pulling the bad leaves from a lettuce. From where she sat in the living room Lucy could see her standing in a pool of sunlight. Her strong brown calves and ankles stood up firmly from open-toed sandals. Lucy looked down at her own slender, white legs. Her mother went brown so easily. It was vexing. Like the way she so deftly pulled the leaves from the lettuce and shouted over her shoulder.

'Do we really need the television on in this weather? Can't you play outside?'

Lucy glanced at the screen. The television was on and she'd drawn down the blinds so that the colours showed up better. But she wasn't really watching. It was a children's programme anyway, one she felt too old for. She leaned forwards to switch it off and then went to open the blinds.

The light struck at her eyes, cascading across the surface of the boating lake. They lived very close to the park and she was used to seeing couples sprawling on the grass with transistor radios, joggers with Walkmans, or solitary men walking their dogs. Lucy whispered the words of the television commercial. So silly that it was mesmerising.

Now you know there's a better way to feed your dog!

She looked through into the kitchen again, frowning at her mother's calves.

A young starling flew down in front of the lounge window and startled her for a second by clawing at the glass.

'Wouldn't you like to go round to Anna's or something?'

Her mother's voice came over the sound of the lettuce being sluiced in the sink. Everything had to be brisk, smart, efficient. Like her little Ford Fiesta that she went health visiting in, parked right there in the driveway.

'Anna's on holiday, remember?'

'Oh yes, where did you say she'd gone?'

Lucy knew very well that her mother hadn't forgotten.

'I told you, Russia.'

'Ah, yes.'

Her mother sounded disapproving and bored at the same time. She always managed to turn the tables on you somehow.

'So what are you going to do today?'

An edge of annoyance was creeping in to sharpen her voice. Lucy wandered into the kitchen and took a cherry from the fruit bowl, biting it around the stone.

'Uhm, I don't know.'

Her mother put down the colander with a sharp rap.

'For heaven's sake, Lucy, you're fourteen years old! Why on earth can't you occupy yourself with something?'

'What's the matter?'

'The matter? Nothing's the matter, it's just that you're so... languid.'

'Languid?'

Lucy was at her most provocative. Her mother snatched up a knife and began slicing it through the stems of rhubarb that lay on the chopping board. There was silence between them for a few seconds, just the rap, rap, rap of the knife and the little scrunch as her mother pressed on, sliding the blade to sever the fibrous skin. Everything about her was brisk and organised.

Lucy took another cherry, slowly and deliberately.

'When's Daddy coming home?'

Rap, rap, rap went the knife.

'When's Daddy coming home?'

She repeated it slowly as if her mother was deaf. She watched her stop chopping and straighten up.

'I don't know, tomorrow sometime.'

'Tomorrow?'

Lucy said the word as if she'd never heard it before. She knew by the way that her mother turned back to the board and crunched the knife through the rhubarb stems that she'd touched her on the raw.

'Where's he gone?'

'Where's who gone, dear?'

Lucy opened the pedal bin with her foot and spat the cherry stone in.

'Daddy, of course!'

'Oh, he's at a conference. About allergies.'

Her mother lifted the rhubarb into another colander – it matched the one that held the lettuce – and rinsed it under the tap. For a moment the water coming through was stained pink from the skins. Lucy's father was Dr Ainsley and they lived in a large house near the park. Her mother was the health visitor at the local Health Centre. The household was run with medical precision.

Lucy ran her finger across the working surface. She was bored. Her mother began to untie her kitchen apron and put on a housecoat. Lucy moved towards the door, anticipating a request for help. She was too late.

'Would you like to dust the lounge?'

'I was just going out.'

'Were you? It didn't look like it to me. Come on, it won't take you long.'

Lucy refused to put on an apron just to dust the lounge. She flicked the duster over the cocktail cabinet, her father's cricket trophies, the ghastly wedding photograph and the one she hated of herself in school uniform. She flicked three dead flies off the windowsill and onto the thick pile carpet. It gave her a secret pleasure to do the job badly, knowing how her mother wouldn't settle until she had personally dusted the whole room again.

She threw the duster onto the kitchen table and shouted up the stairs where her mother was busy in the bathroom.

'I'm going out now.'

'That was quick!'

Lucy didn't answer. She loved the insolence in her own silence.

'Ok, have a nice time!'

Her mother's voice was bright with relief. Lucy slammed the front door, slouching down the driveway to annoy her, just in case she might be watching from an upstairs window.

It was much hotter outside the house. Lucy undid another button of her blouse. When she looked down she could see where her small breasts were gathering into the bra. They were coming on. Her mother, of course, had firm, full breasts that jutted out smartly from her uniform.

Lucy crossed the busy main road that separated the house from the park and went through a gap in the green metal railings. The lake looked cool and peaceful. She picked her way through the couples on the grass. Snatches of dance music wavered in the steamy air. There was a path all the way round the lake, leading through thick stands of rhododendrons. Lucy walked slowly, feeling the sun on her hair and neck. She wondered what Russia would be like and envied Anna. Would it be summer there or winter? She couldn't remember. She decided that it would be summer and swelteringly hot and Anna would be in a troika galloping through the dust of the steppes.

Lucy stopped in a little arbour of rhododendrons that sheltered her from view. She went down to the edge of the lake and crouched down, idly flicking a handful of dust and gravel into the water. A family of mallards, one duck and five ducklings, sailed out from under the overhanging branches to investigate. They pecked at the dust on the water.

'Stupid things!'

Lucy threw another handful of dust and the ducks gathered around it in a flurry, darting and pecking. In the sunlight the ducklings looked like golden catkins dusted with brown pollen. There was a little beach at the water's edge and she threw down a handful of tiny stones there. The mother duck kept her distance but two of the ducklings came closer. Lucy watched them. It was fascinating, the way they had such trust. It might be possible to lure one of the ducklings from the water. She began to trail dust and gravel from her hands, pretending that it was food. The ducklings paddled closer. It was too easy. Soon one of them had ventured from the water and was pecking within a few inches of her hand. The down on its body was like stained fibres of cotton wool.

Lucy leaned forward, taking care that her shadow didn't fall on the duckling. Very slowly she moved her hand over it and made a little grab. She gathered it up, clumsy, struggling, folding the stubby little wings under her fingers. Beneath the fine plumage she could feel its bones, its weird heat. She held it firmly and rolled her hand over to examine it from all sides.

It tried to break free and she had to keep pushing the useless wings back under her fingers. Its life throbbed in her hands, so different from her own, so inexplicable. It was a small machine of feather and muscle, its heart ticking away, its eyes flicking under a pale membrane.

Shuffling close to the edge of the water, Lucy placed the duckling's feet just below the surface. It struggled in her hand again: it was an odd feeling. She pushed her hand slowly under the water and pulled it out again. Water ran off the downy fur, globing into little droplets like mercury. The mother duck swam around, unconcerned, only a few feet away. Lucy pushed the duckling under the water, testing its buoyancy. She pulled it out and then gently pushed it under again, holding it there until its struggles weakened and it fell still in her hand. She brought it out and laid it on the beach.

Two thin rivulets of water ran out from the nostril holes in its beak. It twitched its webbed feet feebly a few times. The sun seemed to evaporate its remaining energy and it began to die, a milky film coagulating over each eye. Lucy watched it, engrossed, as its life ebbed away. Now that it was dead she was afraid to handle it. It had become taboo, an untouchable. She scuffled the little body with her feet so that it rolled over and picked up a coating of dust, pushing it back into the shadows of the rhododendrons.

Crouching under the low branches, Lucy scooped out a little grave from the gravel and decaying leaves and laid the duckling in it. She built a mound over it then fetched some pink blossoms of rhododendron which she laid across the grave. She wanted to cry, scared now, the dead duckling hidden in the earth below her feet. She felt a sudden outburst of love for the creature that only minutes before had been almost incandescent with life. Its mother swam around so stupidly, losing her children and not caring.

Lucy cried in stuttering sobs, swirling her fingertips in the dust in little panicky movements. Then, suddenly, she stopped. She flung the flowers away from the grave and stamped the earth flat so that there was no visible mound. Then she scuffed dust and leaves over it until it was almost indistinguishable from the surrounding earth.

Lucy went and washed her hands in the lake; her fingernails were black crescents, packed with soil. She took out a handkerchief and blew her nose thoroughly. No one must notice that she had been crying. Then she set off for home, threading her way through the people who still lay on the grass, unconcerned. She felt slightly breathless, her heart beating close to the surface of her chest. What if they all knew what she had done? She imagined a secret observer. Someone who had watched her drown and then bury the duckling. She even thought up a story in her defence: how she had found the duckling and realised it was sick and had tried to revive it in the water. It was no good. She had drowned it, killed it, kidnapped it from its mother and shut off its life.

When she got back to the house everything was spotless, every cushion plumped and tidied, no trace of dust on the glass-topped coffee table. There was a note from her mother to say that she had gone shopping and would be back by one o'clock. Lucy glanced at her watch. A whole hour to go. She searched inside her head for something to do, something that would please her mother. But the house was hermetic, organised, sealed up in itself.

Sitting in the lounge, Lucy watched thousands of dust motes glitter in a shaft of sunlight. They turned just as planets turned in the emptiness of space. The tight feeling was there again in her chest. She got up, drew the blinds to keep the sun off the Indian rug, then went into the kitchen to set the table. The telephone rang but she was afraid to answer it. She let it ring, on and on, rapping down the knives and forks to shut out the noise. At last she could bear it no longer and picked up the handset just in time to hear the other receiver being replaced. The line clicked. A steady buzzing set in like tinnitus. Lucy stood there for a long time, holding the telephone, waiting, imagining her father's voice.

The Caretaker

Mary held the child as he was sick into the bath. She felt his ribs convulse. A gush of vomit splashed onto the enamel. He struggled to spit out thick dribbles of saliva and his hair was damp with fever. Mary reached beyond him to turn on the taps. Water swirled into the vomit, its smell sweet and sour and cloying. She almost retched.

'Alright now darling? Alright?'

Mark nodded dumbly, pale faced, unable to talk. Mary gave him a drink with her cupped hands. She massaged his neck.

'Don't swallow, just spit out.'

Mark did as he was told and she wiped his face with a damp flannel. There were faint shadows under his eyes and his skin seemed thin, almost opaque. She led him back to the bed, tucking him in with a light kiss on the forehead as he snuggled down. He was seven years old and only two weeks from his next birthday.

'Try and sleep now, darling. Ok?'

Again the weary nod and the slow drift into unconsciousness from a child who had been ill for days. She stood for a moment watching him. There was a time when he had been carefree, childish. When was it? It couldn't have been long ago, but it seemed so.

Mary went back to the bathroom where she had left the tap running and squirted a thick green liquid into the bath. She couldn't afford to get sick herself. The smell of bile and pine disinfectant was nauseating. There was a throbbing in her head. When she'd finished cleaning the bath she washed her hands then went to the bedroom and looked in at her son. He was drowsing in ragged little snores, shifting under the sheets. One hand lay next to his head, clenching and unclenching. He was dreaming some deep, feverish dream.

Mary walked out to the living room and stood at the large window. Theirs was a fifth-floor flat, one third of the way up the building. She looked down onto the rectangle of grass below, only millimetres of glass separating her from the fall. The road flowed down the hill towards the shopping centre. All the streets there were named after poets for some reason: Wordsworth Street, Keats Street, Milton Street, Browning Street. The lights were still on in the florists, showing a window display of white and yellow flowers. It was getting close to Valentine's Day. It made her want to smash something. Cars went by, cutting through slush. It was beginning to freeze again. The snow on the grass had been scuffed into heaps, leaving green scars.

The sun had dropped down behind the fields and the ink blot of woods beyond the town. The grey mass of steel mills to the north stood smokeless, silent with an eerie vigilance. Gulls steered past the window, stooping onto a paper bag that had been thrown on the grass. The first schoolchildren were beginning to make their way up the hill towards the flats and the streets that radiated from the tower block. Mark was in the third year of junior school now. Normally, he would have been one of them. Mary put out a hand and touched the window ledge. It was made of plastic, not wood. Some polymer, transformed from coal or oil. It had once been a forest. You had to remember that. She moved away from the window.

The whole flat stank of vomit and disinfectant. She had turned down the heating, but still it was too hot. It was claustrophobic. Mary fished her mobile phone out of her handbag and tried to switch it on. Dead. She'd lost the charger a few days ago, though where and how, she'd no idea. She'd turned the flat upside down, but to no avail. Now she needed to go down to the telephone in the foyer but dared not leave the boy. She waited, listening to him stir in the next room. Her neighbours began to arrive home from work. She could hear faint bass lines start up, then voices and theme music as the evening news was switched on in surrounding apartments.

It had appalled her at first, living here in the middle of a tower block with people above and below her, people on all sides. It was a hive, a matrix. Fifteen floors and four flats on each floor. Sixty apartments. But behind the maths were human lives, families. Each evening, she thought of all those minds falling into sleep, surrendering their consciousness. Then all those dreams and desires ascending to the night. Mary had taken the flat out of desperation to get away and because it was close to Mark's school. She still had to face the other mothers and what they knew. They couldn't stay here. Not much longer. In the end, they'd need help to get away. They'd need Des.

Mary went into the bedroom again and touched her hand to Mark's forehead. It seemed cooler and his snores had taken on a more regular rhythm. His eyelids were closed up like white petals. Back in the living room she paced up and down, occasionally putting up a hand to scrape back the strands of hair that had escaped from her ponytail. In each ear she wore a thin spike of jade. Her eyes were a light brown, almost amber. She stared at the crimson sunset, at lights emerging street by street. They defined the town against the coming darkness. Pulling her head from the glass she left the room and shrugged on her coat. The door of the flat clicked behind her. She went to the lift, pressing the button to bring it down. Nothing happened. There was a faint smell of washing powder out here on the landing and the air was cold. The display of lights told her that the lift was at the eighth floor. She tried again. Nothing.

For a moment she was unsure, turning back towards the flat. Then she turned again and was pelting down the stairs, pursued by a cascade of echoing footsteps.

Mary arrived in the foyer breathless and dizzy. Thank God there was no one on the phone. She went across to the booth and dialled the number. Her breath was harsh in the earpiece. From far away she heard the sleek, self-satisfied purring of his telephone. The booth smelled of stale cigarette smoke. The ringing went on and on. Then the receiver was lifted up and a man's voice spoke, faintly.

'Hello?'

Mary pushed a fifty-pence piece into the slot, pressing the receiver to her ear.

'Des?'

'Yes?'

'Is that Desmond?'

'Yes. Who's speaking please? This line's really bad, I can hardly hear…'

The man's voice was hesitant, unwilling, lost in static.

'Des, it's Mary, don't hang up, please, listen.'

There was a short silence. Her heart was sucking the air out of her chest.

'Is it about Mark? Is he alright? If he's…'

'Oh he's been ill, but it's not that. It's not that…'

Then the line clicked and burred, cutting her off. Mary let out a spurt of breath and half turned. She daren't try again. Shit!

The caretaker emerged from his office next to the entrance to the flats. He was wearing black tracksuit bottoms and a rugby shirt with green horizontal stripes, open at the neck where a tuft of blond hair showed. Then his hand was on her arm, his other hand firm in the small of her back. He took the receiver from her and replaced it.

'Mrs Linton.'

The voice was soft, courteous, tinged by a north-east accent that could almost have been Scandinavian.

'Steve! I can't use my mobile, so…'

The man shook his head gently and smiled, showing the tips of perfect teeth.

'That line's faulty. I've been trying to get it seen to. Anyway, what about the boy?'

He took her arm and led her back towards the lift, always considerate.

'I'll let you know when it's repaired. I promise.'

Mary didn't struggle. He was a short man, but stocky, and yet so light on his feet that he seemed to appear from nowhere.

They waited side by side as the lift came down. The lights flashed: *four, three, two, one, ground.* There was a rattle and a bump and the doors opened. The caretaker got into the lift with her. Mary caught sight of her face in the mirror. It was like looking at another woman. A woman that she'd been translated into. She looked at her expression, at the language of her face, but couldn't tell what it was trying to say. The caretaker spoke, making her start.

'How's the boy? Better?'

There was an insinuation in his speech. Always something else behind what he said.

'A bit, but his father should see him.'

Again that gentle shake of the head, almost imperceptible. The lift reached the fifth floor and the doors opened with a faint hiss. The caretaker propelled her carefully into the corridor and pushed open the door of her flat.

'I'll be up at six with some shopping for you. Are you hungry?'

Hungry? She was hungry. It surprised her. Mary nodded.

'Look after the boy!'

With a half-salute and a faint smile he was back in the lift. Its light glistened on his thin blond hair. She saw his head from three sides in the mirrored walls, like a hologram or an exhibit in a museum. She shouldn't have told him anything. But she had.

The lift doors closed in a thud of rubber. Mary went into the flat and locked the door behind her. God, that smell! She paused to listen. All was quiet. Mark had not woken to find her gone. Mary was thankful for that. She went into the bedroom to check and he was sleeping peacefully, his hair plastered down where she had mopped his forehead. She half closed the door and went back to the living room, resuming her circling. Des had no way of calling her back now that her mobile was out of use. Des, the middle manager with his important career. Des, like a small boy let loose, all impulse and regret, oblivious to the hurt he was causing, to their intimacy ebbing away. In the end she could hardly bear to be near him. Especially in bed when he went to sleep at once – or pretended to – and snuffled into the pillow, unaware of everything that was leaking away from their lives. Until the leak became a flood.

They'd been married for nine years. She'd had her suspicions about other women from time to time. Usually when he harped on a woman's name or enthused about a new female colleague. She'd told herself that she was being silly. Things had drifted a bit on the physical side after Mark had been born, but she knew that wasn't unusual. They just needed a bit of time after the nappies and sleepless nights. But that time never really came. Years had passed with only the rarest acts of love. And afterwards he'd seemed almost sheepish, as if ashamed he'd let go with her, or told her he loved her. Somehow Mary thought this was normal, that it would get better, that it would change with time. That way people spent their whole lives hoping for more, when what they have is all there is. And, after all, she had Mark. She also had a degree in chemistry and a teaching certificate and she wanted to work again. One day.

Then Des had started to spend a lot of time on his laptop in the evenings, hunched in the spare bedroom after work. He was often late home. He missed meals. And he'd suddenly become more considerate, even solicitous. There were cups of tea in bed in the morning and he'd drop Mark off at school when she had her period and felt wretched. That made her wonder. She even thought he might be ill and keeping it from her. But Des wasn't the heroic type. When she asked him if everything was ok he just nodded, dropping a dry kiss on her forehead.

Then he'd given her his computer password over the phone so she could forward a file to him at work. Something he'd forgotten, something that couldn't wait. Mary was curious and it didn't feel wrong to look. She found a mail folder marked 'Charm' and in it were dozens of emails from Des to another woman. And dozens back. She wasn't even surprised.

What made her angry, apart from the betrayal, was how bloody stupid he was. The messages were pretty cringe-making and didn't leave much to the imagination. Here it was: the who, the what, and the where. She could imagine the how, but not the why. Never the why, because she'd always hoped. Now she'd simply run out of forgiveness and understanding, remembering all the nights she'd lain there next to him, wanting to be touched. To be held. To be loved in a simple way. But simple things were always the hardest.

Mary saw herself reflected in the window. A ghost super-imposed on the darkening town. She felt like a haunting, not a real person, but something made of ash. A residue. Afterlife rather than life itself. Then she remembered Mark asleep in the next room and felt the tug of love. Des would be missing him. He was probably still angry with her after what she'd done, though he'd never stayed angry for long.

'Charm' was Charlotte Hamilton, an old school friend of Mary's. Someone Des only knew because of her. Because they'd been introduced at a party when they'd all had too much to drink. *Des, this is Charlotte. We were at school together.* And Charlotte giggling with her chalky teeth, making big eyes and pulling her top down over her breasts, pretending to be more drunk than she really was. Somehow they'd connected. And they'd carried on connecting. She'd called him *Taser* in the emails. Which must have been code for something. It wasn't hard to guess. Mary hadn't even been granted the minimum consideration of her husband making love to a stranger. All their friends were bound to know about it in the end. The women who waited for their children at the school gates at four o'clock each afternoon. The women who asked how she was and touched her arm. He hadn't even tried to deny it when she forwarded one of Charlotte's emails to him. But then, how could he?

Mary stood at the window, watching traffic negotiate the freezing snow. Watching the closure of the night. She'd grow old like this. Alone. Time had slipped away from her somehow. She was losing track of so many things. Except memory, which could still cut her with its cruelties. She thought about Des more and more, when that should have been less and less. He was the kind of man who went bald young and still looked good. A crooked grin and close-set ears. Slightly hooded eyes and heavy brows had made him seem thoughtful. He liked to play five-a-side football and have a pint with his mates afterwards. Which wasn't asking much, except that it rarely stopped there. He'd been a bit of a Jack-the-lad in his day. Women liked him for some reason. Why on earth that had attracted her she couldn't remember. Perhaps because he was so different from her father. They'd never got on, of course. He was dad's idea of a waster. Things had come too easy. Des had a Saab convertible when Mary met him, but that had to go after they got married and Mark was born. He'd never really settled down to a Vauxhall saloon and a semi-detached house on a new estate with a lawn to cut and a rockery and the Neighbourhood Watch twitching their curtains whenever they came or went. But then neither had she.

When she'd read those emails and found out about Charlotte – Charlotte Hamilton, of all the stupid, gormless women he had to fuck! – Des had brought her white lilies and asked for forgiveness, crying like a little boy, saying how much he loved her. The flowers had seemed shameless, like exposed pudenda. Their hypocritical whiteness and their faint scent of corruption set off a deep rage in Mary. She'd made up her mind there and then, stuffing the flowers head first into the swing bin in their kitchen. Mark had watched them, wide-eyed. Des took to the spare room, sleeping on the fold-down bed and adopting a bewildered expression whenever they passed in the hallway or she found him waiting for the bathroom in the morning as she hurried to get Mark ready for school.

Before she left, she took a pair of pinking shears and cut the arms from every shirt and every suit jacket in his wardrobe. Then she paired up all his beautiful shoes and recycled them into the Help Africa bin at Oxfam. It was a vulgar cliché – like the emails she'd read – but deeply satisfying. Like writing *Taser* across the bathroom mirror in lipstick then slashing a line through it. Just one small act of revenge that stood for everything that was too huge to heave into words. There was sweetness in it, just as the proverb said.

Mary had already found the furnished flat. She'd packed her clothes and Mark's and a few toys and moved there in a taxi. Then she'd met Mark from school and taken another direction home. She'd led him away to another life, answering all his questions calmly. She'd explained most things. Not everything, of course. And that had felt good, fuelled by the purest rage. But now Mark was sick and there was this other thing. She didn't feel strong any more. Not even anger could last for ever. Not even the satisfaction of revenge, which had just diminished her in the end.

It was almost dark outside. The whole town had lit up into interlocking patterns of lights. Meaningless patterns. And a meaningless thought – as if they could have a purpose or ought to have. Whatever had made her think that? No wonder she was beginning to feel trapped. She'd sent Des the address on a strip of paper. No message. Because after all he was Mark's father. But in two weeks he hadn't been in touch. Not unless there were messages on her mobile that she couldn't retrieve. Today was the first time they'd had any contact. The first time she'd heard his voice. She wondered if he was still seeing Charlotte.

The sunset was extinguishing behind a bank of cloud. It resembled a burning slagheap. Mary couldn't get the other man out of her mind. The pale hair on the back of his hands. Hands that had held her, or rather steered her. His blunt features and cleft chin, his green eyes, his teeth glinting. The way his shoulders tapered to a thick waist and muscular legs. They'd had a nodding acquaintance until that afternoon in the Byron precinct. She'd picked Mark up from school and was heading home when some lads on skateboards had surrounded them. They'd found it funny to circle them, make them huddle against the precinct wall, performing their stupid stunts and laughing.

Then Steve, the caretaker, had appeared. He'd hardly spoken. It was as if the lads recognised him or knew him by reputation. Somehow he'd drawn them into a circle and whatever he'd said or done had sent the lads grovelling to apologise. She'd seen him take the ringleader in his hoodie to one side, gripping his arm above the elbow. The boy had seemed scared. Then the caretaker had walked her home, polite to a fault, solicitous, helpful. He'd called by the day after to see if she was ok, and then the day after that. Then he'd had to check the fuse box or repair the intercom and Mary had offered him a cup of tea. One day, he'd played chess with Mark, as if remembering the moves from childhood. After that, he seemed possessed of some indelible loyalty. Now Mary didn't know what to do. She rose to draw the curtains. It was five-thirty and soon he'd be here again, asking about the boy. Enquiring in his low, insinuating voice. Touching her arm in the way that made her afraid.

Mary went into the kitchen and reached above the gas

cooker for a box of matches. She took a packet of cigarettes from the back of the cupboard and lit one, switching on the kitchen ventilator. Thin strands of smoke swirled and were sucked out through its plastic visor into the night. Cars went by outside, changing gear as they took on the hill where slush was freezing to the road. She threw her cigarette butt into the sink and turned on the waste shredder. The noise was sudden, shocking, a harsh metallic outburst. How easily the blades might take in a hand or arm. It was hard not to imagine that. Faint footsteps went into the flat above. Then a voice on the radio. Somebody had come home. She wouldn't know them. She hardly knew anybody.

It was days since she'd left the flats. In fact it was hard to remember exactly when. Mary went back to the living room and stared out through a gap in the curtains. From the road, headlights flashed up against the windows. The layer of slush had frozen hard. Now and again a car would skid on its way down the hill, veering into the kerb or towards the centre of the road. From behind, a whimper warned her that Mark was about to wake. She took a glass of water from the kitchen and went to him. He was sitting up in bed, rubbing his eyes against the light. Mary offered him the drink. His lips were parched and flaking. The boy took the glass and drank in little self-absorbed gulps.

'Is that better, darling?'

He nodded. His brown eyes seemed huge. They were hooded with drowsiness.

'Try and sleep again, hey?'

He nodded again and she tucked him in, kissing his temple, placing the bedside lamp on the floor to dim the light. There was a soft knocking on the door. She caught her breath, looking down at her son. He didn't seem to have heard. He was sinking back into sleep.

From the corridor Mary could see the outline of a figure waiting outside. Shadowy behind the reinforced glass. It was the way he looked behind the glass door of his office down there in the foyer, the room lit like a chrysalis with something inside waiting to emerge. She paused at the door, her hand on the chain.

'Who is it?'

As if there could be any doubt.

'It's me of course! Steve.'

It was the caretaker's voice. Of course. Courteous and considerate, his impatience a faraway suggestion. Mary unbolted the door and slipped the chain. He came in at once, carrying a large paper carrier bag, brushing past her, stocky as a bulldog. He was still wearing the rugby shirt with its dark-green stripes.

'Warm up some plates, eh?'

She went to the kitchen, realising how hungry she was. Maybe he could smell the cigarette. Hard to tell. The fan was still on. Today he might notice but say nothing. Or he might sniff the air in that quizzical way. You couldn't predict. You could never predict. The caretaker followed her in, unpacking some foil cartons with cardboard lids from the brown-paper carrier.

'Here we are. Fried rice for two, one chicken Chow Mein and one fried beef in black bean sauce!'

He seemed cheerful tonight. Mary tried to look pleased. There was a little vacuum of dread in her chest as she gathered cutlery and plates.

She opened the cartons. They were surprisingly hot. He must have gone for the food in his car. The blue Datsun.

'How's the boy? Better? Asleep?'

His hand brushed her arm and she shuddered slightly. She couldn't help it.

'Better, I think. He's stopped being sick.'

'That's good. Poor little lad, he's had a bad time, hasn't he?'

Mary tipped the food onto the warm plates. In the silence she knew his green eyes were on her. Looking, absorbing her. Sometimes she wondered if he was simple. Unformed in some way. It was the way he'd let his gaze rest on hers without any inhibition. She couldn't discuss Mark with him. He'd offer more help. More ways to make her grateful. Always insinuating. Sometimes asking questions about Des. Why their marriage had broken up, what kind of food or TV programmes she liked. Innocent questions, but with an edge, an undertone. Leading questions that went in a certain direction. Though she never quite knew what that was.

'Here you are.'

She handed him his plate and they sat down to eat in armchairs in the living room. He reached down into the carrier bag and brought out two cans of pale ale.

'I nearly forgot! Got a glass?'

Mary shook her head.

'Never mind. Drink it out of the can. Like football supporters, eh? Lager louts!'

It was cheap pale ale, not lager. But he laughed anyway, balancing the meal on his knees, pulling the ring-pull from his can and folding it neatly back in itself. He tilted his head so that the light fell across sparse hair, taking a long draught of the beer. Then he sighed and put the can down, opening one for Mary and handing it across. It was gassy and metallic, but she drank it. She needed its chill to quell the fluttering in her stomach.

The caretaker ate rapidly, dipping his head down to the fork rather than raising it up to his mouth, and swigging beer from the can. When he had finished, he laid the plate on the floor and rested his hands on his knees. She could see the hairs glistening there like strands of glass.

'I'll just take a peep at the boy.'

Mary opened her mouth to speak. She couldn't. It was hard to get her breath. The man was already rising from his chair, padding softly to the bedroom to look down at the sleeping child. When he returned to the living room Mary was gathering up the plates and the empty beer cans. The caretaker looked at her. Green eyes, like a cat.

'I'll fetch it then, shall I?'

Mary nodded, running the hot tap to wash the plates, squirting washing-up liquid into the sink. That smell and the spicy food made her feel sick again. She turned on the fan again to get rid of the steam, rinsing the plates and stacking them. They'd have coffee later. That was the usual way of it. But not until he asked her.

The man returned, carrying a chequered board and a box. He set up the board on the table and laid out the chess set, carefully positioning each piece. It'd started as a joke, a way of passing the time. He played chess impulsively, making bold and foolish sallies with his pieces to capture a pawn but sacrifice a bishop or knight. It was as if he had no subterfuge. Mary sat down opposite him. He took a black pawn and a white one, mixing them together behind his back and holding out his clenched fists. She chose the right hand and he held out a white pawn.

'Lucky! You go first.'

Mary said nothing. The chequered board made her dizzy. She was short of breath again, moving her king's pawn two squares forward with an effort. The caretaker took his knight and moved it into the centre of the board, taking command. Mary let her fingers stray towards her queen's pawn and then paused. He was looking at her, watching every move, examining her motives. She broke out her own knight. He stared at the board. The hands of the electric clock jerked silently forward on the wall. He leaned over to move a pawn and the intercom gave a screech in the corridor like the scream of a caged bird. She had a visitor. Down in the foyer someone had come for her, someone was waiting to be let in.

Neither of them moved. Mary let her hands fall into her lap. The intercom went off again. She rose to her feet, but the caretaker was quicker, getting between her and the door. She sat down again at once and looked up at him.

'It'll wake the boy.'

The man said nothing. He bit his lip, looking puzzled, uncomprehending. Again the screech, two short ones this time, followed by a whimper from Mark's room. Mary moved forward but the caretaker caught her wrist, his fingernails scraping into her skin. Then Mark was there, framed in the doorway of the bedroom, his eyes glazed and unfocused, unaware of the man.

'Mummy! Mummy!'

She broke free to go to him, but the caretaker got there first, taking him up and hugging him to his chest.

Mary ran to the corridor, pressing the switch that would allow her to speak and release the lock on the main door. The mouthpiece swallowed her cry. It flew out of the room, down the black lift-shaft to the man below. The lock clicked and gave. She waited for the sounds of the lift, for footsteps on the landing. From behind her came the muffled, almost sobbing words of the caretaker as he comforted the boy. She could hear Mark asking for her over and over.

'Where's Mummy? Where's Mummy?'

The man, in a dazed voice, repeating, 'It's alright, she's here, it's alright.'

Their voices meshed. Like the cries of gulls that circled the flats each morning. Mary imagined Des pounding up the stairs with his bald head gleaming and his jacket and shirt sleeves flapping at the elbows. Jack-the-Lad with his arms full of lilies. *Taser.* That was hysterical. But she didn't laugh. She watched the glitter of lights that lay beyond the window, mapping each street. The earth she stood on was slowly turning. Here she was, upright, clinging to the wall. Beyond a single sheet of glass lay the long fall. Glass that was neither a liquid nor a solid, but something in between. Indeterminate, even by the reasoning of molecular dynamics. Glass that had been a mountain, an ocean, a tide of sand washed onto a beach on one day of history. Glass that had been changed by fire, incandescent in an iron crucible, in furnace heat. Now here it was, cool, between her and everything. There was the game of chess, unfinished, each piece staring into battle. There was the lift, rising with her husband inside. There was that stranger cradling their child. And outside was the world. All that treachery. The night.

Why I've Always Loved Fishmongers

I've always loved fishmongers. Ever since I was a child and stood in front of their windows in the town where there was a row of fish shops following the hill down to the market square. I love the red, honest hands of fishmongers and their smeared white aprons. I love the fishy smell of them. And I love their thin, worn-away knives that are so very sharp. The way they slide them along the spine of a mackerel or herring. The way they lift the backbone clean out.

There's something infinitely treasurable to me about the grotto of a fishmonger's window, its cornucopia of the sea. And let me tell you, I hate the bloody mess of butchers' shops. The butcher is a crude mechanic by comparison with the fishmonger's artistry. He shows only parts of an animal: their rib-joints, loins, neck, legs, kidneys, livers and lungs. But the fishmonger offers you the whole creature you're about to devour: head, tail and fins. Though they're dead on his slab you can imagine their lives in the rivers and the seas so easily. You can see them leaping from the phosphorescence of the fishing boat's bow-wave or hurling themselves upwards over the sheet silver of a weir.

I love fishmongers and the clean, hygienic windows of their shops. Their piles of ice like the jewellery of a snow queen, their heaps of winkles and mussels and oysters with sequined shells. Their fans of herring and trout, skate wings and sea-bass, red and grey mullet, the fillets of hake and cod and huss, the fat coils of conger eel or the dull red meat of shark steaks cut from behind a staring, savage head. Silvery mounds of sprats and sardines, sliced whiting and coley, hake and halibut and the slack, gaping mouths of codfish. Lastly the shells of live crabs or lobsters, those anachronistic war machines of rusted iron. They way they stalk blindly about their tanks, the armoured, predatory spiders of the sea.

Let me tell you that this is a love affair that will not go away. Each night I dream of fishmongers unpacking their crates of ice, lifting out the slender, delicate bodies of fish under the moon. Cradling them tenderly in their mercurial slime and bearing them away like lovers.

My father never touched me until I was eleven years old. Then we had a secret and my mother's eyes behind her smudged spectacles stopped seeing. Let's be clear: my father was never a fishmonger and he disliked eating fish, though he spent hours trying to catch them. I remember him choking on a fish bone when I was very small. I held onto my little sister and watched him go blue as my mother pounded his back and the meal went cold. Whenever we had fish after that my mother had to search through it for bones and my father would search after her, probing it with his fork until we felt sick watching him. Sometimes it was cod or haddock rolled in breadcrumbs and fried, but usually it was grilled mackerel that my mother brought home fresh from the market.

Much later, I remember my mother buying fish fingers and cooking them for tea. My father came home and said, *What on earth are these?* and when my mother explained that it was fish with the bones taken out he was delighted. It was a long time before my mother tired of the blandness of fish fingers and we had real fish again. Even tins of pilchards had a spiny piece of bone that caught in your teeth and had to be lifted out carefully from the little fish. I remember how the cat loved those bones especially, mewing like a crazy thing and rubbing against my legs with her ecstatic, hypocritical fondness.

Sometimes we caught sticklebacks in the stream below the house and kept them at home until the water went foul and they died, belly-up and stinking like the worst cowards.

My father came to me at bedtime when my sister was safely asleep in the next room and my mother was busy over the ironing board, pressing his white shirts for work. When he touched me it was like opening the pink gills of a fish and I caught the faint smell of saltwater as if there was an ocean or estuary inside me. Afterwards I could feel it washing backwards and forwards. Backwards and forwards inside me like a wave over strands of slippery weed.

I've got a seashell here in my hand. Faintly pink with dull purples and blues. They lie sleeping in the rough surface until water lights them and they glint with memories of the sea. My little sister found this shell on the beach and gave it to me because I was crying over something. Because my father in his swimming trunks and long arms and hairy belly had got too close and hurt me. The shell whorls into a tunnel like the inside of someone's ear. I called into it for help or for sheer love of the sea where it swayed in green glassy waves. Inside the sea and inside me tiny fish were darting, silvery as those shoals of stars that turn the sky to milk at night.

I remember the first time I put my ear to the ear of the shell and we heard the sound of the sea in each other. The shell pink and clean as the inside of my body, gleaming when it was wet in a hundred subtle colours, which I learned to call *hues*.

He'd spidered his arms around me under the water where no one could see the hurt, just our heads bobbing like corks. It was no use calling out because everyone yells with cold or surprise when they enter the sea.

A fishmonger must lead a strange and beautiful life. Rising early from sleep to drive off and collect his boxes of treasure from the wholesale market. Inside them, on ice, lie the closely packed bodies, the blinded eyes of fishes. Or perhaps he rises even earlier, before dawn tinges the sky. Driving all the way from our town to the coast, walking the quayside, waiting for the fishing boats to come home, standing where the fishermen's wives wait fearfully near an angry sea. There he can choose from the open crates of freshly landed fish, bear witness to the strange, deformed monsters that the sea has made inside itself. Deep down, away from the light that we take for granted but which never reaches the ocean depths.

I can't bear the thought of a polluted sea, its poisons twisting the exquisite bodies of fish that gather there under the waves like dreams. Under the waves where the light of day is only a faint green glow. I can't stand the thought of what we're doing to the oceans and long for the purity of saltwater and wind and passing time.

I've seen my own body like that in other dreams. Tangled in a fisherman's net and dragged out from the deep with my long dark hair wrapped around my waist, my cunt salty with days in the sea, my nipples icy from freezing water. Each time I'm hauled ashore onto seaweed and shingle one kiss on my cold lips would wake me, but no one dares. Instead the fisherman gather and mutter in foreign tongues: Portuguese or Spanish, the exotic vowels of Welsh or Gaelic. They stump around angrily in their sea boots, trying to make a decision, until I'm thrown back into the breakers. Another useless deformity of the deep.

My father kept a fishing rod and a creel of bait and hooks in the garden shed. On Saturdays he went fishing in the canal after his week in the factory office where he added up the company figures and did complicated sums. He spent his days submerged in the teeming shoals of mathematics. Sometimes I or my sister or both went with him at weekends, staring into the water where factory chimneys wobbled in wintry light. Down in his keep-net we'd see the pale flicker of a roach or the dangerous spine of a perch. Their lives so secretive, so different from our own. Their fixed stares, their mouths opening and closing, trying to catch something just out of reach or understanding.

Sometimes my father would take a small fish for live bait, dragging a hook into its body right along the spine, fixing it there as it writhed in his hand, choking on air. The scales would come away on his fingers and he'd wipe them carelessly on his thigh and go piking in the reed beds. I'd watch the poor fish fade and glimmer in the water until it died on the hook, its silvery gleam growing fainter and duller like an electric light flickering into darkness when the current fails. Though sometimes there were monstrous pike stalking that glimmer, seizing it then being hooked on the end of the line, dragging down the red-tipped float.

My father would play them so calmly and cunningly. Giving them line, deceiving them into thinking they'd broken free, then almost imperceptibly reeling them in. Inch by inch, foot by foot. Until he pulled their long, reptilian bodies from the water. Their ugly mouths lined with sloping teeth yanked sideways by the cruel hook. Their bellies sagging and struggling and their goggle eyes glittering with an ancient greed.

My father would drag them in with the gaff hook and finish them off on the bank with sharp blows to the head. He'd tell me how the female pike sometimes ate the male after mating and I'd gladly watch her striped body thresh at the end of the gleaming, almost invisible line.

One year at Christmas my father came to my room smelling of beer and cigarettes. He sat on my bed and told me a story about a lost boy. Long ago and far away in the Old World this boy had chased a runaway kid goat onto a mountain and then had lost himself as darkness fell. He'd heard the goat bleating and found it on a rocky ledge and stayed with it all night singing, hugging it for warmth and playing his flute until the moon had risen in the east to light the pathway home to his mother and father.

Ever after, the goat had been his special friend and people began to think that the boy himself was only half human. His long hair was tied back with a leather thong and the notes that came from his flute were like the bleating cries of a lost kid. When a drought struck the village, withering all the crops, the villagers suspected the boy of sorcery and decided to cut his throat to end their bad luck. But as the angry mob surrounded him and as the headman raised his knife, the boy bounded away from them in the shape of a goat and was never seen again. As my father told me the story I thought of the boy's wicked yellow eyes smiling at me through his words.

After the story, when the goat-boy's eyes faded into the darkness of long ago, my father touched me for the first time so that I wriggled like a fish and loved him for it and would keep the secret forever. My mother would never understand our love, even though she slept with him and knew his warm tobacco and sweat smell, the touch of his lips and rough cheeks. Sometimes I thought about her breasts and I envied them above all else. The breasts I didn't yet have. I imagined them iridescent, like fish scales in the moonlight under the song of the little goatherd, imagined that this was what drew my father to her bed when he left me each night, kissing me on the forehead and asking me to promise never to tell.

Never is deep and final. It rolls in your head in waves that get higher and higher but never break. That day at the seaside I had sand in my nails and he touched me clumsily under the water and hurt me for the first time in my blue swimming costume. Perhaps not meaning to, under the water where no one could see. Just two heads bobbing in that swaying green and the sun glaring on white cliffs and the gulls screaming close, telling everybody who would not hear. That day I found a huge crab on the shingle and dropped a stone onto it, smashing its shell. All week it rotted and stank in the sun and I felt such terrible guilt that I'd killed it. Years later I realised that it was already dead, already scuttling along the floor of some ghostly ocean, its pincers stretched out to grab whatever spectral prey was there.

Some nights I dream of nets wrapping around me like wet hair, of my father's drowned face found under the canal bridge where the tench swam, deep and secretive. That long fish with its thick, rubbery lips. My father had never caught one, his clever hooks sliding empty in water that was shaken by traffic and reflected the sky. Rain breaking those pictures of the world above, pelting onto the surface when they found him near the lock's falling tons of water. My father wanting to be a fish, wanting to breathe water instead of air, his fingernails torn off from so suddenly leaving life. Or from finding out that he was not watery-lunged or cold blooded or fishy enough to live in that sly, suffocating element.

Never is a word without depth or fathom. I wanted them to throw him back into that trembling water-sky to try again. But my mother kept his body in the air and blubbered over his blue face and salted it with tears.

Now I have a glass of water in my hand and on the plate in front of me are three sardines fried quickly in olive oil with a handful of green capers and black peppercorns. I've dashed the vinegar bottle across them and squeezed out a yellow crescent of lemon. I'll eat them with slices of German rye bread and a glass of spring-water from a source in Scotland where the rain still runs pure over the granite and heather of the moor. I picture this with each mouthful of hot fish, each time my teeth meet to crush their bones.

Today the fishmonger smiled at me as he looked up from filleting a brown trout on his cutting block. He threw the guts away and held its skin in his hands and smiled at me and I knew that he was thinking of the countless shoals of fish that dart in rivers and rivulets and oceans. I knew that in the night he would dream of fish as I would. Their golden eyes, their mouths bulging with the purest water, their gills coaxing out its difficult oxygen. That was a trick my father never learned and trying to learn it cost him his life. That the fishmonger had learned it, I knew for sure. He'd smile the same smile as each gleaming fin stroked his face where he lay staring upwards through weed and water at a thin moon polishing the pebbles of the riverbed.

I count out silver coins from my purse into the fishmonger's hand. The irises of his eyes are pale grey, the colour of watered silk. I give him the exact price of the fish, coin by coin. The fishmonger smiles and turns to his window, tipping a bucket of mackerel into trays of ice, lifting a salmon onto its crystal throne. The fishmonger's wife comes to the doorway and scowls, watching us together as if she knows everything. But the fishmonger still wears that secret smile as I put the sardines into my shopping bag. He shows it again as we say goodbye, subtle as a glimmer of sun on water.

Tonight he and I will glide from saltwater ocean to the river's mouth. We'll swim upstream to the foaming edge of a waterfall, smelling out the peaty stream where we were born together as sister and brother. Tonight my breasts will stand out, cold and taut in their nickel skin of fish scales and I'll arch out in ecstasy, leaping above the ocean and the river to fall back gladly into their depth. I'll leave saltwater for fresh, swim in the milt of my lover's sperm, letting out orgasms of fabulous, jewelled eggs as his flanks stroke mine. No fingers or panting breath or hot skin, no secrets to keep or lies to hold. But coming again and again with that electrical pleasure, the shuddering beauty of his touch.

I turn to go and a lobster waves its claws, troubling sediment and sand in the tank where it waits to die, wafting up tiny pebbles that sway and slowly sink again.

I've only told you half a secret, because the rest is unsayable, because no one else can really understand and perhaps they don't even want to listen. They pursue their own lives in the streets, in factories and shops and offices. In cars and in suburban houses where the curtains are drawn at night and televisions blare, blinking blue light at the walls of their living rooms. They go on, day after day, night after night. Immersed in sitcoms, reality television, in stultified marriages, in children who call out for attention from upstairs rooms. Look how the hall lights come on. Look how they leave half-hearted conversations, or the news half-watched, to go upstairs with soothing words and hands. No. They need never know what we know: the fishmonger and me and other water-breathing dreamers.

Sawmill

Dave squints along the beam, sets it straight on the saw plate, then gives it to the white band of steel, pushing from the hips. I wait on the other side to take it. The blade shears through steadily. Its racket rises then falls like a motorcycle circuiting a track. Scraps of blues songs rehearse themselves in my head, chasing round and round beneath the tumult of the mill. This is my third day: I know what to do. Catching the beam as it parts from itself, I hold it until Dave moves forward to take the other end. Holding the two halves together as if it was still whole we carry them to the crosscut where Chris sweats to keep pace, sawing these lengths into arm-long stumps and stacking them.

It's 1978 and I've just graduated from university, the first of my family to get a degree. I'm working in a sawmill in Nottingham, renting a flat in Radcliffe. I'm just another hired hand from the labour agency. Another mug. For three years I've been longing to get out into the world, to touch down, to get real, to escape from libraries and critical theory and the arid discourse around books. I'm a manual labourer, a throwback to my class. I'm living with a girl whose hair smells of cologne and apricots, a girl with hazel-brown eyes and freckled shoulders. We fetched up here for no good reason. Elaine works in a bookshop in town and has a degree in philosophy. Sometimes I wonder if that's why we argue so much. I wonder if she's thinking about me now as the flaking timber tumbles onto the pile beside Chris.

We return to the machine. Beside it stands a chest-high stack of railway sleepers from the country's torn-up tracks. We're making them into pit props now, steadily sawing up one part of the last century to support another. Dave's signalling to me. Words are useless in the din of the two saws. He is already part-deaf, a gesticulating, one-man mime show, nose flattened to one side, cigarette dangling from his grin, jerking in green overalls like a puppet on wires. Together we lift another beam onto the table of the band saw, picking up a hammer and chisel each to dislodge the stones that are jammed into its cracks and bolt holes. Dave grins with crooked teeth. He smacks a gloved fist into his palm, rolling his eyes in horror to show me what they would do to the blade. We lug the beam over to inspect its other side. All is clear.

Through the open doorway of the mill we can see the yard stacked with railway sleepers that still have iron fixings for the rails. Simon and Dan are at work in the pale sunshine, levering off the ironwork and stacking the stripped sleepers. They're both booted, broad shouldered and slim hipped. Simon has a long ponytail and a gold earring. Dan's head is close-shaven with glittering stubble and he walks with a pronounced limp. At the end of every day they climb onto an old Norton Commando and leave in a haze of blue fumes blasted from the backfiring exhaust pipe. Neither of them talks at break times. They glance through the *Sun* or the *Mirror*, impatient, as if they're waiting for something. Killing time on the killing floor. There's something ritualistic in the stark rhythm of their work. All day I watch them silhouetted against the light. They're both graduates of the local gaol, Chris tells me in a whisper.

Dave drags the sleeper across the rollers and lines it up in front of the blade's hiss, its constant flame of steel. He pushes the timber into its blur with a leering grin. In a rogue's gallery he would be the pickpocket, slight and quick, yet heaving the beams into position with amazing strength.

The blade bites in a flurry of orange sparks. It's a good beam and the old, sweet pine divides easily. I press down on to the rollers on my side to ease its passage. We hurry it over to Chris like the last one. He's hanging under his saw with a spanner, changing its circular, shark-finned blade. The next beam feels heavy and waterlogged. There's a fungal stench of decay. It sticks coming through the blade and Dave signals to me to send it back to him. I return the part-rotten halves and we saw each one into four thinner lengths.

I carry these over to the crumbled stack beside Chris. They drag my arms down with their damp, dead weight. I hurry back for the next four, catching them just as they arrive, shedding fragments onto the floor. One of the lengths breaks as I carry it, unbalancing me. *Fuck, fuck!* I'm staggering, kicking the broken halves from underfoot, flinging them onto the heap of rubbish that is piling against the far wall of the workshop. Somewhere down in the city Elaine is pushing her hair from her face, attending to a customer in the shop, keying an order into the till, counting the minutes until her lunch break. She's there in the world of books that I've tried to leave behind. Last night when we made love she tugged at the short hairs on my neck. I can still feel the cool stealth of her fingers.

The minute hand jerks forward on the clock that hangs above the restroom. Dave turns on his heel, touching my elbow to bring me back to the saw. Later in the afternoon we'll begin to saw up this pile of thinner lengths on the crosscut, stacking them on pallets in bundles of four. We work together at this: I lift the wood onto the machine, four lengths at a time, sliding them back up to the blade each time they are cut. Dave operates the saw, handing the bundles to Chris who ties them on a wire binder and stacks them. Dave and Chris work furiously at this since they earn a bonus on each pallet filled. My wage is fixed but I must sweat to keep up with them. That job comes later in the day, in the last hour before we switch off the saws and the mill falls into sleep and we return to our lives.

I get back to the machine, panting, sweat basting my hands. We heave the next sleeper onto the saw. All day, beam after beam, dividing them up relentlessly. As if one might contain a secret. As if we're searching for the living heart of a tree, or a century. We cut through a fragment of stone we've overlooked. Then there's a snick and sparks snap from the blade. It's enough. Dave's face is the tragic mask of a pantomime clown. He holds out his hands, palms upwards and shrugs. His cigarette flicks up sharply, once.

We stop the machine; it slows in a diminishing howl. I tug on a lever on the side that cranks down the tension on the blade. Dave removes the planks covering the sawpit then opens the green metal casing. We ease the blade off the two wheels it rides on: one above our heads, the other below our feet. It's a springy, razor-toothed band of tempered steel, four inches wide and eight feet high. We carry it to the workshop next door and fit it to the automatic grindstone. The foreman shakes his head, tips his cap, and throws a switch. The blade travels, sparking in little jerks as the file puts a new edge on each tooth.

The new blade has a welding scar where it has been repaired. We lift it from two pegs on the wall and fit it to the saw. Now that our machine is silent we can hear the shriek of the crosscut behind us. There's a hiss from the compressed air of the foot switch. Then the blade comes snarling through the slit in the platform, a howling piranha-wheel. It screams into the wood above it, high pitched then diminishing as it drops away. Above the blade is a hoop of girder for a guard. Each night before sleep, I see myself stretched out on the platform, trapped under the hoop as the blade rips up towards my spine. Tonight, I'll sleep with my fingers tangled in Elaine's, listening to traffic die in the streets, to the little catch of breath in her throat. Tomorrow, I'll rise early to work at the portable Olivetti and the stack of poems I've written as she sleeps, her hair massed against the pillow, the dawn stoking itself up beyond factory chimneys and tower blocks. The typewriter was a present from my father, just before I left for university. I'd never seen him cry before.

We fix the blade on to our machine, tension it, and begin again, working more quickly to make up lost time. The foreman drives in with more sleepers stacked on the tines of his forklift. Later the manager appears in his dark suit. He watches us for a few minutes, counting the beams in our stack, flicking his fingers through receding hair, calculating how long it takes us to saw each beam. Dave and Chris quicken their pace. The manager nods to the foreman and leaves, but we don't slacken off. Dave jerks his head, mouths *Bastard!* at me and grins. Jim arrives with more sleepers and drops them beside our heap. Chris and Dave confer over a cigarette, gesturing at the work, at time passing. I think of the blade in the workshop, the snick of the file, each tiny cascade of fire, each tooth ground to a fine edge.

By lunchtime I'm sweat soaked and staggering to keep up. We stop the saws dead on twelve and I take my sandwiches out of the mill, walking through a wilderness of stacked railway sleepers to the canal. I'm deafened by the noise of the saws and everything seems preternaturally silent, even traffic passing on the road. It's a mild day in autumn and I sit by the water to eat my lunch. Yellow poplar leaves are falling all around me. Early this morning the canal had been a ribbon of steam, its water misted with cold. Now it's a calm reflector; murky and placid it heads for the city.

I throw bread pellets for the fish. They sink through the water undisturbed. A barge passes slowly, painted bright red and yellow, making a swell slap up against the canal banks. A man with a huge belly, a white moustache and a chequered cap raises one hand ceremoniously, the other wrapped around the tiller. Below decks, a woman's face passes the steamed-up porthole. The engine putters out black diesel smoke and the barge toils away from me until it's hidden by a slow bend. Today is Wednesday. Half-day in town. Elaine will have finished work now, heading home with carrier bags of food or books. In return, she'll work on Saturday when I'm crashed out in bed or mooching around the flat listening to Junior Parker or Buddy Guy.

The surface of the water has settled back into a dusty still-ness. A moorhen comes bobbing out from the reeds. Half an hour has gone. I get up from the iron bench that has numbed my arse and legs and stroll back through mellow sunshine. The mill is strangely still. Dan and Simon pass me, nodding grimly, pulling on their leather gloves. Dave and Chris step through the doorway to start the machines.

Our overalls are black with dust and tar. Our faces are smeared from wiping sweat with filthy gloves. I have no hat and my hair is full of the scent of tar and sweet pine dust and dirt. I sweep up the sawdust and fragments of wood that have fallen around the machine. Dave presses the red button, cranks it into life.

Sawmill

The long afternoon has begun. That lost afternoon in the first summer of my life with Elaine. It starts badly with a stack of rotten beams that look like the decayed hulls of long-boats. Heaped carcasses with their bellies caved in. Some are covered with white fungus that gives off a sickly stench of corruption. When Dave finds one of these he grins, pretends to fart, then looks round in surprise for a culprit. In his overalls and peaked cap he's lively as an acrobat.

Rotten fragments of wood fall around the machine. I can't believe that these props are meant to hold up the roof of a mine. Only one in four of them is truly sound. I imagine the fury of the colliers as they discard them in the close darkness underground. I watch Dave closely, trying to read his mood. His broken-nosed face is inscrutable behind the fixed grin: a puppet mask, a mechanical toy. Divorced and with a gambling addiction, he could be the hero of any blues song. Away from the machine, half deaf and stammering, he's an easy target for the horseplay of the other men. But the machine jerks him into life, articulates him, transforms him into the nodding, winking demon of the saw. He carries out its will, his body eloquent through its wall of noise. He's a good workman, quick and accurate with love of the machine, guiding the timber through its blade with the steady pressure of his hips.

We work on, making the same moves. Making the same moves, beam after beam. The Lord's prayer comes back to me from childhood assemblies in school: *for ever and ever, amen.* Light falling through the slatted blinds of the school hall onto children's heads, finding copper threads in their hair. *Thy will be done.* The rotten wood is hard going; it slows us down, makes us falter and sweat. Most of it has to be cut into narrower lengths and stacked for later. The afternoon has hardly started when the blade shrieks through a piece of bolt embedded in the wood. We have to change it again, reclaiming the sharpened blade from the workshop, fitting it to the saw.

Dave is working too fast, hurrying to finish this last stack and begin on the crosscut. He lights a cigarette, blows a perfect smoke circle, shrugs, then re-starts the saw.

We lift another sleeper onto the platform, chipping stone ballast from its coating of tar. Sweat stings my eyes. We heave it over; inspect its other side. My arms ache at the elbows as if the joints are pulling apart. My wrists are raw from carrying armfuls of wet timber. Dave nods: thumbs up, all is well. Buddy Guy is crooning in my head. *Five long years and one lonely night and she had the nerve to throw me out.* Dave leans down on his end of the beam and drags it towards himself, resting one end on the roller set to the saw plate's height. He spins a wheel to adjust the width of cut, locks it, flicks fragments of rotten wood from the slit where the blade whistles. A guitar solo peels off into the air, brittle as shattered glass. All is ready.

Dave takes the beam and feeds it to steel, cigarette at an angle, his eye set to the line. Slowly he moves it through, thighs pressed, leaning in still concentration. The beam surges towards me, then sticks on the blade. Dave lifts it, the way you'd lift a lover by the hips. It frees for a second, jerks towards me then sticks again. Dave shoves it forward. This time the beam bucks up the blade and twists it. There's a terrific bang, then a high, high screeching that's uprooting my teeth from the bone of their sockets. The white band of the blade leaps free of the machine and catapults away from me, a twanging blur of light. The saw roars, ungoverned, shaking itself apart, enveloping me in its din. Chris runs up behind me and even through that pandemonium of noise I hear his quiet exclamation.

Dave has been thrown back by the snapping blade. He's tearing off his gloves to touch himself. His overalls are torn across the chest and a red gash has opened in his face. It screams at us like a crude mouth set the wrong way up, running from below one eye and across one cheekbone to his throat. Bright blood is running down, splashing onto his breast. His eyes have gone dumb, his hand is afraid to touch the wound in his face. People come running to support him: Chris, the foreman, the manager. Their faces look as if they've all been slapped hard. Dave collapses into their arms, crumbling like a rotten stake, mesmerised by the machine in front of him. Simon and Dan stare in from the sun.

I've thrown off my gloves, tearing at the overalls, stepping from their tangle of legs and sleeves. Grabbing my jacket, I run from the mill. Out past the stacks of timber, past the forklift, past the yard gates, past the Commando leaning on its side-stand and dripping oil, not stopping until I reach the canal.

Traffic flits along the road. All is supernaturally quiet as I jog towards home. Elaine will be there, waiting for me with a clean bath towel. Her hands will be cool against my neck. She'll kneel in mock humility to wash away sawdust where sweat has pasted it to my back. The scratches on my arms turn her on and she'll graze there with her lips. She'll count the knobbles on my spine then lose count, laughing at my squeamishness as the water cools. I picture her throat rising from her pale clavicle; feel her hands, their tenderness, their elusive touch. I wonder what a lifetime of manual labour is like, the way my parents have lived. The way their parents lived. Then all the nameless generations: the ones who left their villages to work in mills and mines and lie in paupers' graves. I know more about characters from books who never lived than my own people. Their lives, their deaths. *For ever and ever.* Without wanting to, I think about Dave, the way a serpent of steel betrayed him, the way his eyes suddenly emptied of light. *Amen.*

The sun is low behind the factories, deepening its hues through the hazy atmosphere, glowing red in the water. Yellow poplar leaves are falling in a slight breeze. They fall onto my head and shoulders. They drift down into dark waters and float like tiny Chinese junks, like unfinished poems or stories half told, towards the heart of the city.

Friday Night

Stott pulled up the collar of his overcoat and stepped from the bus. The first drops of rain had just begun to fall. Stott felt them smack onto his head where his sandy hair was thinning out. He felt them drip coldly onto his neck. The bus pulled away and he stood for a moment, idling in the street. It was October and the evening light had not quite died. The yellow glow of the streetlights seemed to struggle into existence. Spots of rain were darkening the pavement and drifts of cloud gathering over the town where it stood, exposed on the hilltop. The plain of Lancashire glittered below as millions of lights were turned on in towns and villages across its breadth.

Stott set off walking downhill, into the town. His shoes were new and the left one was rubbing a little at the heel. Still, they felt crisp against the pavement. Positive. Good shoes made you feel good. Stott passed the Gothic town hall, the war memorial, the deserted marketplace where scraps of litter flickered under faint wind and dim light. It was early in the evening and there weren't many people about. He liked to get up to town early on a Friday. It was the only way to make a night of it. He walked past lit supermarkets. Past a fish-and-chip shop, its band of warm air sharp with the tang of vinegar. Hot, battered fish. That's what he'd have later.

After a few pints. A good few. Stott smiled, nuzzling his face against the collar of his raincoat, ignoring the pain in his heel.

Fifty yards further down the hill and he was turning into the Royal Oak, which stood on the corner of Gas Street. It was near to the bus station, perched above the town's gasometers. The Oak had a heavy mahogany swivel door with panes of frosted glass. It was a well-appointed pub that had begun to grow seedy from the brewery's neglect. The bar was u-shaped, built of the same solid mahogany as the door and with identical panes of glass set above it. A few off-duty busmen stood drinking at the counter, still wearing their uniforms. Stott stepped up to the bar. He shook the drizzle from his coat, wrinkling his nose at the faint smell of cat piss that haunted the pub. The landlord looked up from where he was pulling a pint.

'I'll be with you in a tick, Frank.'

Stott nodded at the little man and waited, one hand resting on the polished wood. The pint that had just been pulled stood settling, its head of foam distilling from pale liquid gold. The landlord rang the till and then looked across at him, a glass already in his hand.

'Bitter, Frank?'

Stott nodded.

'Please.'

He watched the beer hiss into the glass with each steady stroke of the pump. The landlord was an ex-collier and pulled one of the best pints in town. He set it down on the bar towel and picked up the money that Stott had put there.

'Is it rainin' yet? You look a bit damp, lad.'

Stott paused with the pint halfway to his mouth, catching the sharp scent of hops.

'Aye, it's just started, bugger it!'

The landlord moved away and Stott dipped his mouth into

the foam, drinking fiercely, exulting in the cool, bitter rush of beer. He took another long gulp and put the glass down with a sigh. The creamy head ran back down its sides, clinging in rings that marked each draught he'd taken.

The landlord was leaning across a newspaper with two of the busmen, talking over a horse race. That was a fool's game. More money than sense, and not much of either, probably. Above the bar, rows of empty glasses burnished the shelves. The trap door to the cellar had a brass ring-pull set into it. Stott thought of the barrels of mild and bitter waiting down there in the darkness. Waiting for him. He sank the remainder of the beer in three long gulps, setting the glass back on the bar. Empty. The landlord looked across. Stott nodded, almost imperceptibly, as if secretively bidding at an auction. He handed a five-pound note over as the beer arrived. The land-lord grinned, fishing change from the till.

'You look as if you needed that! What's up, wife bin' at you?'

Stott laughed grimly, taking the head off his beer.

'No chance!'

They didn't know that he wasn't married. He felt in his pockets for his cigarettes. They didn't know anything about him. Not the terraced street where he still lived with his parents. Not the motorbike that he took apart and rebuilt and brought to life again, riding it on Sundays across the moors where the grass bent away under the wind and lapwings flung themselves skywards. That sense of speed, singleness, release. That feeling of numbness that was part cold in every knuckle joint and part pure thoughtlessness. They knew nothing about his job in the wages office in the mill, about the two women who worked under him, about his boss, that idle fat bastard, Henderson.

Stott flicked open the cap of his petrol lighter and struck down the wheel. The flint sparked but the wick refused to burn. He tried again. Nothing. Dropping the lighter into his pocket he took the cigarette from his mouth.

'Have you got a box o' matches, Geoff?'

The landlord took down a box of Swan Vestas from a display rack behind the bar and laid it in front of him.

'Ta. Bloody lighter's knackered!'

He struck a match and touched it to the cigarette. It was a long time since he'd smoked. The smoke was sweet and smooth. He took another drink of the beer, letting it go down more slowly, taking his time now that the first pint was a reassuring weight in his stomach. He sucked another mouthful of smoke down into his lungs and slowly breathed it out. There was plenty of time. Plenty. A whole night of it. A lifetime.

He stayed at the bar for another twenty minutes, drinking and smoking quietly. At eight o'clock he drained his glass, putting in his tongue to lap at the last bit of foam as it slid down towards his mouth. He buttoned up his overcoat, turning quickly from the bar, saying goodbye over his shoulder.

'See you, Geoff, thanks.'

'Alright, Frank.'

He took up the empty glass.

'See you later?'

Stott doubted it.

'Mebbe.'

He was already halfway towards the door. He put out his hand to swing it round. Stepping from the warm pub into the street was like going through the air lock in a submarine or a spacecraft. The air was chilly and damp now. Darkness had almost obliterated the clouds and freakish drops of rain still blew about. Groups of skimpily clad youngsters were making their way towards the new disco pubs. Ears clamped to mobile phones or texting each other as they crossed the road, making the traffic swerve. Bollocks to that. He never carried a phone. When he was out he was a free man. As for discos, they'd taken one pub, The Cemetery, done it out and called it The Harlequin. The Harlequin for fuck's sake! At least someone had a sense of humour. It was all flashing lights and DJs and alcopops. They were welcome to that. Fucking kids.

The pavements were wet and yellow lights gleamed on them, forming shapes that gulped at Stott's footsteps. He made his way back up the hill into town, the new shoe still rubbing at his foot. He shuddered, huddling deeper into his coat. The beer lurched in his gut.

Stott passed the chip shop and again almost went in. He walked on. Eating now would spoil his drinking. Better save it for later when the pubs had closed and he was really hungry. He walked back towards the town hall, where it crouched above a broad flight of steps. Opposite was the war memorial where a soldier in First World War uniform stood sentinel, pointing his bayonet at the sky. Stott paused. Silly bastard soldier with his arse stuck in the air. He walked on, wincing. Just below the town hall stood the Hare and Hounds. It was a small, cosily lit pub. The sort of place that the older men brought their wives to on a Friday night. It'd be quiet now, but later on there'd be a 60s karaoke and every daft twat trying to sing. Making silly bastards of themselves.

The bar was already half full but Stott squeezed himself into a corner. He ordered a pint of bitter and watched it being pulled, foam hissing into a stainless steel tray below the pumps. This was a different brewery and a rounder, fuller beer. Better for the third pint than the first, less attack and more comfort in its maltiness.

Taking off his overcoat, Stott folded it carefully at his feet in front of the bar. Leaning into the corner, his shoulder against the wall, he watched the barmaid serve her customers. She was around thirty-five, quite tall and slim. But not thin. You couldn't call her thin. She wore a tight black dress and had bleached hair cut close to her head. Her face was heavily made up, almost a mask, but there were crow's feet at the corners of her eyes. The dress was made out of a shiny fabric that clung to her as she swung out her hips to gain leverage on the hand-pumps. Stott was running his hand over her buttocks, over her small breasts. She was liking it, pressing herself against him. It'd been a long time. He picked up his glass and drank, exploring the beer with his tongue, wiping his lips as he set the glass down. She'd be about his age. He grinned, remembering what Geoff had said about having a wife. No bloody chance! No woman was ever going to tie him down.

Freedom made Stott bold. He rapped his glass down on the bar.

'Pint o' bitter please, darlin'!'

The barmaid gave him a sharp look from under the blonde fringe of hair that grew from grey roots. Her eyes were dark, like shiny pieces of coal.

'Won't be a minute, love.'

Her voice was hard behind the glossy smile. Christ, they could turn it on when they wanted to! Stott leaned closer as she took his glass.

'Will y'ave one yersel'?'

Her reply was brisk, evasive.

'No thanks, I don't drink when I'm workin'.'

Stott blinked, then slowly smiled.

'What about afterwards?'

She spiked him with a glance.

'You must be joking!'

'Suit yersel', then.'

'I allus do!'

Stott swayed slightly as he took the glass. Nothing ventured, nothing gained. He'd been turned down for his daring. Given the knock-back. The bloody KB. Some of the other customers had noticed; they looked at him curiously. Sod them all!

Stott allowed the beer to settle, watching bubbles cascade upwards, the amber liquid coalesce below. This would be a slow pint, a lingering one whilst he watched the woman as she moved silkily behind the bar. Drink was the thief of... what? *Discretion.* Was that what they said? Sure enough, she snapped her head up as she poured a bottle of stout.

'D'yer want a photo or summat?'

He must have been staring at her. Some men at the bar laughed. Stott tried to move his tongue; it was suddenly too heavy.

'Eh? Oh aye... a'dunno...'

He flushed. Some men in suits at the bar turned to look at him. Fucking stuck-up cow. The barmaid was muttering to one of the men nearest her.

'Dirty old sod, he's probably married with three kids!'

Stott finished his beer in rapid gulps, forcing it down on top of the other pints. He picked his coat up by the collar, knocking his head on the bar rail, fleeing the pub, stumbling down the steps into the street.

Outside, flurries of rain began to strike against his hot face. He was walking along a street that led down by the side of the town hall to the swimming baths. The town hall facade was all stone, but the wall he steadied himself against was red brick. It was all show, all bullshit. The bricks were rough under his hand. *The bitch, the bloody little bitch!* She'd really shown him up. Him, a dirty old whatever it was. And those bastards standing there in their suits. Laughing. Stott was trembling and his eyes stung. The wall was cold against his cheek. He walked on under the street lamps, seeing his reflection and shadow touch and part on the wet pavement. They were following him across town. Like hit men. He stopped to light a cigarette. Fuck the fucking rain. Smoke burned at his lungs. After a few draws he hurled the butt into the gutter. It went out with a hiss and began to blot up the water, a dark stain spreading across white paper. Stott lurched off down the street until he reached the side door of the Bath Hotel. It was a better pub. Livelier. He'd finished off a lot of Friday nights here. A lot.

The pub was crowded but Stott managed to get himself into a corner of the bar in the little back parlour. A coal fire burned in the Victorian grate. Cosy. This time he found a stool and stowed his coat carefully between its legs. The last pint weighed heavily on his stomach. He ordered a half of mild to give it time to settle. It was a dark beer with a smooth, creamy head. Not as satisfying as the bitter, a little too sweet, but it lay nicely on top of what he'd already drunk.

When he'd been at the bar long enough to own the stool he rose and went to the toilets. They were a lean-to affair, outside at the back of the pub. Two other men stood there, younger than him and got up in dark tracksuits. They were already far gone, reeling gently and rhythmically as they faced the trough. Stott stood next to them. One of them turned to his mate.

'Would yer mind pissin' a bit lower lad? Yer sprayin' me.'

His friend giggled, swaying back a little to alter his angle of attack. He spoke as if he'd just had his teeth pulled.

Friday Night

'Oops! Sorry lad, sorry! Daft twat. Can't bloody see straight!'

He turned to Stott.

'S'right in't it, mate? Too fuckin' dark in 'ere.'

Stott grinned as he pissed into the debris of dog ends and spent matches.

'Aye, that's right, lad. Bloody dark. I'll say!'

The man flicked his spare hand towards the naked yellow bulb, tugging at his trousers with the other. He muttered to himself in a thick, clotted voice.

'Dark? Dark? Iss pitch fuckin' black, never min' dark!'

Stott watched him fumble his way back into the pub. They were just lads. Lads out on the piss. As they should be.

Edging his feet away from the trough, he concentrated solemnly. No good splashing his new shoes. He was still smiling as he re-entered the bar. What had that first one said? It had tickled him. He said it in his head in an old lady's voice. God, it was comical! Pissing all over the shop. But they were alright. They were just lads on the ale. He suppressed a wild giggle as he sat back down to his drink.

Drinking felt good now. He drained the gill of mild and ordered a pint of bitter. The real stuff. It slid down easily. Then another. Pint after pint. Each one consumed in the same easy rhythm. Each one savoured, appreciated, held up momentarily to the light before Stott's low growl of anticipation and the fierce dipping down of his mouth. The hours flowed away around him. The landlord stoked the fire, which flared up, sending out yellow smoke and stabs of flame. The whole room was the amber colour of beer. Stott hardly spoke, except to order more drink. But the conversation went on around him, murmuring like a slow sea, dripping into his ears. It was honey and he was a drowsy bee, heavy with nectar, fumbling towards some golden chamber of sleep.

At ten to eleven Stott ordered his last pint. He had finished it by five-past. It was time to go. Time to go. He reached down for his coat, knocking his head against the brass rail in front of the bar. That was fucking twice in one night. He straightened up, rubbing it, grinning, struggling with his sleeves and collar. Two attempts at the catch and he was through the side door. His pockets were full of small change. Amazing. Shillings and fucking pence. How? He stood for a moment, buttoning up his complicated coat. It was a mystery. All those coins. A dizzer. A real fucking mystery.

The bus stop was at the brow of the hill, next to the town hall. He set off towards it, but his progress was slow, distracted by patterns of light on the wet pavements. He arrived in time to see the last bus pass, hissing through the spray from the road. His hand was half raised. Too late. Again. Cunt of a driver. Paki. Fucking rag-head. A ship in the night. Passing. Like that fucking barmaid. Stott shrugged. He'd missed it before, dozens of times. That last pint robbing him of a warm ride home. He'd never learn, silly bastard. But so what? He'd walk. Fuck the lot, he'd walk. Stott rambled through wet streets. Under the rank-smelling pedestrian precinct where his feet slapped and echoed. Over a patch of wasteland where a mongrel stood drenched in the rain. It yelped at him and cringed away, wouldn't come to his hand. He walked on. Across another side road, onto a grass verge, until he stood at the pavement on the ridge of the hill that led down towards home.

The land spread away in a confusing mass of lights. Far away, he could see one clear strand, a string of yellow beads draped over the foothills of the moors beyond Bury. There were the patchy lights of tower blocks. A few mills lit up like ocean-going liners. There'd been hundreds once. Ships in the night. Neon hoardings and electric signs above the shops. A faulty streetlamp blinking from red to yellow, a wrecker's beacon. Below him the road dipped away, its gleaming tract inscribed with broken white lines. Stott set off to follow them.

It began to rain almost at once, splashing against his face, running down from his nose and eyebrows. Shuddering, he stopped. He needed to piss. On his left was a disused church, a Victorian red-brick affair with wrought-iron railings and a short, ugly clock tower. He went into the yard and round the side of one of its buttresses. Stott pissed clumsily, wetting his leg. Did it matter? Did it fuck. He was wet anyway. He was pissed through. Pissed. He giggled. He'd be even wetter by the time he got home. Home to the silent street. The still house where his parents would already be snoring blindly in their beds.

Stott got back to the road, peering round to make sure he hadn't been spotted. It wouldn't do to be seen. Not in a church. That was another thing, fucking priests. That was something else. He lost the thought. Or it never came clear of the blur of lights. There was something about that he wanted to say. Churches. Priests. But it was gone. Fuckit.

Stott began to amble downhill in a rapid, rolling walk, overbalancing and then balancing again like some ingenious mechanism or a droll circus clown. He came to a chip shop and remembered that he was hungry. Must eat. Must. Fucking starving. There were smells of vinegar, hot food. He spat on the pavement, almost drooling, then stepped up into the shop. There was a queue and he had to wait in his damp clothes. They prickled in the heat. The light was hard. A sign proclaiming *Holland's Pies* blinked at him.

'Fish an' chips, love?'

Stott nodded. The girl had a rose tattooed on her arm and

a silver stud piercing her lip. Her eyes looked huge behind thick glasses. She'd asked him first, before he'd tried to speak. That was clever. His tongue felt numb and swollen. The girl spoke again.

'Salt an' vinegar, love? To eat now?'

The piercing made her lisp slightly. Stott wondered if she had one through her tongue. He nodded again, swaying back onto his heels. Say nothing. Get the money. Get the fucking money. He fumbled a handful of change over the counter, watching the girl pick through it with red fingers and drop the remainder into his hand. She wasn't bad looking. It was just the glasses. She was alright, big tits pressed against her tee shirt. Funny tattoo, though. And that thing in her lip. Why do that?

Taking the packet of fish and chips, Stott went out into the rain. Walking a few paces, he leaned against the wall of the engineering works to eat. Platt Brothers. They were fucked, now. The pride of the town, gone west. Like everything else. On the corner of the street below him the landlord of the Westwood pub was locking up. Stott ate carefully. He'd forgotten to get a fork, would have to use fingers. So what? He broke open the hot fish, slobbering cool air into his mouth as it burned him. Fuck. Too fucking hot, that's what. Cars swept by on the road beside him. The traffic lights at the crossroads changed from green to amber and then to red.

A line of traffic began to gather beside him. There were pale faces at car windows, hands smearing holes through condensation on the glass. In all the gutters of the town rainwater was draining away, its voices hoarse as a man's cut throat. Stott paused over a mouthful of chips, remembering the barmaid at the Hare and Hounds. Those bastards at the bar who'd turned to laugh, to stare, to mock. The way he'd stumbled past them out of the pub. Nearly broken his fucking neck. What was it she'd said? *Dirty*. He couldn't remember anything but that. *Dirty*. Then a hot gush of shame.

The cars began to move off beside him, leaving him alone under the street lamps. Alone under needles of rain that slanted down at him, stinging his face. He dropped the fish and chips into the gutter, lurched away from the wall, sobbing as he went down the hill. Breaking into a shambling trot, he felt his left heel rub where the skin had blistered. His smart new shoes were sodden with rain. His toes squelching as he ran, his legs gathering momentum. His open coat cloaked out behind him, loose change chinking against the dead lighter in his pocket. Down the hill, street lamps ran out in lines and the road ran out, hard and true. Squalls of rain blew into his face, blurring everything. His eyes fused the molten street lamps into the lights of cars as they spilled down the road. His fingers were wet, held out, groping as he ran.

Stott was taken by the sensation of flight, rising from the pavement into the lights that hung above the town, haloed with rain. Light everlasting. He rose in a wild exultation, above and beyond them. He rose into the night where he found an echo for the howl rising in his chest. Then he began to fall. He fell into the confusion of lights and rain. He fell like a star through darkness; fell through all the Friday nights and all the beer and all the emptiness that lay before him.

Mud Bastard

Kevin watched the three boys file into the gully that led down to the culvert. That was where the river came through the railway embankment. Today they had no gun. Once he had seen them shoot a robin with their air rifle. Red blood on the red breast; he'd never forgotten it. They called him Mud Bastard. He'd never found out why. He supposed it was because he was fat, or because he had no parents. Because he was half-black and his dad was a coon. Because they hated him. He was lying on the tarpaulin roof of his granddad's pigeon cote. Beneath him he could almost feel the sobbing cries as they bubbled in the birds' throats.

The roof was black and hot. Kevin half-turned to scratch his leg. In the intense light it looked almost white. He settled back, waiting for the boys to appear again. All around the river grew thickets of willowherb. From where he lay it looked like clumsy purple brushstrokes. It was sending out a fine mist of cottony spores that drifted up into the gardens, setting seed in the more neglected ones. His granddad hated the stuff. *Fireweed*, he called it.

Kevin dug a fingernail into a bubble of tar on the roof. He caught the faint shouts of the boys as they emerged from the far end of the gully and gathered on the little bridge that went over the river. It was so hot that the topmost branches of the big sycamore tree shimmered in the air. He'd peered through a piece of ice once and things had looked like that, but cold. He turned over on his back. Behind him lay fields, the river, railway, canal, farms with cows in their fields. This side, rows of houses followed the old river terraces and the hulks of mills rose above their dark slate roofs. Through a gap in the houses he could watch a constant stream of traffic, which rumbled in and out of the town.

Kevin lived in the end house with his grandparents. His parents were dead, or somewhere else, or he had never had a father. No one had told him, except in the insults they threw. The Mud Bastard. His granddad worked the night shift at the bakery; his grandma did days at the Co-op vinegar works. She always smelled of stale vinegar, as if she was being slowly pickled. Today was a Friday in the school holidays: his granddad's night off, so he was in the pub with a pint in his fist, playing darts or maybe bowls since it was a fine day. Soon he'd be home to have lunch – a bacon muffin or a slice of pie with some of the pickle his wife brought home.

Kevin turned back to watch the boys who were gathered aimlessly, looking down from the bridge. Once they'd tipped some barrels from the dye works into the water and it had turned dark red, like a biblical river running with blood. The roof sloped back towards the house, so he could watch without being seen. The Mud Bastard is watching, waiting. He knows everything you do. Waiting. Waiting for his granddad. Waiting for the boys to leave his territory.

Sliding off the roof, Kevin brushed at his filthy shirtfront. He'd catch it off his grandma. He took the peg out of the fastener and carefully prised open the door of the cote. Quickly, he slid inside. There were six birds, white ones and soft grey ones. Racing pigeons. Sometimes Kevin went with his granddad to let them off. Somehow they found their way back through miles and miles of air, always knowing where they were going, always sure in the emptiness. They clucked in alarm at Kevin's approach, jerking backwards on the perches. Their eyes were expressionless, yellow irises like coloured glass.

Kevin dug his hand into a sack of corn that stood by the door and poured a golden trail into the feeding tray. Like the nuggets that men had killed each other for in the Klondike. He held a single piece out towards the birds, but they shrank back from his hand. They would never come to him as they would his granddad. He stood watching them, the faint sounds of the world outside filtered by the stillness of the cote. Finally bored, he went out again into the blinding sun, fastening the door behind him, shading his eyes to look down the long dirt back.

The sun had drunk all colour, bleaching the walls of the houses. Kevin's granddad was making his way unsteadily along the back where the neighbours threw their ashes. A group of small children who were playing with a skipping rope made way for him fearfully. He was in his shirtsleeves, holding a paper bag of muffins in one hand. With the other he touched the wall beside him, looking straight ahead like a blind man. Kevin saw him wipe the sweat from his forehead, ruffling his grey hair, tearing at the collar that constrained his fleshy neck. As he approached, the boy dodged behind the hut, unsure, watching.

'Kevin!'

It was more like the call of a crow or a magpie than a human voice, harsh and ragged. He didn't answer and the voice came again, muffled this time.

'Kevin!'

When Kevin turned to look, his granddad was pissing unsteadily against the midden door. That's where they'd thrown their rubbish in the old days, when his grandfather was a boy. The dustmen came with shovels, then. Now, he was in full view of the neighbours. A fine spray was rebounding down the front of his trousers, glistening in the sun like dewdrops. He kept throwing out his free hand behind him in little balancing movements.

'Kevin!'

'What?'

'Wha'? Come for your bloody dinner, that's wha'!'

Kevin came round the end of the shed as his granddad was trying to mount the steps into the back yard. He stumbled and dropped the bag. Then stooped forwards to grope for it, falling onto his hands and going up the steep yard in one lunge like a bear. Coming behind him into the house Kevin heard the far-off cries of the boys. Turning, he saw them flicking some dark object high into the air, gathering around it as it fell, a distant black dot. They'd found something: something soft and alive.

In the kitchen Kevin's granddad was hunched over the stone sink with his braces hanging down from his waist. He was retching, his eyes glassy, like those of the pigeons. Suddenly, a belch of brown vomit gushed out. The kitchen was full of the stench of stale beer and sick. The big man spat then straightened up, wiping his mouth with the back of a hand, shuddering. His small blue eyes had rolled upwards, showing little cuticles of white beneath the irises. It was the face of a dead man, blanched as suet.

The boy was afraid. He kept close to the open doorway. There was a streak of vomit across the flagstones of the floor and down the front of his granddad's shirt. A damp patch had formed on his trousers. He took a step towards Kevin, then steadied himself, both hands grasping the back of a chair. The knuckles were white and he grinned in a ghastly, forced way, sweat glazing his face. It was like the way he smiled when the social worker came.

'Dinner! S'ave some dinner.'

He swayed, steadying himself against the chair, resisting the terrific pull of gravity that wanted to drag him down. The bag of muffins lay crushed on the table.

'I don't want any.'

The blue eyes blinked in disbelief. He cocked his ear as if he was listening to the radio, to some faint, crackly broadcast from a far country.

'Wha'?'

'I'm not hungry.'

His granddad took a hand from the chair back to wipe his face and almost fell.

'Nor hungry? Wha' the bloody 'ell, d'yer mean? I've got summat.'

'I don't want owt.'

The glassy eyes blinked furiously.

'Don't want owt is it? Yer kekky little bastard!'

The man lunged forward, aiming a blow at Kevin's head. Kevin ducked, but his granddad fell against him, toppling them both out of the doorway and over the step into the yard. Kevin heard the crack of a head as it hit the yard stones. He rolled free of the bulk of the man and crouched in the corner.

His granddad lay on the yard with one leg still inside the house. A thin trickle of blood rolled down from a graze on his temple. The blood was very dark; his skin was white as fungus and sweated a thin mucus. The man raised his head, eyes unfocused, then started to vomit quietly onto the flagstones. Slowly, semi-conscious, he ceased. His head subsided into the congealing pool. Then he went to sleep, snoring almost at once in raw, shallow breaths.

Kevin didn't dare move. He stared at the fallen man from a corner of the yard. Had anyone heard? Would a crowd of neighbours come rushing to offer help? He dreaded the thought, cringing at the shame of it.

No one came. After a time he stood up, unsteadily, took a step towards his granddad and bent down to listen. The breathing came in steady rasps, like a piece of iron being filed. Kevin touched his shoulder.

'Granddad!'

There was no response. The man had entered oblivion. He tried again, this time shoving at the shoulder so that the body rocked from side to side.

'Granddad. Wake up!'

Still nothing. The boy put his hands under his granddad's armpits and tried to drag him forward, so that at least his feet would come out of the doorway. But his own feet skidded in the pool of vomit and he lost his grip. He was unable to budge the weight of the fallen man. Its sheer lack of life defeated him. He smelled his granddad's sweat on his hands and wiped them on his trousers.

Kevin went down into the garden and unfastened the door of the pigeon cote. The dim light and the soft cooing of the birds made a sanctuary. The thought of the man lying up there in the back yard made him feel hollow, the kind of nausea that comes from a blow to the stomach. Kevin had banged his hip against the wall as he fell. He pulled up his shorts to look at the bruise that was forming. Under his brown skin it would be the same colour as the blue in the plumage of the birds. His granddad's birds; they wanted nothing to do with him. Waiting there, he imagined his granddad's voice at any moment, but there was nothing.

After a while he left the cote and went into the garden. The boys had gone from the stream and there were no shouting voices. Kevin went slowly with his sore hip, down through the garden. Past the neat rows of his granddad's cabbages. Past the rhubarb patch. Two white butterflies went by, interlocked in a wild dance, their wings trembling through the air. There was a paling missing from the garden fence and he was able to squeeze through into the meadow beyond. For a time he sat in the thicket of ferns that grew at the edge of the field, breathing their minty scent.

He watched the gully and waited. There was no one. When he was certain of this, he stood up and went forwards through the waist-high grass, its seeds sticking to his sweaty legs.

Kevin ducked into the gully, afraid of an ambush. He almost ran to the river. A magpie flew out of the scrubby elders, startling him for a second. His heart thumped hard upon his tight chest. For a while he stood on the bridge looking down into the filthy water. Everything seemed still and peaceful. Then he saw the frog laid out across an old car tyre in the full heat of the sun. The boys had thrown it up into the air and let it fall on the path, catching it by the leg and flicking it up, again and again. Kevin had watched the game before, he knew that look on the boys' faces, half-horrified, half-hysterical with laughter as they felt the living thing give and twitch under them. Afterwards they had pinned it down like a crucifixion with a stone on each foot, so that it lay on its back under the terrible sun.

Kevin knelt. He was close to the black mouths of the culvert. One by one he took the stones from the frog's feet. Its skin was baggy and loose. All over its body there were grazes.

Dust and tiny stones had been driven into its thin skin. The frog twitched feebly as he touched it and he drew his hands back, suddenly appalled. He watched it struggle with its hurt. Its long back legs stretched out uselessly. They looked like the pale legs of a girl. He turned and broke off two stems of Himalayan balsam from the thicket that grew near the water. Their foetid smell made him want to retch. Carefully he manoeuvred the frog onto them, as onto a stretcher, and carried it down to a little sandbank that made an eddy in the river. Here he floated the frog out on the stems and watched it being carried slowly away, jerking its front half feebly as its body tried to connect a broken spine.

A flight of six pigeons went overhead. They flew in a smooth circle above the houses, wheeling like handfuls of torn paper. They flew over the man who lay unconscious in the hot yard, the only things he had loved.

Kevin watched them. Had he fastened the door of the cote? Did it matter, because they would return wouldn't they? But for him? Would they come back for him? The thought was like a hot needle, jabbing, jabbing at his brain. Had he? But the voices broke out in front of him.

'Mud Bastard!'

'Mud Bastard!'

'Mud Bastard!'

And the boys emerged one by one from the tunnel, their chanting faces stiff as masks, stepping from darkness into the blade-hard light.

Rain

Jenny could smell dust on the window ledge, sour as powdered acid. Sun burned through the glass and across her face. The cactus plants were arid. Lifeless. There were dead bluebottles on the windowsill and the grain of the wood was bleached white through its cracked varnish.

Dust turned in the light like tiny splinters of glass. But behind her the room was cold and dark; a shadow was falling across her shoulder. In the little garden outside, a row of daffodils was dying back into the soil. Traffic passed on the road. Incessant. Opposite her house an identical terrace of houses stared back. Occasionally a young starling would flurry out from one of the gutters and stand, squawking for food. Their cries came faintly through the traffic, raw with hunger and life. Their plumage was glossy with a hundred shades of the refracted sun.

Jenny was thirty-four years old. She put the book she had been reading flat across her knees, smoothing out the fine cotton of her dress. Egyptian cotton with a thin blue stripe. On a day like this she should be outside. She could almost hear her mother saying it. Almost. It filled her with dread: the thought of the town, the people.

The postman passed, late today, lopsided with his bag of

letters. None of them were for her. Yesterday a letter had come for her mother. Jenny had opened it and found that it was from a credit company offering a cheap loan. She'd thrown it away, imagining her mother's scorn. Thirty-four years old. It had passed so quickly. She'd been waiting for something to begin; now it was never going to. Not here in the house where she'd been born, where both her parents had died, where the days stretched out, holding her, waiting for her. She could have done anything with her life her mother had told her. Anything.

Jenny stood up, careful to avoid the mirror that hung in an oak frame over the fireplace. Her face still hurt, stiff as a mask, parts of it nerveless. The backs of her hands looked like melted plastic. She saw the flames again, blossoming among the haberdashery, replayed like an old film. She smelled the smoke, white and acrid, scalding her lungs. She'd dreamed it all, over and over again. The bell ringing, her bloody tampon in the toilet bowl. Then emerging, amazed, into the inferno of the shop. Someone had left the fire doors open and the flames were sucking more and more air into the room.

It had been a quiet morning, a few shoppers picking aimlessly through the heaps of cloth. That was how the dream started, with those ghostly figures drifting silently through the store. Jenny saw their faces looking at her and then looking away, suddenly, as if they had just remembered something. But they couldn't all be remembering something. She was a plain Jane. Her mother had said that. She couldn't afford to look twice at a decent man. Not that there were any. And none had looked at her. In her dream the handle of the fire escape was painted red and she was dragging herself towards it, on fire, but feeling no pain. The metal bar seemed to glow, incandescent, and all around her bolts of lace exploded into flames.

Jenny walked stiffly into the small kitchen where she switched on the electric kettle. In the back garden she could see a pair of magpies quarrelling near their nest in the laburnum tree. Beyond that, across a few remaining fields, the houses of the new estate tilted their red-tiled roofs at the sun. A greenfinch landed on the bag of nuts she'd hung up. It was plump with good health, its heavy bill snatching at the food. The kettle clicked off and Jenny put a tea bag into the special cup with its plastic nozzle. She still couldn't open her mouth wide enough to drink from a normal cup. Light glanced off the roofs of the new houses, hurting her eyes. She closed them, feeling the lids tighten. That had been the first job, the surgeon had said. He had held her fingers where they stuck out from the white gauze. His hands had been cool, like porcelain, or the touch of water. The first job. As if they were renovating a house, or retouching an old master.

Thirty-four years old. She could have done anything, even if she was a plain Jane. Walking back into the front room she eased herself back into the leather armchair. Into the sun. The dead bluebottles gleamed, burnished by the light like exquisite gunmetal brooches. From the mantelpiece the photograph of her parents faced her. Their honeymoon, on the front at Skegness, the Ford Prefect parked in front of them. Their hair was tousled by the wind and they looked breathless. Younger than she was now. Jenny thought of that: there they were and here she was. Their only child unforeseen, their whole marriage before them, uncharted. She cradled the cup in her hands, afraid of the heat, of spilling the liquid onto herself – her arms, thighs, breasts.

For months she'd been terrified of anything hot. The pain would be unbearable. She had tablets for that, but sometimes it wasn't the pain itself, it was having the pain. Having to have it. Every day was a struggle with disbelief. But then she only had to look down at her seared skin to believe. She needed time. The doctor had said that. He had told her to look in the mirror every morning and say her own name. She'd wanted to laugh, would have laughed if she could have moved her face. Jenny didn't want to look at that maimed somebody else, the creature that looked at her from misshapen eyes. The fire had burned her face away. It had burned away her sins like a mythical fire. The surgeons would rebuild her. She'd be like a phoenix, one doctor had said. A new woman would rise from the flames. In time. Lots and lots of time. But outside, in the streets, in the town, life was happening for everybody else. And it was happening now.

Jenny took up the book again and allowed her fingers to stray across its pages. It was a world atlas, open at Norway. She looked at a group of islands off the northernmost coast. Langøy, Moskenstraumen, Austvågøy, Hinnøy, Senja. Her index finger traced the narrow passage of the Sørøysundet and then moved eastwards to Hammerfest. She whispered the names to herself. They sounded so beautiful, like the words of a hymn or psalm. Like the Song of Solomon. *Behold, thou art fair my love: behold thou art fair; thou hast dove's eyes*. And then that other part about the beloved. *He shall lie all night between my breasts*. She'd found those passages at Sunday school when she was a teenager and they had puzzled her. She who couldn't afford to look twice at a decent man. *Dove's eyes*. Her own eyes stung with the light. The lids felt like shutters jammed with grit.

She looked down at the map again. Hammerfest. One day she'd travel. Eighteen years she'd been at the shop. First in household fittings, then soft furnishings, then as a supervisor in haberdashery. There would be some money. Compensation. Mr Evans had said so, standing awkwardly by her bed in his dark suit. Jenny let her hand fall into the Norwegian sea. Into steep fjords, snow-capped mountain peaks, ice floes moving out to the ocean. The Gulf of Bothnia rippled under her hand as the book sagged. She'd hardly touched the cup of tea. She didn't want it now. The sun made her tired. Her eyelids began to lock shut.

When she awoke almost two hours had passed. Two hours. The sky had filled with fine grey clouds, lit at their edges by a hidden sun. She half expected to hear her mother calling her to work. Up every morning at six and calling to her in that shrill, reproachful voice. Every second spent in the warm sheets after that was a sin. Sometimes she would lie for an extra three, or even five, minutes, tempting the voice to call again, savouring the feeling, touching her body where it lay drowsily awake. Wondering if a man would ever touch her. Whether a man would ever want to. A man she could not afford to look at twice because she was a plain Jane. One day she would be like a bundle of myrrh, with dove's eyes. Her beloved would lie between her breasts. She'd touched them, feeling the soft swelling, the nipple. She'd felt beautiful then. Beautiful. Downstairs she would hear her mother raking the fire, chinking the teacups. Then it was out of bed, her feet pattering on the cold lino, dressing hurriedly for the ride into town, the long day at the store.

They had asked her what she remembered about the fire. Jenny had said: *The pigeons.* Through the smoke and at all the windows their wings had been a tumult, seeming to fan the flames. Often she'd sat in the town square, feeding them crumbs from her sandwiches, repelled by their eyes, by their deformed, toeless feet. Then they had gathered for revenge as she struggled towards the doors where fire was gulping and sucking at the air. Then Jenny had dreamed about them; how they had flocked into the room, mobbing her with smoking claws and wings, their beaks tearing at her. Clawing at the backs of her hands as she held them in front of her face.

Jenny rose from the chair, groggy with sleep, stiff from sitting too long in one position. The grafts on her hands and face were soft. She was afraid that they might suddenly slough away. Sun broke through the clouds, casting the shadows of cactus plants across the faded wood of the sill. Jenny caught sight of someone watching her in the mirror. Someone whose face was not a face. A bus halted outside to pick up passengers, its engine panting. She moved sideways behind the curtains. She couldn't help it.

When the bus had pulled away Jenny sat down again, tracing her fingers in the dust of the windowsill. She'd never wanted to die. Not when she lay immobile and the pain had been at its worst. Not when she drifted in morphine dreams through hospital nights. Not even when she'd seen the look on the faces of the nurses and doctors when they changed her dressings. She wanted to live. But she'd wanted her mother to die in those last days. Cancer of the spleen the doctors had said. Then secondaries in her liver and lymph glands. It was before the fire. She'd gone yellow, withering up like a husk. Jenny had wanted her to die; had, at the very end, wanted that shallow, rasping breath to stop forever. She told the Macmillan nurse who clucked her tongue as if there was always hope. If wishing that was a sin then she'd paid for it. Her transgressions had been burned away.

One day she'd be renewed, like a beautiful bird rising to heaven, like a lark singing high above her old life, which had gone for ever. She could be herself then. Dove's eyes. The windows of the soul. People would not move away from her as they did now. They would behold her. Her love would lie between her breasts. She would look in the mirror and see herself radiant as the clouds that floated now above the town.

Jenny's short sleep had tired her. She was exhausted all the time now. The doctors had told her to sleep whenever she had the need. She still felt guilty, having the need, escaping into the sheets, expecting her mother's reproach at any moment. Jenny pulled herself upstairs and undressed in the back bedroom, away from the noise of traffic. It plagued the front room where her parents had slept. Once this window had looked out over open fields with grazing cows. In the mornings the milk wagon had clattered down the lane with its empty churns. They were Friesians or Holsteins, the cows. Black and white. Now they were gone and the fields were built over. The roofs of the new houses glowed like a kiln in the sun. She watched shadows sweep the tiles, then she climbed between the sheets. The cotton flowed over her like a liquid, almost icy in its coolness.

For a long time she lay there, thinking. Her thoughts were unfocused. Images came, shadows of thoughts, never staying long enough, never distilling into words that could hold them. She fell gradually to sleep. Forgetting.

When Jenny awoke it was dark outside. The faint glow of lights from the housing estate across the fields tinted the curtains. She turned over in bed and lay on her back. The grafts tightened across her thighs. It was impossible to forget. Impossible. She put a hand to her face in the darkness. This was who she was. She lay there for a long time, watching the play of shadow and light on the ceiling as cars turned their headlamps against the house from far-away roads.

When she rose and went to the window, the touch of air was cool against her body through the nightdress. The garden was dark, the laburnum tree almost invisible except for its faintly luminous blossom. Poisonous in every part, her father had said. Street lamps burned on the new estate. She knew this view by heart. She closed the curtains against it. It would be a long time before she could sleep again. Her clothes lay over the back of a chair. Jenny took them and began to dress.

The steps down into the garden were short but steep. The terrace had been built on a ridge of the old river valley. The brook she'd played in as a child had been culverted to make room for the estate. There it was, hidden, the water flowing underground, flowing towards the sea through pure darkness. Under the houses. Under the lives being lived in them. Strange to think of that. Jenny slipped off her shoes and let her feet move over the grass on the small square of lawn. It was too long, the grass. A neighbour's son cut it for her every other week. She gave him a few pounds for doing it. He couldn't look at her. Paul. A nice boy. Dark hair and blues eyes and a quick way with things like the lawnmower and the machine that cut back the weeds with little whips.

On the lawn the grass was damp. Tiny globules of dew were forming across it like seed pearls. She loved the feel of its moisture against her skin. The air was warm outside, warmer than in the house where there was no fire, no heating switched on. The sky was overcast, heavy with cloud; it might rain at any minute. The garden was laden with scent from the lilac trees. Jenny's father had planted them. Near the little garden shed. When she peered through them, its windows were misty with cobwebs. Inside, it was still neatly laid out with his tools. Just as he had left them.

Jenny inhaled the scent. She was being etherised, her head growing light, a floating sensation wafting her away. Like thistledown. Or the spores of dandelions. *A bundle of myrrh is my well beloved unto me.* She put out a hand and cradled the hanging blossoms, feeling the waxy petals under her fingers. She touched the flowers to her lips. *By night on my bed I sought him whom my soul loveth: I sought him but I found him not.*

Letting the blossom swing away into the dusk, Jenny moved off over the soaking grass. A trickle of air began to shift against her face. Like the touch of a fabric, cool and smooth. Cambric or silk. She'd almost gloated over the bolts of silk and satin, had coveted rolls of velvet, the fine weave of white cotton. The leaves on the laburnum tree whispered at the air. The magpies would be asleep over their eggs. She imagined them lying in a nest full of stolen trinkets: silver necklaces, gold rings, strands of tinsel, glass beads. They were a quarrelsome pair, tiresome and self-satisfied, like most couples.

The windows of the houses gleamed with reflections. Lights in the street beyond threw silhouettes of their chimney pots up against the sky. The garden was overgrown, going rank with weeds and neglect. Jenny remembered the cedars of Lebanon, their blue-green needles; their sweet-smelling sawdust. She would like a chest of cedar wood in which to keep white cotton sheets. Sheets that she could lift out and hold against her face and luxuriate in.

Jenny thought of the river and the sea again. All across the world waves were breaking against deserted shorelines. Footprints were being washed away on dark beaches, driftwood reclaimed by the tides. Somewhere there'd be a bottle with a message in it. The glass milky, scarred by years of chinking across shingle in hidden coves. Inside, a scrap of paper, some barely decipherable writing. To get at the message she'd smash the bottle on a rock against which the sea was lapping. She'd hold the glass in her hands, swinging back her arm to hurl it. Then the paper, unfolding under her fingers, written in a foreign tongue, its message incomprehensible and out of reach.

The first drops of rain fell against Jenny's face. She winced. Wind shifted leaves on the laburnum and on the lilacs, bringing another cold flurry. She looked around for her shoes but she couldn't find them in the long grass. Moisture bounded out of the air, liquefying all the scents of the garden in an instant. Jenny stood still as the rain intensified. It was one of those summer squalls that washes away all dust, leaving plants and foliage glossy and renewed. Rain filling the gutters, floating away litter, gleaming across the rooftops of the town.

Rain plastered the hair over Jenny's forehead, dripping down her face, soaking her blouse and running over her breasts. It was drenching her whole body. She turned her face towards the rain. Water splashed softly against her mouth and eyes. She held out the parched palms of her hands for the rain to fall on. Tonight the husks of seeds would swell and split. Tomorrow the first green shoots would emerge, turning slowly to the sun. The earth would be moist and dark and there would be new life stirring in it. New life. She never wanted to move from this moment. Never.

Resistance

A bee entered the purple bell of a foxglove and busied itself
there, smearing itself with pollen from the swollen stamens.
Gustave Peythieu watched it clamber in. He had the urge to
close the end of the flower with his fingers, to trap the bee
inside. Instead, he rolled a thin cigarette. These days tobacco
tasted like shit. It was dry, bitter on his tongue. To get any
decent stuff you had to go to the black market. You had to
deal with Leon Besse and his crew. Those bastards. Even at
school Leon had been a little shit. But you had to be careful
in a village, in a small town. What you said, what you did. You
had to let some things pass by. You told yourself that some
people had it coming. One day. That was all.

Gustave watched the bee fly away, dizzy with nectar. He
blew a stream of smoke from his lips then picked up his hoe
from where it leaned against the garden shed and carried on
hoeing the curé's onions.

The sun was sinking into a patch of cloud. It sent diagonal
rays of light onto the trees across the valley. Gustave paused.
Sweat ran down his sides under his shirt. It was hot. He
mustn't overdo it. Not for the Monseigneur. That fat capon of
a priest. Gustave broke off some stems of lavender from the
rock border and rubbed them between his stubby hands. His
fingers were shiny with oil where he'd whetted the scythe.

Lavender smelled good. It smelled of the earth, it smelled of sex, like the sheets of their bed at home.

He snapped off some more stems and put them in his trouser pocket for Amelie. She was scared these days. Scared of him, of what he might do. But tonight, after the job was done, he knew she'd let his hands wander across the soft skin inside her thighs. He knew that they'd make love and that afterwards she'd ask for a glass of water as she always did. He'd fetch it for her and then kiss her beneath each breast as he always did when they made love. Then they'd turn over and sleep. They'd been married for two years.

It was a hazy day. Behind him stood the church with its square tower and its three bronze bells, green with age, hung in a row. Lower down the valley was the walled cemetery where his parents were. Today mist had never quite cleared from the river. Above it the vineyards were laid out in tidy rows. The vines looked like tightly braided hair. He'd seen a picture like that once of an African woman. A Sudanese. He remembered the way her lips and earrings had glinted in the picture. And she'd been bare breasted, like a whore at her window.

Gustave took a bag of peaches from his jacket which hung from the handle of the scythe. He ate one in quick, sweet bites, stooping to let the juice run onto the ground, then spitting the stone into the water butt. Insects skated away across the dusty surface. Running for cover. Gustave looked up. The sky was still too clear. They needed more cloud for the drop, the merest sliver of moon. The hoe sliced through the young leaves of a dandelion. He wasn't afraid. As for hidden radios and call signs – leave that to others, those who were in deeper than he was. He was used to surprises from people he hardly knew, or thought he knew. The way a loaf of bread was suddenly thrust into your hand in the marketplace, the weight of it telling you there was something interesting inside. To the gendarme guarding the mairie it was just another loaf, another box of eggs.

It was easy and he wasn't scared, even if his wife was. Poor Amelie. Perhaps after making love he'd have a small glass of cognac. Even in this war life was not so bad if your tastes were simple. And if you were lucky. He chased a beetle with the shiny steel tip of the hoe. He was lucky.

Gustave squinted at a buzzard as it circled above the valley. Before the war the gamekeepers had kept them down, but now they were everywhere. Vermin. He saw the bird spiral higher on a current of hot air, flicking its wing tips lazily. A spotted flycatcher landed on a hollyhock, arching the stem like the spine of a leaping fish or the fisherman's rod. It flew in quick circles, snapping up insects then cocking its head with those sharp, dark eyes. A lizard betrayed itself, flickering near his foot then freezing into stillness. It had lost its tail in some encounter and a new one was growing from a pointed black stub that resembled a dab of tar. He looked at the finger on his left hand. The one that had been severed by a splinter of steel early in the war. Sometimes he still felt a tingling in the fingertip that wasn't there. Months of training, then a few days shivering in a slit trench. Filthy underwear and lousy food. Sweat, boredom, then apprehension, then fear. Why kill each other? For what? There was a graveyard full of answers not one kilometre from where he was working. He'd hated being a soldier: everything about it from the stinking pit latrines to blind obedience. Some men took to it. God help them, they weren't really men. A mortar shell had knocked him over and finished it. Then a German unit had overrun the field hospital where he was having his hand bandaged and they'd surrendered meekly. The enemy had even handed out cigarettes. It was a relief. The flycatcher went past him on splayed wings, almost touching his face.

Gustave carried on hoeing. When he looked up again the sun was flaring into the ragged branches of a large pine tree on the opposite ridge of the valley. It was time to head home.

Amelie was washing their sheets in the concrete cistern that he'd built outside the house. Her arms gleamed under the suds. The water here was hard. It never really worked up a proper lather.

'Good day?'

At his voice, she straightened up and touched her coiled hair. In the sun it showed its chestnut lights and she smiled. A tender, crooked little smile.

'Yes, I bottled the blackberries and brought in some plums.'

She bent back down to the washing.

'The meal should be ready when I'm through here. Go and wash.'

But he loitered beside her instead, scuffing the toe of his boot in the trickles of water that spilled from the cistern.

'If you're going to stand there, get hold of these.'

She folded an armful of sheets like bread dough, dropped them into a basket and handed it to him.

'Watch your hands. They're filthy!'

He touched his cap as at a commanding officer.

'Yes, filthy with honest labour. Tilling Monseigneur's holy ground!'

She laughed at him and turned back to the grey water.

'Almost done. Go on. Wash, wash!'

Gustave went into the cool of the house, all its shapes vague shadows after the sun. The rooms smelled of hot fruit. A basket of dusky blue plums had been laid on the table. Jars of blackberries were cooling with their lids off and the big brass jam pan had been scrubbed and left to drain on the sink. He rinsed his hands, working at the stubborn soap. Then he took the sheets through to the back garden and pegged them on the line.

They ate their meal almost in silence, Amelie fetching the food from the stove, even breaking his bread for him so that he could mop up the sauce. She knew when he refused the wine that something was going to happen. That crimping of her mouth told him she was scared again.

'I have to go out tonight.'

'Why?'

She paused with her back to him, carrying the plates to the sink.

'Why? Don't ask why.'

Gustave went up behind her and put his hands on her waist. Her flesh was soft under the apron. He thought of later, when they'd make love. How her eyes would close as his hand slid between her thighs where the skin was unbearably soft, where she was hot and moist and ready for him. He'd surrender to her then. Not now.

Amelie wouldn't look at him as he got ready. She fastened the shutters, locking them on the inside. Then she sat on a straight-backed chair, her face turned away from him, her hands folded in her lap. He held his cap and stood close to her, waiting.

'Amelie.'

Nothing.

'Amelie, you know I've got to go.'

He reached out and pulled her face towards him, gently. She wouldn't look at him.

'I'll be late. Don't wait up.'

She said nothing. Gustave touched his face to hers. He hated her fear. It would make him afraid too, if he let it. He was doing what he had to do. Not what he wanted to. She had to remember that. He murmured into her neck.

'Don't wait up, but don't go to sleep either.'

He saw the sudden glimmer of desire in her face, but she turned it resolutely away.

Gustave left the house by the back door. He walked through the village, staying close to the houses, catching the scent of jasmine in the day's fading heat. It had gone dark quickly. He made his way back to the curé's garden, prising up a flat stone with the broken blade of a sickle that he'd hidden in the wall. He reached down inside the old drain until his fingers touched oilcloth, then metal. When he closed the gate behind him and buttoned his jacket, a cold weight lay against his belly.

Gustave took an old logging path down through the woods. It was overhung with snowberry and brambles. There was the faintest slice of moon that the clouds kept covering. He walked half a kilometre down the slope of the valley and then waited at a fork. Soon he heard footsteps, the crack and scuffle of feet on fallen pine cones and twigs. The feet stopped and a voice whispered four numbers very slowly. No names. Gustave moved towards the man, intoned his own sequence and touched his arm. They went on in silence. Another three kilometres to the drop. It was to be in the meadow of a disused farm down in the valley, where the river had planed enough flat land for a family to scrape out a living. They'd prospered for a time, even building a mill to press sunflower oil. But they were long gone. The miller's three sons had all been killed at Verdun in the first war. Their flabby faces stared out from the family headstone in the cemetery, surrounded by porcelain roses of remembrance. Gustave stumbled and righted himself. He could smell wine on his companion's breath. The fool! He let him walk a few steps in front.

The arrangement was that four other men would be waiting for them. It was their job to take the supplies away. Gustave and his comrade were there to speed up the operation, to dispose of the parachutes and canisters. The quicker that was done and the stuff was separated the better. He didn't know the other men or where the equipment would be taken. But in a few weeks they'd hear rumours of a railway track being blown up, or of a factory being sabotaged. Just rumours usually. He was a small part of the machine: that was all.

The others were waiting at the edge of the overgrown meadow where the ruined farmhouse and mill stood in shadow on the far side. Gustave lay on his back, listening to the river and watching the sky. Around them, grasshoppers chirred remorselessly. The clouds were lit faintly by the pared moon. His companions' faces were vague and pale. A moth landed on his cheek, startling him. It was mostly waiting. Hours of waiting and then a few moments of action. He needed a cigarette, but that was out of the question.

Gustave half dozed for a moment. In that slippage of his senses he remembered the dream from which he'd woken the night before. He'd been in his parents' house, a small cottage built into the hillside with dark, crooked rooms and hams hanging from the beams. His mother had been there, but not his father who was already dead. A red mare had somehow come inside the house. It was nuzzling his face. Its eyes were almost hidden by long lashes and its lips grazed across his forehead, touching him with the utmost tenderness. Somehow it was speaking to him. Or it was thinking words into his head. It was telling Gustave that it was pregnant with his foal. Telling him with such intimacy that its breath was delicate and warm against his face. But there was no smell of horse. No scent of sweat or dung. Then Amelie had been helping the mare to foal and it had let fall a long-legged colt that had lain helplessly in the straw, its coat dark chestnut, streaked with blood and birth-slime. The mare was licking it as it struggled to rise up. He'd begun to panic then, trying to pull it away from the foal by its mane. Amelie had stood smiling, nodding to his mother in that knowing way that women have about such matters. And all the time she'd been wearing his father's best chequered cap.

Gustave rolled over onto his stomach. No use trying to make sense of a dream like that. He'd woken Amelie by muttering in his sleep, but he hadn't told her about the dream. Instead he'd pressed himself against her curled body, finding its shape with his own. Amelie had ignored him, pulling the sheets closer. But Gustave had lain awake for a long time in this state of arousal and only began to doze again when the first light was chinking through the shutters of their bedroom. Then he'd had to rise for work.

One of the men was muttering beside him that the plane was late. He didn't like it. There was silence for a time except for the hoarse, rhythmical chattering of grasshoppers. Nothing happened. The starved moon slid behind a cloud, taking away its remnant of light. Gustave needed to piss. He got up and walked slowly to the edge of the clearing, relieving himself into the bracken. The moon reappeared, sailing between two clouds. In the window of the ruined mill he thought he saw something glinting. Like the suddenly uncovered gaze of a bird. The way that film of skin flickers across its eyeball. He stared towards the gutted windows again. Nothing. But now he knew what fear was, how it pushed the blood from your face and tightened around your chest. Something was wrong.

Gustave stood ten metres from the river that had shrivelled in the summer heat. Across the clearing he heard the faint voices of the men arguing. The idiots! They could at least keep quiet. That was the rule. Gustave wanted a drink; his mouth was dry as leather. He pushed down through the bracken towards the river until he was screened from the open meadow by the trees and the dipping angle of the bank. He followed the water a few metres upstream until he came to a bridge. This was where the road crossed the river before winding up to the village. Pressing his head to the stonework, he heard the faint throb of engines. Not a plane, but lorries far back on the road. He dipped his hand into the river and took a mouthful of water, swallowing his heart with every breath.

Gustave began to run. Upstream, through shallow water and overhanging fronds of bracken. A heavy bird broke out from the trees above and panicked away through the branches. Below him a white tongue of light flickered across the meadow and the sounds of their betrayal began. Engines were approaching on the road. There were shouts. He climbed quickly where the stream fell, running, flinging himself over boulders in the river bed. The moss broke off under his hands and his feet slipped everywhere on the rocks. He had to clamber up onto the bank when he came to a waterfall, taking to the hillside. He knew that he had to get back to the village. Below him a voice was hailing them in hesitant French. Then a small volley of pistol shots. It was answered by rifles and the quick tapping of a machine gun. The bloody fools! Gustave took the pistol from his belt and flung it away into the river. He had to climb the valley, and fast.

To his right lay the vineyards and open land. To his left the forest grew thickly, extending to the meadows that spread below the village. He heard the heavy thrumming of an aeroplane approaching. Instead of following the signal from a torch they would see the searchlight, the muzzle-flashes of the ambush below. The plane banked over the trees and droned away. There was nothing anyone could do to help the men now. Nothing he could do. The twin headlights of a lorry were heading down to the bridge, twisting with the road. There was a shot from the meadow, then another. Then the machine gun, methodical as a seamstress tacking cloth.

Now Gustave ran by instinct. He ran through the forest of his childhood, dodging overhanging branches, finding the footpaths that were soft with fallen pine needles. He ran with a feral cunning. The thought of the men below being dragged into the truck or to the mill where the soldiers had been waiting jabbered in his head. He'd taken a girl there once, before Amelie. They'd picked bluebells in the meadow and seen an adder coiled on a stone in the sun. She'd let him touch her breasts in the disused upper room where they used to store the grain. Then she'd helped him to masturbate, his semen jetting onto her face, hot and quick. His only hope was that they would all be killed.

Gustave's feet were sodden from the stream. His shoes were rubbing at his heels. He limped on. Panting in harsh gasps. Taking a direct path to the village through the meadow, between cows that lay on the damp grass. Here and there were the white faces of mushrooms coming secretively in the night. Gustave leaned against a gate, wiping sweat from his forehead with his cap. He couldn't remember the girl's name.

At the outskirts of the village Gustave took off his shoes and went barefoot through the streets until he reached his house. He got in through the back door, lifting the catch and letting it fall quietly. The rooms still smelled of bottled fruit.

It was the scent of briars and summer lanes. He hid his wet shoes behind a pile of logs in the hearth and took off his jacket, splashing water into his face at the sink. Then he fumbled for the cognac bottle in the dark, taking a swig straight from its neck. The liquid skinned his throat.

When he entered the bedroom his breathing was calmer. He knew from Amelie's voice that she was sitting up in bed. Gustave took off his clothes and folded them blindly onto a chair.

'Gustave?'

He didn't answer.

'Are you alright? You're not hurt?'

'No. I'm alright.'

It was a faraway voice, not his.

'I thought you'd be later.'

'Later than this?'

It was all unreal, even now, just half an hour later. Nothing had happened. He had to remember that.

'Yes, you said so.'

'Well, it's alright then, I'm here.'

He reached under the bolster for his nightshirt but she tugged it from his hand and threw it across the bed.

'Come on, you don't need that.'

In the bed Amelie was naked, softly enveloping him. Her tongue was hot inside his mouth, her breasts firm against his chest. Gustave arched himself above her, his hands curved around her shoulders. Then he sank slowly down between her outspread knees.

After they'd made love she asked for a glass of water and he brought it to her. She lit a candle, placing it low on the floor so that the light couldn't show. A lorry went past the house, rattling the shutters, travelling at speed towards the town. Then another. They kept going. Gustave's heart measured his pulse in steady beats. He stood listening intently. Amelie's hair was spread down behind her, against the pillows and the oak bed head, gleaming in the dull light. He saw that his cock was slick with her blood, something they'd always celebrated.

'You've come on!'

'Ah, so soon?'

Amelie reached for a square of cotton waste and pressed it between her legs before examining it.

'Oh, yes.'

She looked up shyly.

'I thought it'd be another week.'

'You're a clever girl!'

Gustave handed her the glass of water, allowing his hand to linger on hers. Then he kissed her once under each nipple. When he climbed into the bed beside her the sheets smelled faintly of lavender.

Finding the Rocking Stone

The rocking stone was in Spooky Wood. It was accessible only by driving off the road that ran down from the head of the valley and onto a rutted track. The track curved sharply, climbing past the old railway cottages and onto the moor where there was room to park beside a ruined limekiln. That was next to James' house. Lucas drove onto the patch of rough ground, pulled up the handbrake and elbowed the car door open. The ground was soft underfoot. He leaned back into the car to drag the keys from the ignition. Not that anyone would steal it up here.

To the south, the bulk of the fells rose in a hatchwork of shadows and soft afternoon light, forming a flat-topped escarpment. Limestone was overlain with a layer of gritstone that had stopped it from eroding, from dissolving under centuries of rain. Lucas turned his head, hunching from the wind. He hadn't brought a scarf or hat. His hair that had once grown in dark curls was thinning at the temples now. He took his bearings, leaning both hands on the top stones of a dry-built wall. There it was, Spooky Wood, way down to his right where the sun would eventually set. A patch of larch trees sprawled on the moor, as if the wood had picked itself up to flee, then fallen.

The house looked deserted, except for a wisp of wood

smoke. That evocative scent. After James had died, his younger brother had turned up to dispose of the house and studio. No one even knew he had a brother. Half-brother, someone had whispered, significantly, at the funeral. The house had been quickly sold and just as quickly gentrified. Instead of white plastered walls and stripped-wood floors and a filthy electric cooker, it had an Aga, floral wallpaper, discreet lamps, chintzy curtains, a Range Rover in the yard, a chestnut pony in the paddock. James would have hated all that. And Elena had moved away without leaving an address, without saying goodbye to anyone. Not even to Lucas. At the funeral she'd stood gaunt and silent, dabbing at her nose and wearing one of James' old coats.

Lucas zipped up his jacket against the chill and buttoned the neck-flap. What was he doing here? Each year a feeling grew in him, a kind of yearning, and he made his way back. Sentimental, maybe. Perhaps he would always return like this. The past was important. But it needed keeping in its place. It was good to come back, so that things didn't grow in your mind to overshadow the present. After all, that was how regret began. That was one thing he'd learned from James: regret nothing.

He climbed the stile, gripping the damp timber to haul himself up, the breeze nipping at his bald patch. Low fells sloped away to the north, so that he was walking gently downhill towards the dark smudge of the wood. *Spooky Wood.* Not its real name, but the name he and Elena had given it when James was alive. James who had seemed so bohemian, self-sufficient, ageless. When he fell ill towards the end and Lucas was visiting he'd send them out together: *Go for a walk, get Elena into the fresh air. Go, go!*

Lucas glanced back at the house. The first time he'd come

here was to look at some of James' paintings. He'd just set up a small commercial gallery in Ilkley after curating for Leeds city art galleries. He'd cut his teeth there, made the necessary contacts. That was long after studying at Falmouth, long after he'd given up his own ambitions to be a painter, of course. He'd decided that his talent was in showing the work of others. Commissioning, procuring, talent spotting. And he'd been right. He'd done well, building a solid reputation throughout the north of England and even further afield. But then the art world was a small world. An unforgiving world if you got things wrong. These days art was an investment and his customers expected to buy something beautiful *and* watch it grow in value. They hadn't learnt the greatest pleasure of any art form – that one wants but does not need it, that beauty is useless but not meaningless.

That wasn't true of the artists of course. He'd been put on to James Essien by a dealer in Amsterdam. He'd been astonished to find a painter he hadn't heard of living close by in Yorkshire. And one whose reputation – whose value – was rising. But all that had come out later, when he knew James much better. There'd been a phone call first, some tentative remarks, then James sweeping all that ceremony aside, his fruity public-school voice urging Lucas to visit. A few days later he'd driven up through Airedale and Ribblesdale. He'd found the track and then the house – squatting on a ridge under grey clouds – with difficulty. He'd knocked hesitantly and James had answered, dressed in a torn blue sweater and khaki trousers, larger than life, a smudged glass in his hand. Lucas was taken into James' studio and plied with Bulgarian wine. Fluent in three or four European languages, he'd peppered his conversation with authentic pronunciations: *jouissance, chiaroscuro, pointillist*, the names of great artists flowing from his tongue as if he'd known them all personally.

Lucas had been impressed, a little intimidated, a little repelled. Elena had been there in the background somewhere, listening to the radio in a distant room then appearing at the window as Lucas drove away. There was already something wistful about her pale hair and skin, the fine turn of her neck.

Lucas had found some of James' work bombastic and overstated. But most of it had hit the mark with what he felt was a kind of searing veracity, an unmistakable authority. The kind that time would judge. The kind you had to take a hunch on. He'd bought two huge watercolours, landscapes that had been abstracted from their original forms into patches of colour that seemed almost motile, changing with each angle of view. He'd sold one but kept the other for himself. The painting surprised him every time he climbed the stairs at home to find its colours warping the lit space of the landing. Then he'd exhibited other work for commission, making frequent trips to visit James and look through the latest stuff. Or James would simply call him when he had something new to offer: *Time to visit, my dear.* They'd become friends. Of a sort. Friends who were useful to each other. Well, come to think of it, that wasn't entirely fair. Friends ought to be useful to each other, after all. There was a genuine fondness, too, a mutual admiration that went unremarked but was nevertheless gratifying. Whenever Lucas drove away from the house after a visit he felt more generous, more talented, more fulfilled in his work. James had that knack.

Now there it was behind him: the house where James had lived on cheap wine, stewed tea, Dutch cheese, sardines, oranges and brown bread. He'd bought it for a song in the seventies when he'd given up lecturing. He'd set up a studio, thrown the key over a wall and never locked the door again. Except he'd never lectured anywhere. That was part of the myth. The rumour was that James had got caught up in a forgery scam when he was in his twenties. Lucas had heard that it was early French impressionists but, more authoritatively, he'd also heard that it was Dutch work from an earlier century. The Delft school. Hals, Ruisdael, Cuyp, de Witte, van Goyen, Saenredam. One thing was for sure: you needed technique to get away with that kind of thing. Though he'd never known James work in oils or even acrylic. He was a water colourist through and through.

One dealer had told him that James had done time after being caught out. Another that he'd simply skipped across to the Continent and got by on the family money. He was a German-Belgian Jew by descent; his father had been an industrial chemist, eventually settling in Manchester. Long-standing Anglophiles, they had already sent James and his brother to school in England. The elder brother who'd been killed in Burma right at the end of the war. Lucas had never asked about any of that, of course. But it was a strange feeling to wonder if James was sometimes imitating himself, whether his work was some kind of double take. Fakery. Impressions of impressions. Pastiche. But then what else could it be? It was art, and like all art both inauthentic and true.

If you visited when James was away – which was often – there'd be a row of notes on the kitchen table, each weighted down with a knife or the pepper mill. Every message from a different friend, saying how sorry they were to have missed him. Lucas lived alone. Whenever he left the house, locking the door reminded him of James. The very action seemed pinched, ignoble, as mean-spirited as pension schemes, insurance policies or burglar alarms. James' generosity had always seemed so effortless.

It was November. Two o'clock. Already the light seemed faint against the limestone. It would be cold later. A thin moon. A horn of ice. Lucas set off along the sunken path. It descended the fell side in a glitter of mud. On each side, exposed peat showed the depth of the bog. To his left, the escarpment shouldered upwards. Ahead was the wood. It grew on a limestone pavement raised above the surrounding fell. Three acres of wind-blitzed trees. A hare broke from cover, ran a few yards then paused to watch him. It lowered its ears and he saw the wind parting the fur on its face. Once, only a couple of years ago, he'd come here in summer on a calm evening, the sun basking in the apex of the valley. He'd been half-expecting to find her there. Elena. Instead, a tawny owl had terrified him, gliding out of the wood's green-golden light. That was all: just the crackle of branches underfoot, the rasp of breath caught in his chest, the scent of larch trees.

He climbed another stile, clambering over slabs of stone set into the wall. The stile was new, the stone curiously familiar. When he bent to look under the steps he could see inscriptions etched in cursive script. They were recycled headstones. The National Park had restored the pathway and the stiles years after James died. But how on earth had they got permission for this? Perhaps the dead were so distant that no living relative had complained. They'd been taken from one of the chapels converted to a dwelling now because the farmers and villagers no longer needed God to fill their empty time. Once they would have thought nothing of walking ten miles to attend services twice on a Sunday. Now even the stones commemorating them had a new utility. Lucas paused with his hand against the slate. Here they were: the names of the dead put to new use, cold under his hand.

The wood was closer now. He could see the edge of the limestone pavement, the trunks of larches splintered where westerlies had harried and broken them and bent them over. *Spooky*, Elena had said. Because it looked like a crouching animal. A wolf or a bear. She'd touched his arm. Blonde hair and pale skin, her eyes almost grey they were so pale. *Truly, it's a wolf*, she'd said, *it's alive! Look!*

They'd found the rocking stone together, set into the pavement, shaped like a flattened torpedo. James had told them where to look. It had become too far for him to walk after the heart bypass that had left his skin grey and baggy, his legs wasted. Sometimes, on warm days, he'd sit with his shirt open, showing the livid scar on his breastbone where they'd opened him up. *Like a tin of fish.* And he had another scar the length of one leg where they'd taken a vein for grafting. So he'd slouch around the house and wave Lucas and Elena away as if they were a couple of children. The stone was there, just as he'd promised. They'd straddled it and swayed their hips until it began to move, knocking against the rock on either side until it was booming along the length of the wood. Once it was moving, it was possible to control it by flexing the ankles, working in harmony with your partner to create a shared rhythm. *It's a sacred stone, a shrine!* Elena had said, her accent thick and husky. Hoops of gold gleamed in her ears. Her small teeth glistened as she moved in rapture to the swaying weight of the stone.

Afterwards they'd gone back to the house and sat with James in front of the fire, sipping whisky and cracking walnuts with the poker. That was soon after he'd fallen ill. After the operation and the long stay in hospital. He never complained about pain or breathlessness, treating the whole business as just another adventure. There he was, waiting for them when they got back, smiling, congratulating them. On what? Elena's face had been abstracted, almost elated, as if she was still on the rocking stone, sending out its primeval boom.

She'd whispered to him as they clambered down from the wood, *Nothing has changed here.* She'd said it fiercely, plucking at his sleeve. *Nothing has changed!* He hadn't really known what she'd meant. But he'd often thought about it, re-running the words in his mind until his memory of Elena triggered them always.

The approach to the wood was tricky. You had to veer off from the path then clamber down from the edge of the moor, which petered out in a low cliff. Then you had to clamber up eight feet of limestone that reared into the wood. Lucas slipped and half fell, banging the heel of his hand. There was a dead sheep lying on the grass below him. Its head was bent to one side, the reddle mark fresh on its rump where the tup had been at it. In the hawthorns at the edge of the wood, a flock of long-tailed tits were stripping the berries. Lucas stepped up onto a ledge, stamped down some strands of wire from a rusted fence and stepped over. He gripped the edge of the rock and then pressed down with the flat of his hands, wincing, mantling upwards.

He was in. The light was filtered by wintering larches. Hart's tongue glistened everywhere. Ferns had died back, a rich russet. There were deep grykes in the pavement and you had to be careful because the stones were covered in moss. A few rowan trees had been planted in protective sheaths to keep away rabbits or deer. The damp rocks were treacherous underfoot. He remembered how he'd taken Elena's hand, how she'd fallen against him and he'd felt her breath hot on his neck. She'd flushed and laughed it off. But he'd felt his chest go tight. And he hadn't really known anything about her. She was Hungarian. She'd come to live with James. *My painter,* she called him affectionately, touching his arm. She was thirty years younger than her painter, four years younger than

Lucas. But then James had always been good at cultivating young friends. That was what he'd called Elena, his friend. But there'd been gossip down in the village. And when they sat together his hand covered hers and lingered there. Then he'd glance up at Lucas with that little smile, half-surprised, half-amused at his good luck. But always sure of his own worth and generosity, his unmistakable largesse.

Lucas' hands were stiff with cold. The veins stood out in blue ridges. He cupped them and blew into them, flexing the knuckles slowly. From the edge of the wood he could hear the ragged cries of rooks or crows. Everything was still: just the tips of larch branches stirring. Elena had been right. Nothing had really changed here. Except those new trees showed someone was taking an interest. Trying to make sure the wood survived the wind and the long winters. Maybe the same people who had mended the stiles and pathways.

Lucas moved deeper into the trees. Larch branches dipped down, trailing on the earth, which was brown with fallen needles. The rocking stone had always been tricky to find. He'd been here a couple of times before and failed. Some-times it was as if it simply wasn't to be. At others, he went straight to it, guided by something. Instinct perhaps? Odd to feel that way, because he wasn't the least bit mystical. The wood seemed timeless, but other things had changed. James had fallen ill again, emerging from hospital gaunt and exhausted, his eyes dark with a wounded look. Elena had nursed him when he was unable to work. Then James had died – died in his sleep of all things – and Elena had gone away. Coming here had seemed pointless at first. He'd felt uncomfortable parking the car at the end of the track, right outside the house where the newcomers lived with their Range Rover and pony and their children, who he saw playing on a swing in what had been James' vegetable patch. He was chasing a memory, a lost moment, his own failure and foolishness. Knowing that gratified him at some level; failure itself was piquant, an indulgence to be sipped like a decent malt. Savoured without regret. So he'd returned every year. And here he was again.

Lucas moved in a slow circle through the wood, testing each slab of limestone before placing his weight on it. The rocking stone wasn't very deep into the wood: he knew that. And it was some way to the left of his entry point: he was sure of that, too. He was sweating under his winter jacket. He glanced at his watch and the luminous hands showed him four o'clock. It'd be getting dark soon. But even at dusk the wood was lit with an ambient glow that rose up as if the stone was burnished. He remembered the glint of Elena's earrings, her hot breath, her pulse moving under the pale skin of her throat. Then the way she'd cracked walnuts with a firm whip of her wrist and thrown the shells to the fire. James had watched them from his armchair, his trousers and sweater smeared with paint, his smile enigmatic, a little triumphant at the new frisson between them.

Quite suddenly, the stone was there under his feet. He'd strayed onto it without noticing. Odd that it was so elusive yet so unmistakable once you'd found it. He flexed his waist and threw himself sideways to begin the motion that would make the rock sound out. Nothing. He checked the stone again. It was surely the right one. He braced a leg against a tree stump and pushed again, straddling the stone. Nothing. The stone that had been poised on its sternum was locked. The boulder that had rocked here for centuries was frozen solid. Maybe a sapling had taken root there. Or a piece of stone had fallen into the gryke to chock it. Lucas knelt on the damp surface and ran his hand carefully around the rock, jamming his arm to the elbow. He could feel nothing and the light was fading. The stone had been silenced, its heavy tongue clamped into jaws of rock.

James glanced at his watch again. He must go. Before darkness came down to hide the path. He pushed on through the overhanging branches of the larch trees and out of the wood. *Nothing has changed here.* What had Elena meant by that? The wood *had* changed; it was changing all the time. He'd been a fool to expect that the past would be waiting for him. He'd been a fool not to reach for her and kiss her as she swayed there on the stone with him that time, letting its boom fill the space around them. She might have wanted that. For all he knew, she might have wanted him. But somehow the moment had passed and James' proprietorial air had come between them. Moments had passed, then years. One slipped almost seamlessly into the other and you hardly noticed.

The escarpment solidified from mist as Lucas made his way back up the path. It was dark, but limestone reflected the last light. His knee stung where he'd slipped again and grazed it climbing down from the wood. It lay behind him now, crouched, bristling like a wolf or a bear. *Spooky.* It was a childish word and he felt a childish fear tug at him as darkness fell. He wanted to be home in his empty house. To light the fire, sip hot tea, sit with a good book or an exhibition catalogue. He wanted to pass the painting on the landing and feel its faint tug of surprise again. Surely that was enough? Lucas hurried on, head down against the wind, against the gathering night.

When he reached James' house, he smelled wood smoke again. At the old limekiln he felt in his pocket for his car keys.

He turned to the house once more, loosening his neck-band, unzipping his jacket. All the lights were on and Lucas was almost sure he could hear children's voices quarrelling in an upstairs room.

The Beauty of Ice

That year the autumn was dry after a summer of drought. In December the lake was low and the first sub-zero temperatures of winter froze it hard. The water didn't look solid at first because the ice remained clear like a fine skin. *Pellucid* was a word I found for it. But at the edges it was at least four inches thick. That was when we started to hear of the accidents, in the papers and on the radio news. How a girl had chased her dog onto a lake and first the dog, then the girl, then two men who tried to rescue her fell through the ice and died in the terrible cold.

I remember the talk of suspended animation, how a body can stay alive without a flicker of a pulse. How drunks found frozen in shop doorways sometimes came to in hospital beds and reclaimed their lives. Some of them experienced ecstatic visions whilst unconscious. Others had miraculous conversions to religion and featured in those evangelical Christian magazines that come piling through the letterbox with free-sheets and advertising brochures.

But not this time: the girl, the dog and the two men were all drowned. That got me thinking about water, about ice. The way it was all so clear, so deadly: so purposeful.

I used to go walking by the lake with my little sister, Annie.

I was twelve and old enough to be sensible, or so my mother thought. Annie was only seven. She looked up to me, I suppose. One day, after the lake froze over, we went walking along the gravel path under the fir trees that came down almost to the water's edge. I remember Annie was excited. She kept running ahead shouting.

'Katie, come on, Katie! We've got to get there!'

I wasn't sure where we had to get, except to the end of the path at the top of the lake where there was a green-painted cabin selling cups of tea to tourists. Then she gave a gasp of delight and knelt down by the lakeside where the big yew trees grew.

The trees were sombre green. Their branches dipped down into the lake and curved out again, just like someone testing the water with their elbow. The way my mother used to gauge hot water in the enamelled iron bath at home to make sure it was safe for us. The level of the lake must have fallen after it had frozen because there, suspended above the surface, were these exquisite candelabra of ice glinting on the yew branches. Annie was reaching out over the ice to try to catch hold of one and I had to drag her back by the hood of her anorak. That got me thinking about water too. About the way ice could be sculpted by freeze and thaw. It got me thinking about the beauty of ice.

The cold weather didn't last long and soon the ice had melted and the family of coots that were breeding on the lake were busy again. We had mallard as well, occasional moorhens, even grebe. Once I'd seen a red-throated diver plunging into the dusty water under the evening's early yellow moon. But that was special and in the day-to-day run of things the coots were my favourites. I loved their white foreheads and the way they sculled along so quietly, jerking their necks, leaving a vee-shaped wave of water behind them. The way they suddenly dipped down their heads and dived until they were totally submerged, swimming below the surface. So unlike the mallards that had to upend themselves and stick their backsides in the air. Especially, I loved their cries, like fine porcelain teacups chinking on thin saucers.

At the bottom end of the lake, nearest to the village, was a series of low meadows that spread down from the hall. In one of them was a little boathouse built of rickety planking that stood on stilts over the water. We'd been warned never to go near it because the water was deep there and the planking rotten and unsafe. I knew that in the boathouse was an old varnished rowing boat. Bob, the under-gardener at the big house, had shown me one day when I was out in the van with my father delivering groceries. I remember because it was late afternoon on a summer's day and I sat close to my father on the big bench seat, our shoulders jostling as he steered. The Spanish chestnut trees along the driveway were all in bloom, filling the air with scent. It was a strange smell, intimate as perfumed sweat. That night there was going to be a party at the house and the driveway was full of long, expensive cars. I could hear the sound of a dance band tuning up somewhere inside the hall.

Whilst my father was in the house the gardener took me for a walk down to the lakeside. He explained how the squire's family had used to row out onto the lake just for pleasure, no other reason. He showed me where the oars were stored and the brass rowlocks that fitted onto the boat so that the oars could be moved about in the water. Night after night I dreamed of that boat, of gliding over the face of the water, staring down into the depths where huge fabled trout swam and the faces of the village people drifted. Those who'd given up the struggle and given up hope to drown themselves there.

Dying for love or despair or grief. Their bodies had been pulled out and laid streaming on the bank, but their spirits still spiralled in the dark waters, each one a tiny silver fish drawn to the moon's reflection.

Those were the stories my mother told me to keep me away from the water and its fringe of yew and turkey oak trees. To warn me of its danger. But I loved its dark mirror. The way such a black element on a December day could spurt flashes of silver light when a flight of mallard touched down from the skies.

You'll think that I'm beginning to romanticise, that I'm pretending that all the days of my childhood were like that. I'm not. The village was no idyll and I knew it. Even so, there were days when the glory of God stood in the air like something absolute and tangible. Days when I almost wanted to weep, without knowing why.

Like all children we explored, gradually widening the circle of our curiosity. In the woods on the squire's land we discovered a kind of larder dug into the earth above the house. I asked my father about it and he told me that before the war the squires had used to boast that they could eat game birds from the previous shooting season the night before the new season began, so perfect was the cold for preserving them. The larder was packed with ice broken from the lake and then filled with birds that had been shot down in the woods and on the moors. I could never bear the thought of a bird being killed and hated the other village children who went birds' nesting or beating for grouse on shooting days.

The winter when we discovered the icehouse was the same winter that the lake froze over. It was the winter of voices. They started in the night when Annie and I lay huddled up in our double bed. Voices downstairs, coming up through the floorboards. Voices from my parents' bedroom. Sometimes the voices were very quiet, going on and on through the night like machinery left running. Sometimes they were loud and violent and I had to hold Annie and hug her and stop her tears, even though I couldn't stop my own.

One morning, after a terrible night of voices, I went down into the kitchen where my mother was cooking the porridge. I noticed that she had a dark bruise across her cheekbone. When I asked her how it had happened she told me, sarcastically, that a bad angel had brought it in the night. I knew all about bad angels. At least, I knew about this one. I had to shush Annie up when my father came in. I remember that day because he kissed my mother and made a special fuss of her as if nothing had ever been wrong. Then it was quiet for a few nights, just the creaking of the beech tree outside the window, the hissing of wind through the power lines that sagged over the rooftops of the village.

We had a quiet Christmas Day that year with no visitors. My father brought home Italian chestnuts from his green-grocer's shop and we found tangerines and oranges and tinsel in our stockings where they'd been draped over the bed. On Boxing Day, my two uncles, Norman and Alfred, came with their wives and their children, my cousins Robert, Anita and Colin, who spent the day quarrelling, bored with the countryside. The uncles were my father's brothers; my aunts were loud and brassy and their kisses tasted of cigarettes. My mother's family lived too far away to visit, though we had once been on a train to Aberdeen to see our grandmother and had watched miles of heather go past the windows, just like our own moors at home.

After Christmas, the lake thawed and the beck turned peaty brown, swirling and muscular with meltwater. Gradually the days lengthened so that the light lingered on in the afternoons.

Birds began to sing again and the rooks formed into pairs, ready for the mating season. Outside our house was a broken oak tree that had been pinned together with an iron bolt by some forester ages ago. The tree's split trunk had healed and each year a family of jackdaws was raised in a hollow in one of the large branches.

One February day, I was off school with a sore throat and a high temperature, all alone in the bedroom with a coal fire burning in the grate. That fire was only ever lit when we were ill and smelled of fallen soot. My mother brought me a cup of tea after taking Annie to school, and through the muzziness of my fever I saw my father standing by the bed. I remember him putting the back of his hand to my forehead. Outside, sunshine alternated with terrific storms of snow that whitened the hillside through the window. The sheep huddled, dirty yellow, chewing on bales of hay that the farmer had dropped into their feeders.

That day, my father came home from work for his lunch and the voices started, just like they did in the night. It was strange and frightening to hear them by day. I couldn't make out the actual words, but caught the bass of my father's voice and the whip-like replies of my mother, sharp with spite. I crept from the bed and put on my nightgown, huddling on the landing above the hallway. The voices were coming from the kitchen, my mother saying over and over, *Go to her, then. Go to her if that's what you want. I don't care anymore. Just go.* She spoke as if she had iron in her throat. I couldn't make out my father's reply, but it was low and harsh. I felt dazed, huddled there with snow blowing outside against the window, obliterating the sun.

It was years later that I found out my father had another woman whom he visited when he was out with the grocery van. And it was years after that I learned not to judge him or the woman or my mother for their lives. It takes a long time to learn how love can bloom unexpectedly and then wither just as suddenly. It takes too long to learn not to be wise after any event or to know how little good it does.

I know that I lay listening to the voices until I couldn't bear any more. They were wearing me away, unmerciful tongues licking away at me as if I might dissolve and fade. I remember getting dressed and creeping downstairs, putting on my overcoat and shoes, stepping out of their blizzard of words and through the front door and into the day that had gone on without me. My father's van was still parked outside our house, the gold lettering of his name gorgeous against scarlet paintwork. Years later, I realised why everybody knew what was going on.

I ran through the village to the woods, skirting the bottom edge of the lake and heading over the ornamental bridge that led to the hall. It must have stopped snowing because my first impression of the woods is of pale sunlight striking against tree trunks, glowing on their sleeves of ivy and moss. There was snow on the fallen leaves and pheasants pecking underneath it, cackling alarm as I went by. And there were tracks in the snow: cloven deer tracks and the footprints of pheasants placed one behind the other, precise as if they were walking a tightrope. I could see where a rabbit had hopped and squatted, then the longer, cantering patterns of a hare.

A thin wind sang in the uppermost branches where some rooks were beginning a nest. The sky was dizzy with blue space and white clouds. As I ran, the light glanced away through the trees, a blinding ricochet. Flurries of snow began to wet my face. It was terrifying how quickly the snow set in, taking away everything with its stinging mist. I was stumbling through the flat meadows then. The hall above me was faintly lit, its rows of windows almost invisible. Below me, to my left, I could just make out the little boathouse with its crooked planking and sunken roof.

I remember running. Running with snow blinding me, snow freezing my face beyond all feeling. I remember the stink of creosote, my numbed hands dragging the boathouse doors open, then entering a sudden absence of snow. Inside was the smell of old rope, dust and dank water with its depth of rotting leaves. Through the open front of the boathouse the lake was choppy, almost lost in even fiercer gusts of snow. Fever was in my head, blurring everything. Blurring this memory. But I must have got the boat down somehow and into the lake. Must have taken the oars and fitted them to the rowlocks as I'd once been shown.

Whether I rowed or drifted out onto the lake nobody knows, but in the legends that were told afterwards I did both. There was one moment of clear sunshine where my head was close to the water, its little waves brilliant with light and wind. And there were two coots sailing towards me, their pale foreheads serene, their black bodies rocking in the wind.

Then everything was taken away by snow. I remember watching my hands holding onto the varnished gunwales of the boat, blue as swallows' wings. Later I heard how a servant from the hall had seen the boat on the lake and how the game-keeper had gone down to the lake with his field glasses. How running down to the village for help he'd seen my father, who'd already started to look for me. He told him that a child was on the lake and my father had begun to sprint through the woods towards the boathouse and the jetty. Now I think I remember voices shouting, a man's hands parting the water towards me where the boat was sinking lower and lower. His dark hair is bobbing, his forehead pale, his mouth spitting out the lake into the sudden sun. I'm already too numb to feel the water take me, or the man who is my father take me.

When I awoke I was burning with fever. Blurred faces above me where I'd been laid on the grass, my father sobbing in a blanket close by. Then faces wavering above the bed in a room where there was a fire burning in the grate and a glass bottle of medicine on the cabinet. Days of fever followed where hot dreams came every night. Dreams in which everything was cut from the burning beauty of ice. Dreams filled with brilliant light and space. And dreams of darkness where the feathered bodies of birds were packed into crystals of ice, the golden rings of their eyes still moist and alive.

The days went by, the faces came and went mysteriously, the doctor's visits lessened, until I found myself alone and able to hear the songs of birds building in the trees outside. The sounds of things beginning again.

Then at night, and sometimes dozing by day, I dreamed of the lake, of those shoals of faces below the surface. Of yew trees dipping their arms into the water, of the beauty of ice. If life is a thread, then I must have reached for it and pulled, hauling myself back towards the days. The days that would continue to pass, the days I knew I had to live in somehow.

One morning, I was woken by a touch on my forehead and I saw my father standing over me in the flickering shadows that the firelight cast out. He was crying and his hand was hot and moist against my head. Days later, when I was well enough to sit up and spoon down a bowl of soup, I remember how my mother came into the room and placed a kiss against his cheek and touched his hand. Then how his face gave up a brief spasm of pain or grief as he pulled away from her.

After a moment of silence, Annie came in, laughing and secretive, holding something behind her back. She leaned over me, smelling of cold wind, of spring air and of the earth, placing a bunch of snowdrops on the pillow next to my head. All day they lay there. Burning paler than flames of the whitest fire. Greener than the heart of the fractured oak tree outside our window. That tree where the jackdaws made their home and called out and flew onwards, shaking the light like crystals from their wings.

Smokehouse

Leo awoke to the sound of gulls screaming outside the window. He could hear the churning of a diesel engine in the harbour, the clang of iron on the dock below the cottage. He didn't want to get up. Leaning from the bed he reached for the glass of water that he'd put on the floor the night before. It was empty. Spilled. A wet stain had spread underneath it, a blob of protoplasm rising from the blue-grey carpet. He lit a cigarette and blew smoke out over the bedspread.

Helen had gone. He felt for the empty space on her side of the bed and remembered that. She'd stayed a couple of days to settle him in. Making sure that he had things to eat, things to read. Things to take his mind off what dismayed him on a daily basis now. The day she left they'd driven to Robin Hood's bay and had lunch in a quaint little pub and Helen had bought him a cheese dish from the local pottery. It was painted with frail blue flowers and the top fitted snugly onto the base-plate where a ceramic mouse lurked cheekily. All the way from bay to bay the hedgerows had been white with blackthorn blossom. Lapwings dipped over the fields and Leo had smelled the earth stirring under the sun's warmth; it had all depressed him beyond words.

He'd bought Helen a pair of silver and jet earrings, which he'd caught her admiring in a shop window. At least he hadn't lost his touch there. But all the time she'd been eager to get away, to leave him to his misery. None of that was any secret. He was actually glad when he waved her off and she drove down to Manchester, leaving him alone at last.

A ship's hooter went off below the window. Another reproach. Leo pushed back the sheets, stubbed the cigarette into an ashtray of dog ends and clambered from the bed. The gas boiler was neatly hidden in the bedroom cupboard and he peered in at the blue pilot light that had watched over him all night. He turned up the boiler to warm the house and heard the sound of gas igniting like softly torn fabric. When he opened the curtains a glaze of light vibrated across the mud flats of the Esk where lines of boats were moored. The light lay like dazzling skin, a skin that seabirds tore at and screamed at and hungered for. Immature gulls flustered in shabby brown plumage and adult birds slick in suits of grey and white, the red spot throbbing at their beaks as they stared in at him. Herring gulls stalked the mud; they called out from the chimneys above the window where he watched. They called with the sound that had woken him from a dream he couldn't remember.

Leo dressed quickly, stumbling to the bathroom to confront his fleshy face in the mirror. He needed to lose weight. To take control. He was alone now. He could do that. Without hindrance from Helen. Without interference from anyone.

He'd stopped using hair dye after his mother's funeral and now his curls were turning grey at the roots and temples. He'd look distinguished, in time. The light from the window was too bright in the mirror. It lit soap spots on the glass. It lit his face, showing bags sagging under his eyes, lines engraving his cheeks. This light wasn't like stage-lights, which hid everything, which tucked the years away under pan-stick and artifice. Before his mother had been buried, powdered and rouged by the undertaker, Leo had looked into the coffin and he'd known that he was going to die. Not today, not even tomorrow, but some day. The thought had tugged at his guts and spilled them.

When his mother had passed away, back there in October, wasted by cancer, the thought had wormed its way into him. He'd nursed her unselfishly, everybody said so, even Helen. And of course we all have to die. But knowing and feeling are different and the worm lay coiled in his heart. Finally, he'd cracked up. Couldn't face work, couldn't face the stupid repertory audiences, couldn't stomach another pantomime. In the end Helen had rung his agent to say that he'd been told to rest by the doctor. Not true, because he hadn't even been to the bloody doctor. The truth was he couldn't face anything anymore.

They'd bought the cottage in Whitby ten years before, when he was still doing quite a bit of TV work. When things still looked promising. Before Helen had become more successful than him. He'd been a celebrity then. Almost. The cottage had been a manifestation of their success, of their expectations. It was the last in a row that clung to the east cliff below the abbey. It was small, but they had no children, didn't need much space. They'd ripped out the interior and built a new kitchen, installed gas central heating, painted the walls a naive Van Gogh yellow and hung old photographs and prints of the town there. It was charming. But then they'd hardly used it, partly because Helen had become a senior partner in her law firm at last and partly because he'd been too busy. Mainly it was because they'd grown tired and careless of each other. Too tired to pretend. So they'd lent it to friends. Theatrical friends, indigent writer friends, even some legal friends – those tight-arsed bastards. But they'd never taken any money for rent and as a result the place overflowed with gifts: bric-a-brac, kitchenware, bottles of good wine and excellent single malt whiskys. The cottage was the embodiment of goodwill and friendship, of their worth and popularity.

Leo rinsed his spectacles in the sink and wiped them on the towel. He went downstairs and spooned coffee into the cafetière, letting the kettle sing over the radio news. He noticed that a slug or a snail had gone across the carpet in the night, leaving a trail of dried slime. *Nacreous.* That was it. A strange word. Something to do with pearls. Nacre. He scuffed at the silvery line with his stockinged feet until it vanished.

Helen had stayed two days then she'd gone back to work. Two days to settle him in. He hadn't really talked to her about what it was. What it was that left him sitting up in bed, sleepless and full of dread. He'd never really talked to her at all. Or not for years. There'd been too many other women. So many that it had become a way of life. It had become a reflex, to seduce a new woman with every production. Then he'd slept with his TV producer and that had blown back on him. The bitch had wanted more than a quick one-nighter with an actor who was almost, but not quite, a household name.

She'd dropped him like hot iron when she found out about the others. Then she'd dropped him from the series, where his character was killed in a sudden car crash. She'd even rung Helen at work, hysterical, but Helen had laughed in her face. The stupid cow. But she'd stung him, sent him packing back to repertory where he'd done everything from Priestly to Bond, Becket to bloody Shakespeare. After his mother's death the thought of the pantomime season had sickened him, finished him with the whole thing. He was supposed to be playing in Peter Pan in Leeds, but he'd junked the contract and fled.

Leo left his breakfast plate and coffee cup in the washing-up bowl. The plumbing was playing up again and there was still an inch of greasy water left in the bottom of the sink. He'd have to take the U-bend apart again to clear it. As if it mattered. Fuck that.

He took his coat and went out. It was windy and bright, an early spring day with scudding clouds and light blazing up from the harbour and the sea. Gulls were perched on the masts of the boats where they lay at harbour, watching him with greedy, flat eyes. Leo went along the front of the terrace of cottages then took the path behind it up towards the abbey, avoiding dog shit that strewed the tarmac. Behind the house was a little shantytown of pigeon huts where the birds wheeled and men in caps called them down, rattling tins of corn. The men exercised their dogs here or burned rubbish in old dustbins, prodding it with sticks. Pigeons blew out like smoke in the wind, swirling up above the fields. When they returned they wheeled and fluttered in rapid circles before suddenly settling on the cote. Leo couldn't understand it, how the whole flock suddenly decided to settle as one. Maybe there was some signal in their flight which he'd missed. But then why should he understand it? Or anything else for that matter.

Leo strained up the hill against the sea wind. From the east cliff the town and its pincer-shaped harbour lay below him. He could see the faded hotels, the gateway of erect whalebones and Captain Cook's monument above the cliffs opposite. He could see the North Sea, flat and grey, mingling with mist at the far horizon. Gulls hung in the air above the cliff, spiralling and calling out and skimming low over the headstones in the churchyard. The smell of kippers curing in smokehouses under the cliff drifted up to him as he watched boats sailing from sea to harbour, from harbour to sea, taking the tourists with their rods and lines. Where the coast curved away in front of him, the spray from heavy breakers blew like fog. They came to the beach, sucking at sand and rocks, surging up around the harbour walls.

The sea dragged everything back to itself in time. The wreckage of iron, stone, timber. Everything. Leo watched a black Labrador running along the beach, hauling a huge branch. It was followed by a stout woman who struggled against the wind like a lamb with the staggers. They stumbled along, tiny figures growing smaller, sand-devils blowing around their legs, disappearing into the mist and spray.

Suddenly hungry, Leo turned and went down the long flight of steps on Donkey Hill and into the town. That day he bought some plaice from the fishmongers, fried them lightly in olive oil, added a slice of lemon for garnish and ate them with crusty French bread. He slept for part of the afternoon and, that evening, read a few pages of his novel and drank a bottle of Italian Chardonnay before going out.

The next day Leo woke with a bad hangover. He lay very still beneath the quilt. Under the cries of gulls. The clanging from the docks vibrated through the house and in the roots of his teeth. He shuffled a deck of images from the night before, trying to lay them out in their proper order.

He'd gone to the Endeavour early in the evening, after drinking the bottle of wine at home. He remembered picking his way down the crooked flight of steps, then entering the pub. The snug was already too hot, a coal fire piled up in the grate. The bar room smelled of fried meat and the fishy coats of seamen who drank there. He'd ordered a Guinness. Then another. Then at the bar he'd run into Big John, a self-styled local character. Trapped at the counter, he'd accepted the barstool that John pulled out for him.

'How are ye? How yar doin'?'

'Fine thanks.'

'Are ye behavin' yesel?'

'I'm tryin' to.'

John had thrown back his head and produced a stage guffaw. More theatrical than anything Leo had ever dared.

'I'm John.'

He pushed out a huge hand and Leo had taken it firmly.

'Leo.'

'They call me Big John.'

'Leo Roderick.'

Big John's eyes narrowed, he pulled at his beard with his free hand.

'Ye've a strong grip, Leo. Strong.'

Leo let go of his hand.

'Stan' up!'

He stood up and the big man raised himself from the barstool. Leo wasn't a small man. He'd always regarded himself as rather imposing, but now he pretended to be impressed.

'God, you must be six-four if you're an inch!'

'Six-four, bollocks man, I'm six-six and a quarter, but what's a quarter of an inch between friends?'

Again the stage guffaw as he gripped Leo by the arm. Leo needed a drink to sit through this. He drained his glass.

'Like another?'

John nodded his assent casually, as if it was beneath him to use enough good manners to say yes. He rolled a cigarette in swollen fingers and licked the edge of the paper with a yellow tongue.

'Pint? Half?'

'Half?'

The big man growled and spat out a fibre of tobacco.

'Can a bird fly on one wing?'

He winked at Leo who ordered him a pint, smiling when the barman shook his head disapprovingly. But Leo wasn't fooled. He was in for a performance and he didn't mind parting with a few drinks in return. Fair was fair. And Big John would do all the talking. He'd do the talking and the laughing and the backslapping for both of them.

An hour and several pints later they took the plot to its climax. Leo and Big John seated across a table from each other surrounded by a ring of men and a pile of banknotes weighted down with a beer glass. When they took off their jackets and solemnly joined hands across the table Leo had wanted to laugh. When he looked across into the other man's eyes they were dark brown and held nothing. Nothing but hollowness that the sea had put there.

When the contest began he saw surprise spark into their vacancy and the big man's face had sagged. Leo had slowly forced his hand before his, pushing it down towards the table. Without pity and without hate but with coldness filling his belly. He'd once watched ice cascade from that machine that stood near the fish market on the dock and it felt like that. It felt good. Coldness gushing into him, until Big John was losing it. Losing his grip. The men around them pressed closer, stinking of sweat and fish and tobacco smoke.

'Fuckin' hell!'

'Come on John, what's up wi' you?'

'Come on, man!'

'Jesus!'

Leo had no intention of letting up. None. Big John strained

his hand from the table top but Leo forced it mercilessly back. No intention at all.

'Christ, he's gunna do him!'

'He's gunna best Big John!'

'Why, the canny bastard!'

And down went the big man's hand as the men muttered around them in disbelief. Leo shook hands and bought drinks all round with his winnings. Then he drank himself stupid. Drank himself into oblivion. He couldn't remember leaving the Endeavour or what had happened to Big John or how he'd climbed the hundred and one steps up to the cottage before falling into bed.

The day of the hangover his arm and his head ached all day. He dined on kippers, filling the house with their fragrance and washing them down with large glasses of malt whisky until the headache went. He loved the smokiness of the kippers mingled with the peat flavour of the whisky. He thought about the kippers curing, slowly sweating out their oil; greasing the walls of the smokehouse below the cliff. He imagined himself entering there naked, like a Sioux brave pushing aside deerskin hangings to enter the sweat lodge. Then the shaman greeting him, healing him. The shaman with his inscrutable smile, his bony hands touching Leo's body. Naked in the reek of the smokehouse, squatting among piles of smouldering sawdust, breathing vapour deep into his lungs. Immortalised, his skin would turn brown and ageless.

But Leo wasn't ageless. He was mortal. He knew he was going to die and he couldn't cast the worm away where it turned in him. That night he went from pub to pub. The Endeavour, Duke of York, Black Horse, Jolly Sailors, The Board. Twice he was recognised and asked to arm wrestle;

twice he refused with the charm of a professional actor. The imperturbable charm that nothing could shift and that he was famous for. Almost.

Walking home, he paused on the swing bridge to stare at the river that glittered under him. It stank of death. Everything did. He needed a woman, needed to fuck away all thoughts of decay from his mind. Helen had carried on making love to him despite everything. But he'd never touched her to the quick. Never after that first betrayal, never again. Every time she'd left him with a sense of failure, the sense that he had never and could never satisfy her. She'd sucked the spirit out of him. That had driven him back to the women who wanted him, who'd gasped for more as he pleasured them and clawed his back, but left him feeling just as empty and lost. So much of that was Helen's fault, the way she'd pushed him away.

Leo spat at the river and watched the globe of froth spin and pock the surface below with a small slap. No, he didn't need a woman after all. It was needing women that had made him like this.

Leo slept soundly, without dreams, and the next day felt better. He dined on fillet of rainbow trout fried in butter and black pepper, washed down with a bottle of Chilean Sauvignon Blanc. No pasta, no rice or potatoes to pile on the weight. He was doing alright, feeling better each day. That night he read for an hour then climbed up to the churchyard below the abbey where Dracula had lured poor sleepwalking Lucy Westenra. Where he'd leaned over her as she swooned in a trance and pierced her throat with his eyeteeth and sucked her blood. Leo sat among the weathered headstones and stared out at the grey waves of sea and sky. He smoked idly, listening to the cries of invisible gulls.

The next day Leo sat for hours at the quayside, watching cormorants dry their wings in the sun and trying to remember his mother's face. His father had left home before he was born. Because of that he'd been an only child. Maybe that was why he'd needed women like he'd needed food or drink. He'd slaked himself with women and after the first flush of cocksureness, they'd meant nothing. There'd been the odd one that he thought he might leave Helen for. Once he'd even packed his bags and threatened to walk out. He'd ordered a taxi and stood waiting in the hallway, but her mocking laughter had kept him there. Her contempt had trapped him somehow in its snare. He still couldn't understand that.

Leo remembered that he was hungry. He left the dockside and went to the shop under the cliff to buy kippers, staring for a long time into the smokehouse where the gutted herrings were strung in rows. He walked home slowly through the town with the fish wrapped in a newspaper bundle. He fried two kippers for lunch and settled them with two bottles of Guinness.

That evening he took a whisky bottle to the harbour and drank from it as he leaned against the iron railings, watching tones of grey overcome each other as night crept over the sea and lay there. He tasted salt spray mingling with the whisky, felt it stiffen his tangled hair. After a while he felt sick and threw the bottle towards the lights of a fishing boat. He took the steps up to the parish church, walking along by the abbey, its ruined stonework lit by spotlights. Then he went out along the cliff road with the wind on his face, until night came on deeper and he wandered back towards the town.

He'd keep away from pubs now. He'd been made wary and wanted no more challenges, no more celebrity. It hadn't even been that difficult. Not faced by such hollowness. The trick was done by going snake-eyed. He'd been shown it by an old

stuntman years ago. Snake-eyed and ice-bellied he'd forced
that big bastard's hand, licked him and swallowed him whole.
Never underestimate an actor and a gentleman. Never.

Not knowing how he'd got there, Leo fell asleep on one of
the benches in the churchyard. At two o'clock he woke and
vomited into the grass. He was cold and drizzle had begun to
blow across the town which wavered below him in a mass of
blurred lights as he walked home, cursing and fumbling for
his key.

The next day he rose feeling ravenous, breakfasting on
kippers and toast. The postman came to the house and he
found a card from Helen asking why he hadn't rung and was
he alright? There was no phone in the cottage; that was the
good thing about it. He read the card with a cynical, staged
grin. Peter Helman, his agent, had been asking when he might
be fit for work again. Sod Peter. He'd always rather despised
him anyway. But maybe he was lucky, being queer. Maybe
that was the best way – love and friendship between men
and no other. Maybe. Leo tore the card up and scattered it
on the floor. He wasn't interested in friends anymore and he
wasn't interested in work. He felt oddly optimistic, as if he
was close to the edge of something. As if something new and
invigorating was about to happen. That was how he'd felt
when he'd taken a new woman.

Leo lived almost entirely on kippers now, frying them up
twice a day until the house stank and drinking whatever their
friends had left in the cupboard – Cabernet Sauvignon,
Merlot, Zinfandel, Chardonnay, Pinot Noir, Pinot Grigio,
Syrah, Sangiovese, Montepulciano, Balbera – somehow they
all seemed to go with kippers. And he drank whisky, especially
the peaty Islay malts – Lagavulin and Laphroaig – for which
he had a particular longing. He drank as he picked at the

delicate flesh of the fish, crunching their fine bones with a shudder of pleasure.

Leo stopped shaving, deciding to grow a beard. He stopped washing, enjoying the stink of sweat when he ducked his face under his tee shirt, revelling in the itch under his foreskin, the crusty feeling between his buttocks. All his life he'd been scrupulously clean but now he enjoyed the squalor of dirt. He piled up unwashed dishes until the house reeked of fish and the decaying contents of bin bags. Rancid water greased the sink, which hardly drained at all now. He stank and he enjoyed this unique sensation. He loved the revenge of it, tenting the bed sheets to smell his own acidifying body odour. Even the bathroom began to stink of piss where he'd swayed at the toilet after too much drink and missed the bowl.

The next day, another card from Helen asking him to call. He relished its hint of annoyance. She didn't really care. Didn't really give a bugger. For years she'd sucked the life out of him, for years she'd driven him away. Even when she'd wrapped her legs round him and made him come inside her she'd been distracted by other things in her life. Legal matters or something else more important than him. And his gasped, *Was it good, darling, was it good?* was merely irrelevant and sad, like her superior little smile of assent, as if she was humouring him. What did it matter how it was? Somehow she'd made him suffer and he didn't quite understand how. Though he knew why.

More and more he thought of the split herrings hanging in the smokehouse, dripping out their own grease and slowly purifying. Walking home from town he'd catch the scent of them blown against the cliff-face or up into the ruins of the abbey and he thought of the shaman pressing a hand against his chest. The shaman naked, just as he was, oily-skinned and elusive, pressing him backwards into the reek of oak shavings where they smouldered in darkness.

The day after, Leo stayed in bed and couldn't be bothered to eat. He took an Australian Shiraz and the faithful whisky bottle with him, smoking and drinking quietly all day. Listening to the clanging of the harbour, to passing traffic, to the cries of gulls outside the window. The day passed in drifts of cigarette smoke. Leo stubbed their wine-stained filters out onto the blue carpet, watching the play of sunlight across the patchwork quilt where his legs lay. He'd run out of kippers and he'd run out of clean socks and underwear days ago. He hadn't washed and he hadn't shaved. He stank. He who'd always been spotlessly clean. And it gave him a frisson of pleasure. It sustained him, this sense of dirt and unworthiness, the foetid stink of his body under the bedclothes.

That night the moon rose early. Not a full-blown moon, but a three-quarters moon, a gibbous yellow fruit that glowed in its incandescent rind beyond his window. Above the orange lights of the pedestrian crossing where they winked on the road below. Over the white jawbone of the whale across town. Leo bathed in the moonlight, quite drunk now and sleepy, but not quite asleep. He stretched in the bed, intoxicated by the light. With each hand felt the smooth skin of his arms, felt their beauty and kissed them as if they were the arms of a young girl. Gradually he fell asleep.

At one o'clock Leo woke up, noticing that the moon had moved out of his window. He reached under the bed for the whisky bottle and drained the last inch. Then he finished the dregs of wine, throwing the bottle against the wall and leaving a streak of purple down its yellow emulsion. The lights at the pedestrian crossing blinked on the road below. Leo got dressed, struggling into his underpants and trousers.

He pulled a shirt over his head, enjoying its barbarous stink of sweat. Being close to himself was like being close to something feral. A fox or a badger. Or a bear that wakes from its winter sleep. He ran his tongue over his teeth, rough with neglect and the fur of days of drinking. He remembered the taste of a woman's nipple, the wet sensation of pushing his tongue into a woman's mouth. The way they'd put their tongues into his, whimpering with desire, pressing against him. It had all been an act. They'd fallen in love with his performance and he'd hardly even noticed theirs. It had meant no more than that. Like shooting a flare, an SOS which burned briefly and then fell into the sea below and was extinguished.

Dressed, Leo went downstairs and out of the house, leaving the front door wide open. He clambered down the steps that led to the main road, striding over the pedestrian crossing and the swing bridge towards the harbour entrance. The moon was there above the sea, misted now by faint strands of cloud. Here was the river, dark and oily, slapping up against moored boats and the stone of the quayside. There was hardly any traffic at this time of night, though seamen still moved about on their boats and there were lights far out at sea. Leo walked into the sea breeze, past the Magpie café and the Dracula Horror Show, past all the other cafés and chip shops and amusement arcades that littered the front. He walked down onto the beach and his feet sank into damp sand. The tide had abandoned pebbles which lay stranded in little dimples of water. Leo could smell the sea. He could hear it, could just make out its grey band where a trail of moonlight lay.

Leo took off his shoes and socks, loving the cold grit of sand between his toes. He heard an oystercatcher call out close by and loosened his shirt, tearing off buttons and dragging it over his head. It stank of him. Half naked, he broke into a run, trotting towards the sea, eager as a child. Feeling the breeze on his skin, he paused to take off his trousers and then went naked, the wind raising gooseflesh as he ran, his penis flapping against his thigh. He laughed at the thought of its helplessness. It had governed him all his life and now there it was, flopping about uselessly.

Leo ran until his feet hit the waves where they boiled at the shore. Until water was breaking against his buttocks and thighs, until his balls retracted at the shock of cold. He ran until water lifted him from his feet, until his ears were drowned in the sound of waves tearing themselves to pieces against the harbour walls. Leo ran until he could run no more and then he swam. He sculled out with slow, powerful strokes, his arms beautiful in the moonlight. For a moment he thought he could smell smoke skirling down over the water, thought he could hear faint music. But he swam on into the sting of the sea, ducking his head, spitting salt, following the faint silver pathway before him.

Yusef

When Marie came up with Pendeen as a holiday venue I must have looked surprised. So that curious look came over her face. Well, I was surprised. I hadn't been there for over thirty years. Which made me feel old, to say the least.

'Pendeen? How do you spell that?'

She looked surprised now, squinting at the map. We were having breakfast and the kitchen table was scattered with coffee cups and plates. The gas boiler was grumbling and there were a pair of greenfinches upside-down on the bag of nuts she'd hung from the washing line.

'P-e-n-d-e-e-n. It's near St Just. Pretty close to Land's End. Heard of it?'

'I was there in '74 with Yusef. '73 or '74, must've been…'

'Yusef?'

'A Persian – *Iranian* – guy I knew at university.'

Marie coiled her ponytail and pushed in a hairgrip. It was going from auburn to grey now.

'You're a dark horse.'

I wasn't sure what she meant by that. She'd found a holiday cottage on a website and wanted to go ahead and book it for September when the kids had gone back to school and the beaches would be quiet. Not our kids. We'd got over that. But kids in general. Other peoples' kids. She raised an eyebrow.

'Yusef?'

'He was a mining engineer. He'd had a placement at the Geevor mine for a few weeks. Loved it so much he wanted to go back and dragged me with him.'

I was trying to remember a name.

'We camped outside this pub… the Radgel.'

She looked bemused now.

'It's Cornish for fox or fox's den or something.'

'And…?'

'Can't remember much about it. Great pub. Cornish pasties and beer for breakfast. Nice place. Lots of mining along the coast from what I remember, but that's probably all gone now.'

She was folding the map.

'What kind of mining?'

'Tin. Copper. Mainly tin. Geevor was the last mine to close. There was a big accident there in eighteen-something.'

'Ok… right… and so?'

She looked at me and then back to the map of Cornwall, draining the last of her coffee. I wanted to get to work.

'Come on, *vamoose*, or we'll be late.'

Marie rummaged in her bag for the car keys. I put the breakfast things away and stacked the plates in the dish-washer. It smelled of biriani from the night before. And something else. Something backing up in the drains. I dialled in a hot rinse, still musing about Yusef as I followed Marie out. But she was already at the door, pushing her arms into her jacket, lugging her overstuffed briefcase to the car.

★ ★ ★

Yusef standing by the roadside, legs apart. Tight Levi shrink-to-fits. Though mine never did. His cowboy boots are scuffed and he's facing the traffic. Bold as brass. His hair is straight and black, falling across his forehead above jay feather blue eyes. He cocks his thumb and grins at each driver as they pass. I stand beside him, half a foot shorter in hiking boots and ex-army pants. I've never hitched before. It's seven-thirty in the morning. Cars surf Manchester's rush hour and the early sun melts their windscreens as they move towards us. Yusef chants his mantra of the road: 'Come on stop, you bastards, give us a break, eh? C'mon baby. C'mon baybee....'

Then dipping his thumb ironically as they pass.

'Yeah fuck you, too. Fuck you madam.'

That was Yusef. Easy come, easy go. He didn't mind the endless hanging around trying to bum a ride. He didn't even mind the shite-awful food in truckers' cafes and motorway service stations. I was new to the game and felt vaguely embarrassed at asking something for nothing. Yusef didn't give a monkey's.

'Man, we are *entitled*!'

His blues eyes crinkle like underwater lapis. Now he's racing down the slip road as the first car stops. Slim in his perfectly fitting jeans and Led Zeppelin tee shirt. He has a gold pendant around his neck in the shape of a half moon. He hasn't shaved and his teeth sparkle a grin at the driver from dark stubble. I mean it. They *sparkle*. I watch the smooth brown skin on the back of his neck as I sit cramped in the back of the car with the rucksacks and tent. Yusef chats to the driver. His father was so rich that they'd once owned a private plane. Then the Shah kicked them out and they'd fled to England. The driver is a pigeon fancier of all things and Yusef is talking to him about racing birds. How does he know this stuff?

The first lift gets us as far as Cannock and dumps us on the

M6. Yusef is happy now. He takes a swig of water from the canteen and sprays an arc into the dust.

'Perfect! We'll get down there in a day. Just takes *charisma*... and balls!'

He grins and hoists his crotch. Then he's slapping me on the shoulder, squaring up to the drivers who trundle out from the lorry park, the sun blinding them as they change gear and squint down at us. Miraculously, they stop to pick us up, dazzled by Yusef who pierces their loneliness. He interrupts their lives of endless driving: service stations, junk food, that solitary early-morning shit with strangers in the next cubicle, dirty roller towels, sleep-overs in the cab, the chance of a woman in a strange town, then sudden, cholesterol-induced death.

★ ★ ★

Marie booked the cottage and we drove down in mid-September, just as planned. Most of the traffic was streaming the other way and we couldn't help feeling smug. It took us three hours to reach Exeter where we did some shopping at the enormous service station and then hit the A30, which runs right down the centre of the peninsula to Land's End, close to where we needed to be. Way past the signs for Jamaica Inn – which rings a sunken bell of memory – we see a sign for Pendeen and I hang a right. The road winds through fields of heather bordered by walls built from huge granite boulders. Ragwort is flowering everywhere. Marie's been dozing but she rouses herself for the last leg.

'It's poisonous.'

She's pointing at the hedgerows, splashed with yellow.

'What? Ragwort?'

'Yes. Gorgeous, though...'

There's fuchsia and montbretia and ox-eye daisies nodding in the slipstream of cars. A buzzard slips across the windscreen, wing tips curled upwards as it wheels then rears like a crucifixion. We enter the village almost without noticing we've arrived. I recognise nothing. I feel nothing. The Radgel is still there, at right angles to the road. There's a row of new houses opposite that couldn't have been there when I camped with Yusef. I park the car on the roadside and snap on the handbrake.

'I'd like a pint.'

'I'd like to get there.'

'I know. It's not far.'

'You don't know that.'

'I do, it's close. I've driven all the way. A pint won't kill us will it? C'mon. It's a holiday, remember?'

'Ok, ok.'

We climb out of the car, legs stiff from the drive. The sea smells sharp and clean. A line of washing blows about in the back yard of the pub.

The first thing I see in the bar is a black-and-white photograph of a stout unshaven man in his sixties. *Wally.* The name comes back effortlessly. Wally was the landlord who'd let us pitch our tent in his back field. Yusef had charmed him into it as soon as we arrived. I can't remember how we got there or that final lift, just the hours we spent at Bristol in a queue of other hopefuls. Here's another photograph: five lads in tweed jackets and long hair, two of them with shotguns broken over their arms. They look like they might have been around when we were. A couple of terriers are pulling at their leads and Wally's there again, younger, wearing a collapsed pork-pie hat and a grizzled smile. The same faces looking ten years older are there in the Pendeen cricket team.

Marie's in the loo as I take a quick look round. A thin guy with a ponytail is watching me from behind the bar, drawing on a roll-up. He's got dirt-blue fingernails and Celtic tattoos twining on both arms. The pub's familiar in a forgotten sort of way – a long bar with an open fireplace, a back room where we drank with Yusef's tin-mining mates. But that's all. Why can't I remember anything else? It's weird. There's no detail, just a sense of familiar space, vague faces crowding around us.

We take our pints of Tanners outside to where a couple of benches catch the sun. There's a car park beyond and beyond that a small field that looks familiar. Below that the cliffs and the sea. We sit down and Marie gets into conversation with a pleasant-looking guy with sandy hair and a generous beer gut. She's friendly like that.

I was a lifeboat man thirty years, I was. Then my back went. Now I'm a lorry driver. Go all over the place, I do. I saw Britain from the outside from the boat, like, so I reckoned it was time to see the inside. Everywhere from Leominster to Glasgow, Penzance to Manchester. I reckon I must have travelled halfway round the world by now, rightly speaking. But life on the boats was great. I can't knock it. Not for a moment. Can't knock it.

A wasp hovers above his pint glass, a tiny hyperactive ingot of sun. He whisks it away. His speech sounds rehearsed, as if he's said it a thousand times. I imagine him picking up women as he travels the country, seducing them with his beery breath and easy body.

I leave them to it and walk into the little field. I have to duck under the line of knickers, striped pinnies and baby's nappies. I can just see the lighthouse down to the right on the cliff. It's disused now, but it used to blink in the middle of the night, its rhythmical light slicing the dark. That, at least, comes back to me. Groggy with sleep and groping outside the tent to piss. And in the morning, tankers clinging to the blue-grey heat of the horizon. We'd had perfect weather, ten days of sunshine. The only rain had been that night we got smashed on scrumpy.

* * *

Yusef tossing back his hair and laughing as I try to drive in the tent pegs. They hit stones buried under the soil and bend uselessly. The sun's burned the back of my neck and my tee shirt's chafing. He drags the little gas stove out of his rucksack humming 'Stairway to Heaven'.

'C'mon Yusef, give me a hand, you're supposed to be a fucking engineer.'

'*Mining* engineer. That's civil engineering, man!'

And he's laughing again, his teeth shining, his eyes alert, singing… *and she's buying a stairway to heaven*… another moment of air guitar, then he's holding the ridgepole for me as I tighten a guy line. He smiles.

'Gotta stay cool, Tim.'

'It's too fucking hot to stay cool… it's alright for you…'

He doesn't like that. Frowns.

'What, 'cos I'm Persian? You cunt! I was born in fucking Croydon, man!'

And he's laughing again, tossing peanuts into his mouth, necking the pint he's carried from the pub. He pushes back his wristwatch and I see a paler band of skin there under the fine black hairs. *Ginger minge.* That's me. The sun brings me out in freckles and sweat. My feet are sticky in my desert boots. Gritty. I need a wash. Yusef's cool. So fucking cool.

* * *

The cottage we've hired turns out to be at an awkward corner of the road. We have to park a hundred yards away on the village green and lug our bags. Marie scans the instructions she's printed from the website and finds the key. It's under a bay tree in an earthenware pot in the tiny front garden. The door opens directly into the kitchen. There's a table, a cream-coloured Aga that doesn't work any more, an electric cooker, some ramshackle handmade cupboards and a faint musty smell. The main bedroom and bathroom are downstairs. You can step through French doors from the bedroom to the garden and there's a wooden bench that faces the sea, just big enough for two people.

Upstairs is the lounge with a large screen TV, a dining table, shelves of romantic novels and some brochures for local restaurants. The owner has left the visitor's book out for us. Marie shrugs, wiping her finger along a shelf to check for dust.

'It's ok, I suppose. I've seen better.'

'It'll do. Bit smelly... gin?'

'Gin.'

I find some old ice in the fridge – the kind that's blind with frost – and mix two large G & Ts. Marie puts a couple of Marks & Spencer's lasagnes in the oven and opens a bag of rocket.

'These'll be about twenty minutes.'

I'm setting out two plates and she's smiling at me. Dark-green eyes, with pale creases at the corners where the sun's caught her face. She tosses back her plait, takes my arm.

'Come on. Let's try the bed.'

We take our drinks into the bedroom, draw the curtains and undress. Her nipples taste faintly of lavender water. Her eyes close and then open, showing the whites, slightly startled. They close again and her hands touch against my chest before gripping the iron frame of the bed. She's silky against me as we make love. Afterwards we open curtains, clink the ice in our glasses; watch the sun sink over the sea. The buzzer goes on the cooker. Marie pushes me out of bed then follows. I turn to cradle her breasts from behind, warm as two birds in my palms.

* * *

Yusef twisting into a wave on the beach, his body lost in breaking foam. He's shouting for me to join him.

'Come on you soft twat!'

A man walking two red setters jerks up his head disapprovingly.

'Come on in!'

Yusef laughs, his white teeth perfect as a film star's. I still feel self-conscious about undressing in public. I'm cowering behind a rock, trying to get into my swimming shorts without filling them with sand. Yusef's hair is slicked to his head. He flicks water at me as I tiptoe in.

'C'mon ginger bastard! It's cool.'

'You mean it's fucking freezing!'

Then he's dragging me in. The shock of cold makes me gasp and grab his arm for balance. We stagger into the Atlantic, wave after wave swelling to the shore, sweeping the sand into underwater clouds, knocking the breath from our chests. Our bodies slip against each other. Our mouths are stung by salt. Yusef's skin feels smooth as oil. The gold pendant glitters and bounces on his chest where black hair curls against dark skin.

Afterwards we lie in the sun watching a family of jackdaws squabble on the cliff. There's sand stuck to Yusef's face, tiny glittering particles of quartz. His eyelashes tremble, long and thick. A tanker labours across the horizon, fuming into shades of blue and green. To the south, the leakage of iron oxide stains the sea dark red.

* * *

The next day, Marie and I drive into St Just for provisions, wandering past the little art galleries and bric-a-brac shops, drinking morning coffee with the newspapers in a café run by a couple of middle-aged hippies. Middle aged like us. Old ladies with tattooed arms pass us in the street. They must have been beatniks once. Dreamers, freedom seekers. But whatever you try to get away from follows you. And maybe that's us: invading the peninsula with thousands of others every summer; then leaving them to the winter.

Everyone's friendly and welcoming. Maybe that's just good for business. We buy bread at the bakers and two colossal Cornish pasties, then drive back to the cottage and sit with the ordnance survey map. Marie has her heart set on the coastal path that runs the length of the peninsula and we set off after lunch with a shoulder bag, camera and binoculars, driving to Pendeen, then finding a track that takes us down towards a small bay. We park at a farm, drop a pound coin into the honesty box, then follow a track that winds through gorse thickets and hedgerows tangled with blackberries and rosehips.

The bushes are full of songbirds and the weather is bright with a steady breeze from the sea. Hot gorse releases the scent of coconut as we pass. The old mine workings appear on the cliff top to our left, then the blue curve of the bay begins. The path crosses over a small stream. I ford it, yards ahead of Marie, and find a notice warning that the beach is full of old metal from shipwrecks and mining. I remember a trickle of blood running from Yusef's heel. *It's nothing man, I didn't even feel it.* His blood seemed unbelievably bright, deeper and redder than any blood I'd seen. Now Marie's calling from behind. I turn to watch her stumbling over the stream I've just climbed out of.

'…a what?'

'Well you might bloody wait…'

She's caught the sun already. Her skin is lightly tanned, gleaming where her hair is pulled back. She catches up, panting slightly, cargo pants tight around her hips. The backs of her hands are freckled.

'A meadow pipit, I think, could've been a skylark.'

I don't answer her, but take her arm and walk a few yards before having to let go because the path is too narrow. Then the beach is there and the Atlantic: green, blue and turquoise, sending cream-topped breakers to drag at the shore. The sun is high, the air astringent. A family with five kids are making a moated sandcastle where the stream fans over the beach. There are a few walkers on the sand, tiny in the distance. A fat guy tackles the waves on a surfboard, cheered on by his wife and daughters. His shaved head gleams like bronze.

Marie wants to paddle. She always does. Her chest is glazed with sweat, her nipples tight against her tee shirt. The light catches her eyes. Hazel-green.

'What's that?'

She's pointing above the cliff where a dark shape is hovering. At first it looks like a kestrel, but when I lift the binoculars it has that unmistakeable moustache.

'It's a peregrine!'

Marie's never seen one before. I hand her the binoculars and she fiddles with the focusing wheel.

'Here, like this.'

'Shit! You have them. I can see better without…'

I take them back and re-focus. The bird has swooped lower, away from the sun. It's flying into the wind, plumage flustering, tail fanned, wing tips flickering, its breast striated, its body rocking on the air. Its head is fiercely alert, gimbaling from side to side. It slackens and sinks lower, trembling in the streaming air. It folds its wings and dives, stooping into bracken. Marie is touching my arm.

'It's got something!'

'Yeah, a meadow pipit, probably.'

She slaps my elbow and the bird rises again, steering away down coast.

We walk barefoot at the edge of the sea, letting the waves wet our trouser hems. Afterwards we pull on our walking shoes and follow the coastal path up through the cliff, a circular route that winds to the Levant mine through heather and granite, then back to the village.

By six o'clock we're outside the Radgel rubbing sun cream into our arms and drinking bitter shandies. Then a tedious last mile to the car, our feet aching against hot tarmac. Before we leave, Marie pulls a plastic bag out of the boot and we pick blackberries, feeling for the fruit amongst the briars and nettles that have grown into the hawthorn hedge, pricking our fingers and staining them with juice. When we leave we have a pound of fruit and a good few stings. I remember my mother telling me how she'd picked rosehips in the war to make jelly for the soldiers in the hospital where she was a nurse. I'd taken her blackberries and stewed apples a few days before she died, spooning them into her mouth. But she was too weak to care by then.

Marie and I drive back to the cottage in sun-stunned

silence, watching robins and wrens break from the hedgerows, then shadows stretching from the pithead wheel.

There's a bottle of Australian Chardonnay cooling in the fridge. We open it after taking showers in the cramped bathroom. When we make love I push my tongue against Marie's breasts, feeling them tighten, nuzzling her throat as I enter. She takes me with half-closed eyes, letting her fingernails graze my back. Afterwards we doze, then wake to the dark, to half-empty glasses beside the bed. A thrush is singing outside in short, cascading phrases. Marie stirs and kisses my chest. Her hot breath sighs across my skin but I can't tell whether that's longing or satisfaction.

★ ★ ★

On the last day we hitch to the Blue Anchor at Helstone to try the beer they brewed on the premises. A young clergyman picks us up in an ancient split-windscreen Morris Minor. I sit in the back as usual, whilst Yusef fields his questions. There's a Welsh Springer behind me, asleep on an old blanket.

'So where are you lads from?'

I remember Yusef telling me he was born in Croydon and tense myself in the back seat.

'We're at university in Nottingham.'

'Oh yes. Studying…?'

'Mining engineering.'

'Mining? Oh yes….'

The young vicar looks surprised. I pipe up from the back before he says something stupid.

'English.'

'Ah, yes, English.'

He seems to approve. Yusef raises his eyebrows and sends out a dazzling grin. His eyes are deep blue in the light that's falling through the windscreen. The dog farts, filling the car with the stench of rotten meat. The clergyman chuckles and winds down a window.

'Sorry gents. Don't mind Waffles. He's getting on a bit now, losing his manners…'

I see Yusef frown. He doesn't do dogs. He turns to me behind the clergyman's back, making his fingers into a gun and pointing them towards the Springer. We don't speak much after that until the vicar drops us off.

In the Blue Anchor we drink four pints of the dark bitter that's brewed on the premises and then reel out into the light. The sun is blinding. Yusef blinks theatrically.

'Fuck, that was *schtrong*.'

'Yeah. Good, though. Where now?'

Yusef has spotted a good hitching point on the way in, where there's a broad verge beside the road. We walk into open country and start to thumb. Progress is slow. We end up climbing over a gate to piss against the hedge. I start to feel slightly nauseous in the heat, the beer dragging at my belly. The sun's blistering my face and my nose is peeling. We don't reach Pendeen until gone six. When we get into the bar of the Radgel, Yusef's greeted noisily by some of his mining chums. We feel great. Triumphant. The night begins.

Hours later, and before I realise it, we've switched from beer to scrumpy. I remember Wally going into the back room, emerging with the dregs of the barrel. Two pints of scummy pink froth. The broken-toothed grin of Beaky saying something dirty in his clotted Cornish accent, so close I can smell his armpits. Yusef's chuckling. The room is dense with laughter and blue cigarette smoke. I want to heave, but hang on as everything dissolves. The room turning on its lost moments like a fairground ride. We're drinking sour candy floss. Then, mysteriously, we're out in the Atlantic rain, struggling with the zip of the tent. We stagger in the mud. Laughing, cursing. Nylon cracks in the wind. Then a voice mutters inside the tent. Which isn't ours. *Fuckfuckfuckit.* This one has a zip that runs round the edge. Ours has a centre zip. Clawing our way through rain, we find our tent behind. Then I'm throwing up into the rain, the lighthouse blinking, Yusef's hand on my neck.

Somehow there's a fight with clothes and sleeping bags. I'm sipping water from the plastic bottle, pissing in the rain, dragging off my wet tee shirt. Body heat. The sweet sharpness of sweat. Yusef's skin smooth under my own. He's laughing, his lips against my neck, his body arched above me. My hands feel his spine, his hips, the curve of his arse. I've still got my socks on and reach down to take them off, but Yusef gets there first, pulling them over my feet. The taste of salt. My face hot. Then sleep. Then waking in a tangle of clothes, rucksacks pushed against the side of the tent where they've let rain percolate. Yusef naked on his back, his pubic bush gleaming, his cock limp against his thigh. Faint snail trails have dried there on his skin. He smells of marzipan and bleach and beer all mixed together. I dress quickly, crouching, careful not to wake him. Though he might already be awake. I step outside onto wet grass into startling sunshine. The couple in the tent in front of us are just making breakfast. I smile sheepishly, but they're cool and smile back. It's the smell of bacon frying that brings Yusef to the door of the tent, growling with a hangover, tousled, flashing his best smile at the couple who make us both a cup of tea.

★ ★ ★

Every day we choose a different route to walk, sometimes taking lunch, sometimes stopping off at a pub. We see Cape Cornwall, Land's End, Sennen Bay, Porthcurno, Mousehole, Carn Goose Promontary and those tiny islands, The Brisons, where cormorants are crowded together to dry their wings against a glittering sea. We swim on the beach below the Minack Theatre and doze on a strip of white sand. In the evenings, I cook or we go to a restaurant. In the mornings we wake and I make tea in the little kitchen, enjoying the early morning scent of gas, the feeling of being alone before the day begins. After dinner, we watch the sun from the upstairs lounge, going down through torn cinema curtains to the sea where the tankers tack backwards and forwards. We stew the blackberries and keep them in the fridge, adding a dab of clotted cream. Their colour is deep, rich as blood in amber. We read in the evening, then lie with clasped hands each night listening to last traffic on the road that runs past the house to Land's End before we sink into sleep.

One day we find Priest's Cove, making our way down past lobster pots and floats and beached fishing boats to the concrete jetty. The beach is formed from smooth boulders, mysterious as blank skulls. Three elderly ladies are getting into their swimming costumes. They flip-flop to the sea, splashing their shoulders, sculling towards sunset, their arms breaking its tilting mirrors. Walking home, we find the pink flowers of campion bobbing in the wind.

★ ★ ★

Things got awkward with Yusef. For two days he hardly spoke. When we headed north again he didn't carry his shoulders with the same swagger and left me to do the hitching. We came most of the way home in a furniture van.

Driving through the night, side by side on the bench seat, our legs touching, a yellow cheese of moon looming over Somerset. When we got to Manchester the city was still asleep. We said goodbye in Piccadilly Square, under the statue of Queen Victoria. Yusef swung his arm and let his fist hit me lightly on the mouth. Not a real blow, but real enough.

'See you Ginge.'

I was too stunned to speak, lips stinging from his fist. He turned away, hoisting his rucksack, his heels striking the paving stones. He looked over his shoulder and smiled and said again.

'See you.'

But I didn't see him. We went our separate ways and I never saw him again. I heard that he'd gone to Manitoba to mine copper. But maybe that was just a rumour. When I got home and needed to wash my clothes, I found his pendant stuffed into the pocket of the spare jeans in my rucksack. I've still got it somewhere.

★ ★ ★

That's a lie. A lot of stuff is lies without meaning to be. Marie and I set off home on the Saturday, hoping to get a decent breakfast in Warminster. We end up in a greasy spoon with a bacon sandwich, drinking instant coffee. The best England can offer at 8 o'clock on a Saturday morning. We'd had a good week: walked miles of coastline, seen dozens of wild flowers and birds, felt the sea pulling at the land, slept in the peculiar darkness of the Cornish night and made love there. We'd got close again. So why did we drive most of the way back in silence? Once we found the road home, after Exeter, we hardly spoke. Something had thickened around us like a misgiving or mistrust. It was hard to say. It wasn't just sadness at our holiday coming to an end. It was something else beyond that. The stuff you grope to understand but words fall short of. Maybe it was the lives we could have led. I don't know.

When we finally get home and drag our bags from the car and up the garden path, the front door is jammed with the weight of stuff behind. Letters, bills: all that junk mail piled up on the mat. I get my arm inside and fling most of it down the hallway. The door opens, but before I can step inside, Marie touches me on the temple, brushing back the hair. She looks as if she's about to cry.

'I love you, you know. Whatever you might think.'

I don't know what to say, squeezing into the house, Yusef's pendant pressing into my chest where it's buttoned into the pocket of my shirt. Why did she say that? It's as if she knows something about us that even I don't know.

Then I'm piling up the mail, watching the answerphone blink and ignoring it, switching on the kettle as Marie pushes the kitchen windows open. The house is chilly with absence. I carry our bags upstairs and place them side-by-side on the bed, ready to unpack. I wonder where Yusef is now, where in the world he can be. I stroke the tanned skin on my arms and it moves in tiny wrinkles under freckles and goose bumps. Marie's calling me down for tea, saying something about the back door key, and I'm suddenly happy. Glad that he's never grown old.

Charcoal Burner

The woman made her way deeper into the forest, pushing aside the branches of a willow that blocked her path. Dried leaves broke off and fell under her fingers. The branches sprang back like whips. Then the scrubby trees in the outer reaches of the forest gave way to a mixture of oak and beech, scattered through with ash and sycamore and the silvery trunks of birches. Here and there a marshy dip and the glint of water. She toiled on, burdened by her swollen belly, by the duffel bag that hung behind her. The strap cut into her shoulder. Sun reached through spaces in the foliage and dappled her face. She stopped walking, gasping, becoming pale as a contraction tightened her womb. The first ones had come early that morning as she left the city. The shattered roofs of houses had gaped under smoke that scrawled itself across clear sky.

The spasm passed away and she pushed on, oblivious of everything except the quickening pains in her belly. She trudged through gold and copper leaves that littered the earth, kicking up the underlying mould. Dead seasons enveloped her. The forest was closing in.

Shadows under the trees grew denser; stray sunlight intensified, slanting down in thin wands. All around her were the strange sounds and heavy scents of the forest. High above were bird cries; the wings of birds flapping through topmost branches. She wiped sweat from her forehead. A robin flew past, needling the air with its notes. It was late in the year and fungi sprouted lavishly: sulphur-yellow horns ringing the roots of trees, honey fungus spreading up their trunks. Then funnel caps and the scarlet heads of fly agaric. Sometimes there were luminous puffballs and mushrooms that she knew would be good to eat. She had not eaten for a long time, but now the thought of food sickened her. The air was laden with the stink of decay; sunshine gleamed like old gold and leaves spiralled into autumn's shadows.

The woman toiled onwards. Somewhere, far behind, the city was burning. The shelling had become heavier over the past days, mortars, rockets and then artillery rounds systematically delivered. Buildings were pockmarked with shrapnel and bullets. Shoppers had been killed in the marketplace. She'd seen soldiers sluicing away blood and broken glass. Day by day the city was encircled. A few people she knew had escaped. They'd gone further west, to safe havens that were never really safe. They could just as easily be traps. Traps for rats. All that hatred. It was everywhere, demolishing their lives. Shells sucking out the church windows, smashing statues of the Virgin. Water mains gushing into the street, lit gas pipes scorching the air. All for nothing: all because of jealousy or fear. All of which turned to hate because of history working away below the surface of things.

Yesterday, she'd stumbled from her shelter in the church crypt to find her quarter of the city burning. The house next to hers was smouldering, its window holes blackened, its roof tiles spilling into the attic. She'd gathered up her things and left. Anything to get away from the stink of fire. On the kitchen table she pinned a note for Martin in case he came home. But she'd had no letter, no word for weeks. Instead of queuing for bread she packed a few things and walked towards the suburbs, dodging through streets where snipers were at work, mocking the population with sudden death, executing strangers through telescopic sights. It was like the eye of God watching. Even God had gone mad here.

The driver of a lorry ferrying drinking water had given her a lift out of the city, past the shells of buildings and bullet-pocked houses, the overgrown gardens where starving pigs foraged. He was a dark-eyed, furtive young man wearing a sheepskin jerkin. His hands were pale and his long fingers drummed at the wheel. There was a blue diamond tattooed on the back of each finger. She had felt his eyes on her, but she was safe enough in her condition. Even the militia wouldn't rape a pregnant woman. Though she'd heard rumours. He'd left her on a wooded hillside, near the burned-out shell of a black saloon car. A pair of women's patent leather boots were standing on the roadside, as if someone had meant to collect them. Then she'd walked past them to the forest, entering its cathedral of stillness. Behind her the city was burning. She didn't care. It was all blurred now. Blurred by sleeplessness, by the daily expectation of loss. The child inside her was a stone, weighing her down. She pitied it: that was all.

The woman came upon a narrow game path winding through the trees. It was a relief: it must go somewhere. She needed to lie down and give herself up to the pains. They were assailing her with greater and greater frequency now. Beneath her blue headscarf a lock of black hair had fallen loose, tumbling against her pinched face. Her eyes were brown, large and afraid. It was her first child and she'd cut herself off from all help. Not that there was any help to be had. Not here. Not back there, where lives were broken in a moment by the crack of a bullet, a knock on the door.

The trees began to thin out, allowing sunshine to splash onto the fallen leaves. It was filtered by the foliage above, flickering and swimming in a dizzying motion. She must rest. Her mind was numb with fear and fatigue. Her body was not her own. It was aching, thrusting itself forward to the birth, building a wave that would wash her aside. She wanted to give herself up to it. First, she had to find shelter.

There was a broad clearing littered with the stumps of cut-down trees. It was divided by a stream that spread itself into a pool of sunlight at the far end. A few yards from where she stood, built in the shelter of a holly tree, was a crude lean-to of logs and piled earth. In front of it lay a heap of grey ash where a fire had been. A sudden gust caught at it, whipping dust into the air and scattering it across the grass. The clearing held the scent and haze of woodsmoke. On its far side lay two large mounds of earth. One of them smouldered sullenly, spouts of smoke drifting from its flanks. The other had grown cold and was being excavated by a man, naked to the waist, who shovelled charcoal into sacks.

The woman walked slowly over to the hut and sank down where the fire had been. The charcoal burner was aware of the woman even before he saw her: a cracking twig, the swish of her legs against ferns. He was black from head to foot from his work. Sweat made pale streaks down his trunk. Someone had entered the clearing. He turned about, gripping the shovel to face the intruder. It was rounded at the end and very sharp. In the trenches they'd fought with these on raiding parties, killing each other in the darkness of dugouts and shell holes. They'd fought and died like beasts. Now, near his hut, he saw a human shape. He ran to the stream, leaping it easily, holding the shovel at the ready. He'd kill if necessary. That was easy now.

The man came close to her and she saw that his filthy hair

was blond and spiky, bristling up from a high forehead. He was short and broad and his eyes were pale blue in a face twisted by rage or fear. She was indifferent to her fate now. She sank down and couldn't move. A new pain cramped her and she bit her lip.

The man stood in front of her. He watched her face as a spasm drew in her cheeks. She didn't look at him, but at the hard-packed earth. He saw her swollen belly under the loose clothing and understood, letting the shovel fall. He waited, hands on hips, watching until the pain left her. When he spoke his voice was quiet and deep. It had an odd, caressive tone, at odds with his hard body.

'Who are you, eh?'

She looked up at him. Her voice was bitter.

'A woman.'

He stared at her, not understanding.

'Where from?'

Questions. She roused herself, leaning on one elbow, not looking up.

'I came from the city. They shell it every day now. I've no people left, no husband. No place to stay. I came to the forest.'

He nodded slowly. Her eyes had a feverish brightness, but her voice was dull, hesitant.

'You?'

The man swept his hand round the clearing, a gesture that included both it and the forest beyond. He grinned briefly, ironically, showing pointed teeth. His eyes were a scorched blue.

'A man.'

She shrugged. So what? It was enough.

'Your time...'

He moved a hand up to his face, as if unused to words.

'...it's very close?'

She nodded, putting her teeth to her lips and tasting blood. The man turned suddenly, abrupt in all his movements. He beckoned her into the hut where some blankets were laid out on a mattress to make a bed. It was dark inside; it smelled of woodsmoke and earth. She lay down, resting for a few moments, then struggled upright to unpack the things she would need from her bag. Baby clothes and a shawl bought in a city shop.

The charcoal burner left the hut and appeared a few minutes later carrying some live coals on his shovel. He knelt down before her and began to kindle a blaze from a pyramid of wood chips, wafting the embers with a leaf of wild rhubarb. The sunlight was beginning to draw back, allowing shadows into the clearing. They darkened it stealthily. A faint chill was beginning to ride on the air. She was glad of the fire.

The man brought her a drink of water from the stream and gradually she sank into a state of drowsiness, almost without consciousness. Before the war they'd lived their own lives. Lives with distinct memories and a future. Her childhood in that same city, her mother walking her to school through dirty snow with the broken melody of a song going through her head. Then years later, a day with Martin when they'd taken a boat out across the river and picnicked on an island. They'd watched a cormorant diving, knifing into grey water, emerging with tiny fish in its beak. In the evening swifts had chased insects above the treetops, screaming in wild gangs. And they'd made love, fumbling like adolescents in the dusk. That was before the fighting, before neighbour had cursed neighbour, before the warlords and militias. Before fear had annulled everything. Fear on the surface and more fear buried under that.

She turned over, moving from side to side, the ache in her back deep and persistent. It made the pains more bearable to drift like this in the shallows of sleep. Her breathing assumed its own rhythms, quickening and falling away with the cramp in her belly. She lay half-conscious, half sunk to sleep. Images of the forest and the city crossed her mind and re-crossed it and then were shut out by new pain. Pale fungi, flickering foliage, shattered houses, smoke coiling like a rope slowly flailing the sky. Once she opened her eyes to find the man watching over her. He'd washed the charcoal dust from himself and squatted with the firelight on his hair and skin. He gave her a wry smile of encouragement.

Now the intermittent pains were being taken over by waves that made her grunt with shock. She'd never felt her body like this, had never been so irresponsibly afraid. The birth was dragging out another layer of darkness. She had to close off her panic, couldn't surrender to it. The antenatal books she'd read had told her how to relax, how to breathe though the contractions. But the pain was a tide dragging her, swinging her legs apart. This child would kill her to be born. The colossal weight of it was pulling at her like gravity. With a terrible effort she roused herself for the birth.

The man heard her owl-like moans and felt scared. Afraid of this after all he'd been through! That was strange. He held a wet cloth to her head. Flames glanced across her dark, occluded eyes. With each cry the child moved down, the head crowned, then emerged like a strange planet, plastered with blood and hair. He brought a light and got ready to take it. It came in a gush with the woman's final gasp. He took the cord in his hand and cut it as she'd told him. The tiny mouth opened in the child's puckered face and it gave a wail. He wrapped it in the shawl and handed it carefully to its mother.

'A boy!'

She nodded, exhausted. Minutes passed in which she soothed the child at her breast. There was no joy, just bitter milk flowing from the pain in her breasts. She was at the very frontier of wakefulness. Another spasm. Then another.

'Take the cord... gently!'

He twisted the slimy umbilical around his hand and waited until the afterbirth came away. It lay there, wounded and raw. The woman sank back with her child and the charcoal burner took the thing and wrapped it in a square of cloth, carrying it to the edge of the clearing where he flung it away into the trees.

When he returned the woman had already fallen asleep with her child. It was a boy and had given a single, thin cry of life, its lungs filling under his hands. It was a boy. He felt glad; he didn't know why.

The man built up the fire with fresh logs. A new moon was sailing above the treetops, casting a faint light into the clearing. Wind hustled through the branches, making the leaves shiver. The stars were spangles of frost glittering against darkness, infinitely far yet almost close enough to pull down and sift through a man's fingers. The Milky Way stretched across the heavens, star after star sending its light. Existing even after death. A huge and slowly turning illusion of light. The road to heaven. They'd watched the same stars from dugouts on the frontline. And falling stars that came and went in a blink like tracer rounds. Then white-hot bullets had ripped in overhead. He'd seen what a round of hot metal could do to a human body. That wet thwack of contact. A neat entry wound and a gaping exit, leaking entrails, blood, shit. Then necrotising flesh. Gangrene. He'd seen the eyes of men who knew they were going to die. He'd witnessed their disbelief at the way a split second could change everything.

In sleep the woman's mouth had sagged open and a lock of hair had fallen across her face. It was dark, like the wing of a bird. Firelight flared upon them: the crouched, expectant man, the sleeping woman, the newborn child bundled beside her. She had his blankets for her bed. He reached forward, moving the lock of hair aside, watching her breathing come and go. The woman slept a deep, narcotic sleep. A profound unconsciousness, beyond dreams, beyond the danger of memory.

When she awoke it was sudden, startling. The light had shocked her awake. She felt the warmth of the bundle in her arms, but hardly dared look at the child. She was sore and stiff. Her thighs felt caked with blood and dried birth slime. She changed the cotton pad she'd placed between them the night before; the bleeding had stopped. That was good. She longed for a bath, to be washed clean and under fresh sheets. Already the clearing was hazy with sunlight, though the air was still chilled and damp. Dew glistened on the grass, pearling a fine tracery of cobwebs.

Across at the pool, the man was bathing. He was kneeling by the water, naked to the waist, alone with the morning. His body was pale as a birch wand when the bark has been cut away. He threw the water up over his head and shoulders and it fell back in splinters of light. His fair hair gleamed like wheat. All his movements were wary, contained, like a creature that has escaped capture. But not free, not yet. The child woke beside her and began to cry. She sat up and put it to her breast, wincing as it sucked. Its strength was amazing, its need to take from her. Its puckered face was red and angry with life.

The city was burning. That was the only certainty. Martin was out there somewhere. The father of this child. He might be dead or alive. She had no way of knowing; her past hardly seemed real. That had been someone else, somewhere else. Another life. Vague, distant, without meaning now. And the future? That was wiped away so that she existed in moments only; her only identity was through sensation and fragmented thought. A song thrush hopped near the hut and began to call out, puffing up its breast and stabbing the earth for grubs.

The man returned, buttoning his shirt, suddenly self-conscious. His face was shiny and alert and she saw that it was heavily pockmarked. His eyes were less pale next to clean skin. He looked down at the woman and child, shy to enter his own living space.

'You'd like something to eat?'

His voice hummed, soft with unexpected bass notes. She nodded and he brought brown bread, toasting it on the fire and spreading it with meat-paste from a jar. The woman ate, gulping down the mug of coffee the man had poured for her. She felt hollowed-out by hunger. She smelled of fire. The charcoal burner squatted before the burning logs, allowing his face to absorb the weak sunlight. She put the child to her other breast drawing her blouse close around it.

'What's your name?'

The man started, her question unexpected.

'Peter.'

'Peter?'

She repeated the name like an incantation, touching the baby's forehead with her finger.

'I'll call him Peter, then.'

The man laughed abruptly, a short yelp of embarrassment. He shifted on his haunches. A gust of wind rolled a heap of leaves through the clearing.

He rose and filled a bucket with water, hanging it over the fire so that she could wash. Her child had taken life in his hands, between his hands. The charcoal heap emitted thin plumes of smoke, a scent of heated earth. She fell gradually asleep again, dozing with the child, vaguely aware of the man, busy around her. The fire had grown dull again, whitening to ash. The charcoal burner took his axe and went to fetch more logs. It was a keen, fresh morning. He filled his lungs with air, the awakening scents of the forest, alert to every sound. He came to a heap of sawn beech logs and began to split them. Where his mind had been empty or slumbering the woman now lay. He remembered the lock of hair that had fallen across her face. Like a black wing against snow. He had touched her, then.

Resting on the haft of his axe, he stared into the sky's deepening blue. High above, the fuselage of an aircraft glinted in the sun. Its engines droned. Dead leaves drifted around him, rustling their incomprehensible speech. Winter would soon be here. He'd need to rebuild the hut, to seal it against snow and wind. He swung the axe high above his head, balanced it for a moment then brought it down upon the log. It split cleanly and fell into two halves. The woman would stay.

Touch

The light at the wing tip tilts as the plane circles. Its bright planet had seemed fixed at the horizon. Now it scribes a wide arc as the plane banks into darkness. Local time in Nairobi is 6.05am. The aircrew bring a tray of hot towels. Miles wipes his face and hands. The towel is almost too hot to touch, but cools quickly. The plane tilts again and the porthole shows the dawn coming. The sky is still black above the wing. Below, it falls in shades of indigo, folded drapes that sink to a line of smoking orange where the sun is splitting the horizon.

Miles dozes, then feels the plane lurch again as it hits turbulence. The seatbelt light beeps above his head. Below the wing the land is dull khaki. Dark hill ridges come into view, an avalanche of grey mist frozen into each valley. Light strengthens from the widening band of crimson at the horizon. Then a flat, parched landscape etched with settlements, the circles of old kraals scarring the veldt. A few tiny lights flicker, forming lines, squares, rectangles. Dawn chill is waking the villages and farms below. Miles imagines the people beneath them. Hearing the choir of engines through sleep. Glancing up from kindling a fire or guarding cattle to see a silver fuselage and vapour trail. Yet the plane gives little sensation of flying, just this turgid droning progress. He stares down as the land rises under its dipping wing. The bare peak of Mount

Kenya appears to the left and recedes, a glowing cone of rock that is lost as the plane slips into cloud.

When Miles looks up from his book for the last time, they're skimming the outskirts of Nairobi. The plane shudders and sinks lower, passing over a road lined with industrial units and neon signs. Then it's circling Jomo Kenyatta airport. Scrubby fields and flat-topped acacia trees and blue perimeter lights pass under the wing as they touch down.

★ ★ ★

Carol is still dozing. Maybe it's the heating coming on – water creaking and clinking into the radiators – that finally wakes her. Maybe it's the call of a jackdaw on the chimney pot above the bedroom. Every year a new brood is raised there. She sits up and notices the empty space in the double bed. It's not a surprise, but there is still a small tug of disappointment. She slips on her nightgown and opens the curtains. A thrush is busy on the lawn, thrashing a snail against one of the stones in the little herb garden Miles planted. It's not yet dawn, but there is a pale intimation of day beyond the silhouette of hills. Carol pulls the bedclothes back over the warm place where she has been sleeping and pads downstairs into the empty house.

★ ★ ★

Miles sits in the Java Café with a cup of black tea, fishing out his mobile phone to send Carol a text to say that he's arrived safely. There'll be no network from now on. Not in Uganda. He finishes the tea and makes his way to Gate Eight. The attendant frisks him half-heartedly. Then he's climbing aboard a small jet that will take him over Lake Victoria. It's just one hour's flight to Entebbe. He dozes most of the way, lulled by the sun where it seeps through the porthole. When he wakes, his skin itches with a papery sensation.

He'll get a couple of hours' rest at the hotel. Then he'll walk down to the office in Nakasero for the first briefing. He feels light headed, drunk with light. A group of small islands goes by on the lake, covered in oil palms. He sees the faint trails of fishing boats written on water. Now the light is almost unbearable. His head is a gourd that's been scoured with salt. The water below is beaten copper, a gleaming brown patina. He pulls the shade down and tries to sleep.

When Miles steps down from the plane, the runway is already heating up. Uganda wraps him in the scent of wet foliage, scorched earth, charcoal smoke, burned hide and rotting fish. Unmistakeable. The lake glistens beyond the perimeter fence and the undulating bush. There's a steady, warm breeze. Then he's squinting at the pink immigration form, entering his address and passport number. The officer in the glass cubicle looks up listlessly and stamps his visa. Now he's waiting at baggage reclaim, his palms damp and prickly with heat. A stray dog is jumping on and off the carousel, which keeps jamming as the bags lurch into view. He finds a trolley and heaves his holdall from the conveyer belt. He chooses the Nothing to Declare exit and walks on. Jjuko, the driver, greets him and takes his bag to the Land Cruiser. Then the forty-kilometre drive to Kampala along the Entebbe road. These days the road is safer, but still brings a twinge of apprehension. And they avoid it at night.

Miles becomes almost preternaturally alert. Everything seems astonishingly bright. Even at this hour, vehicles crowd the road. New hotels are being built for the Commonwealth summit. They appear at regular intervals, festooned in bamboo scaffolding. Since his last visit, houses have appeared where there were little gardens, or shamba, before. In Uganda there are two rainy seasons and a family can feed themselves from a small patch of land. They pass little roadside markets tended by women in bright gomesis. The stalls are piled with pyramids of tomatoes and peppers, mangos and oranges, sweet potatoes and passion fruit. Dusky branches of green plantain are piled on the red earth. Sacks of charcoal and bundles of sugar cane are slung across old-fashioned bicycles, which are pushed along. The roadside bars, pharmacies, beauty parlours and pork joints look like pigeon cotes nailed together from random timber and sport racy, hand-painted signs. They pass smouldering brick kilns, stacks of pottery, workshops making lurid sofas, wooden beds, coffins and stacks of metal security gates. They're caught in a stream of white Toyota saloons, ancient lorries, sugar cane transporters, mini-van matatu taxis, mopeds and bicycles fitted with tasselled seats to carry passengers. They drive inside a haze of fumes, passing under jackfruit trees and broad matoke leaves. Closer to the city, a few high-rise buildings come into view above the Omo and Guinness advertisements. A moustached troubadour grins with his guitar from the Bell brewery hoarding. *Bell lager shares your passion.* Miles tries to remember if he's ever met a Ugandan with a moustache.

Then they're stuck at the roundabouts below Nakasero. Tyres grind diesel fumes from the oil-stained earth. Teenage boys flit between cars, matatu and lorries, hawking bags of coffee beans for the drivers to chew. The bags are made out of banana fibre. Boda-boda mopeds flit in and out of the traffic, their female passengers riding side-saddle. Women walk beside the road, balancing jerry cans and baskets of plantain on their heads. The traffic lurches forward a few feet, spurting smoke. Hump-backed cows and skinny goats graze by the roadside. A few black kites circle the Hindu temple, watching the city below. The temple dominates the market-place, a marquetry puzzle of cream-coloured stone. Then Miles is dozing again, his head knocking on the window in the sun. When he looks up, a marabou stork is sailing just above the windscreen, its pink gullet swinging as it wheels into blistering air.

★ ★ ★

Carol is cupping a mug of tea in her hands, watching a fleece of mist drag itself across the fields. The hilltops are already clear. She can see a stack of yellow pipes, a scar of clay running across the fell. They're putting in a new pipeline to bring Norwegian gas right across the country. Every pub and B&B in the area is putting up fitters who've come to weld up the pipes and bury them from coast to coast. It will always be known as the year of the pipeliners. Though she'll remember it for something else.

She puts the cup down among the interlocking rings that lace Miles' desk. The skin on the back of her hands is faintly mottled. It creases like vellum when she stretches her fingers. Sunflowers are drooping in the garden outside. A spider has tied its web from the corner of the shed to old bean canes tangled with brittle growth. The computer is switched off and she can see herself, ghostly on the flat screen. She could check for messages, but it's too early. Uganda is two hours ahead. Was that right? Ahead or behind? Ahead, she's sure. In which case she should switch on, but she'll be late for school.

Miles had told her not to worry about hearing from him until later in the day. Carol has never been to Africa, has never wanted to go. Except maybe to Zanzibar. The name is beautiful. It draws her, somehow. *Zanzibar*. Centre of the ancient spice trade where clove-scented zephyrs blow off the land to the sea. It was the centre of the Arab slave trade, too. She has to remember that. She can almost hear Miles correcting her, placing suffering where it belonged.

On the wall of the study is a small camel-hair prayer rug from Mali. It's flanked by four Congolese masks, their dark wood carved into grim faces with slits for eyes. They make her flinch every time she passes. Carol sips at the cold tea, slips her hand into her nightdress and grimaces. She dresses, eats a bowl of muesli, packs her briefcase, then leaves, pulling the front door shut behind her.

★ ★ ★

On the fifth day, Miles is woken by rain pattering on attic sky-lights. If he stands on tiptoe there'll be a view of green fells and grazing sheep. Carol's body is warm, just beyond his. He pushes the sheet away to reach for her. Instead, the Hadada ibis fly past, squawking over the hotel with crude, throaty cries. He remembers them now. How he's seen them on the parkland with the storks and cattle egret. Close up, they look like huge, iridescent curlews.

Kampala rain pours like sacks of rice emptied against the metal roof. Water is slapping down from the eaves, gurgling and draining away in the compound. It's a cool morning. He twitches aside the mosquito curtain and peers through the mesh in the unglazed window. There's a blue Mercedes parked next to a white pick-up truck. A man in a boiler suit is carrying a jerry can of water. He's wearing gumboots, stepping across rivulets of red where dust from the road is draining across the tarmac. Purple blossom from the jacaranda tree is being carried away by the rain.

The thoughts of home are a dark thicket, impenetrable now. He catches sight of himself in the mirror, naked. He's slept under one thin sheet, stuffing the coverlet into a cupboard. And the night had been cooler, too. It's the second wet season, when the day starts with rain. He breathes in slowly, watching his chest inflate above the bush of pubic hair. He's lost weight and his stomach looks sunken. His penis feels inert. He pulls his foreskin back and sees the glans, moist as a seed in its pale skin. The blue vein is mysterious, a quiet river, his own blood tattooed there. Under a layer of low cloud the light is strengthening, silvering wet leaves. Brown parrots are squabbling in the trees outside. The gates open and the blue Mercedes pulls away.

Miles pushes a Malarone tablet out of its blister pack and swigs it down with bottled water. He's been bitten on the ankle by a mosquito and it itches maddeningly. That's despite long trousers and desert boots and Jungle Formula sprayed on his arms and face. Mosquito repellent and Bell Lager – that's the smell of Kampala nights for him. Bitter and intoxicating. When he gets dressed and pulls on his boots he finds a split in one of them where the welt has pulled away. He'll need to find a new pair back in England.

Today is Sunday. His first day off since he'd stepped from the plane. He remembers the wing tilting as they circled Nairobi: scrubby fields with thorn trees, then the slum-lined railway line and runway lights below. When he crossed the tarmac there were swifts flickering over the airport buildings. The same birds that fly from Spain and North Africa to breed and then scream in gangs over his roof in Yorkshire.

Miles picks up his spectacle case and goes out to breakfast in the enclosed hotel garden where a waiter is drying rain from the chairs. He picks up some pineapple, sweet bananas; a slice of watermelon. A plain yoghurt spooned from the carton. A slice of toasted bread with a dab of butter. Then coffee, weak, insipid and unforgivable when Ugandan beans are so good. The fat American he calls Big Mac is booming familiarly to the hotel staff.

'Hiya Freddie, how're ya doin'?'

Freddie is the Kenyan who works at reception and serves breakfast and breaks eggs on a hot griddle. He looks about seventeen. The shambling American dwarfs him.

'Be-yootiful day. Whaddya got?'

Freddie obligingly opens the silver tureens to show bacon, sausages and tilapia.

'Summa that and summa that and… yeah, eggs over easy.'

Traffic hoots on the road beyond the perimeter wall.

'Yeah, yeah… be-yootiful, more-a that Freddie… and gimme summa those….'

From behind him come the smooth, unbroken tones of the Brits who sit at breakfast tables in safari suits with their lap-tops, stirring their coffee.

…well, you can only ask these people and see what they say… safeguards? don't make me laugh…! well you'd think so wouldn't you…? so much of the stuff goes missing as soon as it's put down… you'd think that they'd respect the fact it was for their own people… they don't see it as stealing… well, we call it corruption, but they'd call it something else… looking after the family, I suppose… blood being thicker than… absolutely hopeless… dispir-iting in the end… my predecessor actually tried to put a stop to it, but to no avail. Ah well… do you think Jjinja would make a good base in your experience, of being there, I mean, or Makerere, actually on campus?…really? on the campus? Joseph Mwiine, oh he's very …entirely plausible… very nice chap… oh yes, we take delivery on Wednesday… and eventually they'll take over…. At the end of the day we can only try to help with logistics… when Isabelle comes we'll check that… oh, she's very able… terribly able…

Miles watches the American push food into his big face, blinking wretchedly as he does so. He watches the Chinese postgraduate student making an entry in his diary, column after column of neat black characters. He sees a pied crow alight on the jacaranda tree in the compound, its eye round and bright as agate. The thin girl, Mary, is wiping red dust from the steps that lead into the hotel, working in bare feet, her orange nylon overall riding up her thighs. He sees the American delve into his ear then examine his finger. Freddie watches impassively from behind the griddle. Mary flicks her rag into a bucket of dirty water. Miles rises and passes with a quiet *thank you* and slips into the gloom of his room to pack his laptop.

★ ★ ★

Carol is in the staffroom, lost in the drift of conversation. It's almost the end of lunchtime. A stack of blue exercise books stands in front of her. She puts the pencil down and clasps her hands, pressing down on the tabletop.

'Carol, are you ok?'

It's Maddy, the head of English.

'Yes. Sorry, just daydreaming.'

Her mouth is sour with the taste of staffroom coffee. The table is digging into her.

'What's next?'

'3C. Speaking and listening. I'm doing that passage from *Kes.*'

'Ok, sounds good. Best of British with that lot!'

Carol rises and gathers the books into her locker. She picks up her bag and makes her way through to the corridor, to the smell of school dinners and the yells of children in the playground outside her form room. She might get two minutes to herself without anybody asking her anything. She looks at the faded map of the world and finds England. She finds Europe and then Africa. She finds Uganda, Lake Victoria, Kampala, tracing the creased paper with her finger. It's like old skin. Elephant skin. Then the door is forced open and the kids spill in upon her.

* * *

The Shangri-La hotel and the Shanghai restaurant share a compound with the Kampala sports club. Tonight, Miles decides to eat in the restaurant instead of going out. The traffic is so bad now that taking a taxi is slow and means suffocating in diesel fumes. By seven o'clock, the power has failed across Kampala and all the bars and shops are lit by candles and kerosene lamps. Load-shedding. All because someone built a dam in the wrong place. Miles sits at a balcony table under lights that ebb and brighten. The generator throbs somewhere. He's finishing his fried rice and is sipping soda water when a white rabbit appears on the lawn below. It's nibbling the coarse grass and looks up, seeming to watch him. The faint light makes it look like a mythical creature, a golden hare fallen from some constellation in the night sky.

Later, Miles is trying to send an email from the hotel's business centre. It's maddeningly slow. He sees that all the tables in the hotel garden outside the window have candles burning on them. The email system crashes over and over. He waits for a connection, watching plasma crawl across the bar at the bottom of the screen. Then a voice floats up, husky and plangent. A woman is singing, solo. He strains to hear the words… *Oh God thou art a light to me…* She is joined by other voices, male and female, swelling confidently into harmony.

He watches the tiny hourglass blink on the screen. The voices sink and rise and go on. There is a lull filled with conversation and laughter and sudden ululation. Then one voice hums, picks up a melody and words, until the whole garden resonates in three-part harmony. They sing in English, yet it is quite unlike anything he has ever heard. This language has the thickened tone of loss. Or maybe he imagines that. Candles flicker in darkness beyond the mosquito netting. The connection fails again.

When Miles goes into the compound to breathe the humid air, the night-watchman greets him softly. *Good evening, Sah.* Miles answers awkwardly, smells the rain; sees the moon parting silver clouds. It is rising like the head of a bright mushroom. He thinks of Carol under the same moon. He misses her now. He is alone but not lonely. He is wherever he goes when he is this far from home, somewhere beyond loneliness. He feels beside or beyond himself.

★ ★ ★

Carol's school is six miles from the village. It's a five-minute drive from the house to the main road. Today she's late and gets stuck behind the school bus, which stops at every lane end and farm gate and village to pick up children who clamber aboard in their dark-green uniforms. Even at this time of year hardly any of them wears a coat. A group of third-formers crowds the back window of the bus and waves at her. She waves back, trying not to smile at their delight.

A tract of mud spreads across the road where the traffic for the pipeline has crossed. She slows down for the temporary traffic lights, watching a yellow digger slew out a wave of clay as it turns in the field. It's hard to imagine the landscape ever healing. A group of Charolais bullocks are crowded by a gate as she slows for the roundabout just before the school. The bull is silhouetted against the horizon, shoulders hunched into its massive neck. Its balls hang heavily beneath, swinging as it lunges at the grass. A pair of crows rises from something on the road.

By the time Carol gets to school the bus is already empty and pulling out of the gates. The driver is an ex-pupil. He has a head of blond, almost white hair, fine as cotton strands. One of those boys for whom school was a waste of time because he already had employment with the family firm. He'd had a job as soon as he was born. She feels old, watching him turn the wheel, watching him pull away into his new life. Ironically, it brings him back to school twice a day. Carol pulls on the handbrake, checks her lipstick in the mirror; drags her briefcase from the passenger seat. Another day. She wonders what more there is beside work. The school bell peals its din of hammered iron as she climbs the steps. Inside, she sees her face gliding inside a glass cabinet of silver cups. She hurries on.

★ ★ ★

Now he's on Nile Avenue, the Sheraton to his left, the Grand Imperial and the Speke Hotel on his right. It's already dusk and traffic is swarming. The air is dense with diesel fumes and the dirt paths beside the road chock-full of school kids on their way home. He's passed the woman with her sick baby laid on the pavement. He looks straight past the cripple who clings to a cut branch. There is something biblical and stark in the crudely hewn crutch. A legless man sprawls on a square of cardboard and Miles finds something of interest in the towering blue panes of the Workers' Building that dominates Nakasero. The road dips down and becomes dual carriageway. He crosses over and turns right at the Uganda Broadcasting Corporation where boda-boda riders gather and a woman sits under a parasol with cigarettes and bags of sweets and newspapers laid out under pieces of glass to tempt office workers on their way home.

He's had a long day, checking serial numbers on the second-hand computers they've imported from the UK against the recorded numbers, assigning them to schools, arranging for new software to be installed. Miles works for a UK-based NGO, Computeraid. He works mainly in Harrogate, but also in Uganda, Malawi and sometimes Kenya. He retired from the bank at fifty, bored but with a decent pension. Then he replied to an advert in the *Yorkshire Post* and a new life started. An unexpected sense of purpose. He'd never been out of Europe before that first trip to Nairobi. Now his passport is full of African visas and he has a life that no one else knows about. Not even Carol. A life that he doesn't talk about, because he can never quite find the right words or the right time. But it's part of him, growing relentlessly, pushing at his other life. In the space of that first drive from Entebbe to Kampala something had changed for good. Or for ever, it was hard to tell.

Miles thinks about a walk around the craft market and a beer in the National Theatre before eating at the Chaat house on De Winton Road. But he's skipped lunch, so goes straight to the restaurant. He orders a Nile Special, spiced lentil cakes with yoghurt and a mutton and spinach curry with garlic naan. The restaurant is just a small café, really. There are a couple of Asian families in there and three Australian backpackers with rat-tail dreadlocks. The waiter remembers Miles from his previous visits. He welcomes him – *Hello Sah!* – brings the beer first and snaps the cap off. The restaurant is Indian, but all the waiters are Ugandan. There is still tension between them, a hierarchy that leaves the Asians on top. Miles has come straight from the office and forgotten his insect repellent. He rolls down his sleeves and buttons the cuffs, then takes a sip of the beer, breaking pieces off his pappadom and scooping up chutney and chilli sauce. He drinks the cold beer too fast and orders another. The starter comes, swimming in spiced yoghurt. He likes this place. It's familiar, scruffy, safe from ex-pats for the most part.

Miles walks back through darkness to the Shangri-La, passing three prostitutes on a street corner who smile at him. The dusk of diesel fumes burns his throat. The boda-boda riders beep at him enquiringly. But he shakes his head and walks on, stumbling and narrowly missing an open manhole. A woman passing murmurs, *Oh, sorry!* He rights himself, murmuring, *It's ok, thank you.* He remembers the bag of needles and sutures he carries, as recommended. They're back at the hotel. So what use are they? It's hard to say. Just that it's advised to carry such things in Africa. In any case he doesn't fancy a visit to Mulago hospital.

He walks on. Three small girls surround him in the road, their mother waiting nearby. He gives them some change and waves them away when they persist. He's heard they are Karamajong women widowed in cattle raids. AK 47s have replaced spears and sticks and the northern tribes are slaughtering each other. On his last trip he met a German tourist who'd had his Land Rover stripped of its tyres, so that the warriors could make sandals.

On the pavement near the Sheraton a small boy sits alone in the dark, almost invisible, holding out his hand.

'Sah, Sah!'

His voice is a mere susurration. Miles finds a five hundred shilling coin and presses it into sticky fingers.

'Zankyou.'

The boy smells of shit and sweat. Miles wonders if he's being watched? Whether a bigger boy will take the money? Where he'll find shelter for the night? Earlier, outside the theatre, a Down's syndrome boy had politely begged a few shillings to buy a Fanta. Why had that affected him so much? The trick is never to look. Last year in Kano he'd been stuck at traffic lights and his car had been surrounded. A couple of ragged men without legs clinging to home-made skateboards, others pressing their stumps to the windows. Where to look? Away? Nowhere? That was the trick. The driver was impassive, flicking his head to one side. One of the men had dirt on the stump where his hand should have been. Miles could never get that out of his mind. He'd earned his thousand-yard stare.

Back at the hotel Miles switches on CNN news. He watches the slaughter in Iraq where the insurgency is out of control. American troops drag bloodstained bodies to a flatbed truck, a man's head bouncing as he is dropped. Miles runs a bath from the trickle of water the tap produces. He lies in a few tepid inches, working the soap, hearing TV's blare down the corridor. He towels, cleans his teeth, sits on the bed, flicking through his notes for tomorrow. He can hear the smack of squash balls from the hotel sports club. He'll remember that too: the inane flapping of rubber against cement. A gecko is broached to the wall above the TV. He waves at it ironically, pulling the sheet over himself.

Miles switches on the lamp and gets up to root through his jacket. In his wallet, tucked between his credit cards, he has a photograph of Carol taken at Widdup Moor just before he came out that first time. They'd had lunch at the Pack Horse after a long, boggy walk. She'd had her hair cut short. The pale roots were just showing. A purple scarf, a wistful smile.

Maybe that was just impatience at his incompetence with the camera. Her way of saying, *Get on with it, Miles, for God's sake.* She'd always been better with a camera than him. She's fifty-two. Hard to believe. Apart from those lines running from the corner of her eyes, she looks just the same to him. Strange, how he'll always see the girl in the woman. Grey eyes, like her mother's. Beautiful as the light catches them. And she'll be ok, after all. She'll be fine, because maybe it didn't hurt to be apart. Maybe that was a good thing.

Tomorrow, he'll go to the craft market on Buganda Road and find her some tribal earrings, a matching bracelet, maybe an unbleached cotton cloth for the kitchen table. Today, he'd like the fridge in his room to work so that he can drink cold water. He'll ask Freddie to look at it, knowing that Freddie has no fridge, that Mary will never have a fridge. Still, he'll ask them to look into it.

In the small hours of the morning he's woken by the clatter of heels from the room next door. Then voices. A woman politely thanking a man. A man laughing. The male voice is low, its tones almost indiscernible. When he peers through the curtains, a girl in a short dress, deeply scooped at the bosom, is talking to the night watchman and blowing smoke from a cigarette. The moon casts her shadow onto curled jacaranda leaves.

* * *

Carol sits on the edge of the bath. Her feet are touching each other and the enamel is cold under her thighs. A chill is seeping through the windows, though the gas boiler is rumbling in the kitchen below. She'd been woken in the night by mewling cats. Their cries were eerie, visceral and frightening like the hunger of babies. She shifts along the bath, reaching for a towel, remembering how the girls had cried in the night, pulling them from sleep. From each other.

Dawn is a bubble of gold melting onto frosted glass. The shelf above the sink is a jumble of shampoo bottlers, conditioner, bath oil, shaving foam. She notices some dark snips of hair at the base of the taps from the last time Miles shaved. She's wearing a pair of his old pyjamas with the cuffs and trousers rolled up. They don't smell of him exactly, but of *them*. She'd worn them the last time they made love. He'd undone the buttons so gently, one by one, a kiss for each. Then he'd touched her belly, kissed it in little circles, his lips pressed against her, grazing her skin.

A bird brushes against the window, a shadow from the world outside. She unbuttons the collar of the jacket and slips her hand inside. It's cold: a stranger's hand or a doctor's. The little lump under her left breast is still there, like a marble under the skin. She undresses, switches on the shower, steps into heat and steam.

★ ★ ★

On the way to the office, Miles sees half a dozen police at the Nakasero roundabout with capes and rifles. There is a tree on which five marabou storks have settled, flapping that dry drum-skin sound. It's the sound of hunger, the sound of appetite or desire. He sees the woman begging with her baby and crosses over the road, having no change. Then white clouds puffing up at the horizon in giant thermals. Kites and storks circling; a black wheelbarrow filled with purple blossom. He sees school kids hand in hand, with their green uniforms and satchels. A man lies asleep or already dead on a piece of open ground beside a termite mound of red earth. His skin is shiny as polished wood. Three women in bright gomesis with puffed shoulders sweep dust from the pavement with brooms made of bound twigs. A truck full of soldiers in olive uniforms and steel helmets goes by.

Miles sees the pavement, broken and crazed, the drift of dust across his shoes, the crystals of minerals glistening where the rain has washed them into the road. And when it starts to rain he sees a tall woman dressed in a grey two-piece suit stepping from the offices of the Stanbic Bank wearing a black carrier bag over her hair. Then he sees that he is already outside the Computeraid office and enters to make calls, check records, enter data, arrange transport. To do whatever needs to be done to make a difference.

★ ★ ★

Carol sits at Miles' desk and switches on the computer. Miles' sketchbooks are neatly filed on a shelf. Her hand falls to a tin of pencils that he keeps on the desk and opens it. Derwent Graphic. They range from 9B to H, each one a dark chocolate colour with an orange stripe. Each one ranked in perfect order. She clicks on the email program and watches it load. She clicks on the inbox. Get Mail. She waits. There is a stain on the beige carpet, almost the shape of Africa. A message appears silently with a blue dot beside it.

Darling, I'm working late in the office so firing off a quick message before I sign off. It rained all morning here and then it was very hot all afternoon and the aircon broke, so it's been pretty sticky. The Ugandans are lovely to work with – especially Agnes and James – but we seem to have lost half a dozen computers that were meant for Taibah High School. Hard to get to the bottom of things here, as you know. I hope you're ok. Missing you and home and this time of year in Yorkshire. The leaves must be turning now? Say hello to the girls and tell them I'm ok and thinking of them.

    Love, M

    PS I've got some Kigezi coffee beans from Bancafé, so looking forward to our next breakfast together.

Carol presses *Reply* and then sits for a long time watching the cursor blink at her, its small pulse lost in the machine.

★ ★ ★

The ninth of October is Ugandan Independence Day and a public holiday, so Miles has some free time. He'd intended to hire some transport and go somewhere, Jjinja or Entebbe maybe, but he's been sleeping badly and the tiredness has accumulated. Most days he's woken at dawn by the muezzin's call to prayer at the local mosque. Most nights he turns in before ten and sleeps for a couple of hours, then lies awake listening to a mosquito that has got in through the torn window mesh. He thinks of Carol, the girls, of Yorkshire in October, of home, of the next day's work.

He thinks how things never get any clearer in Africa and that maybe he shouldn't be here. It's as if the real problem is always undefined. Or it undefines itself. Things are hard to explain. Things that go missing or that don't get done. The Kampala office has the best team he's worked with yet, with the most thorough records. But things happen at the edge that are inexplicable. Things – even people – simply disappear. They fall away. He's learned to accept some things: unpunctuality, silence, disappearance, even early death. Those are the unspoken things that lie beyond beautiful manners and perfect decorum. He's learned not to probe too deeply for reasons. It's like learning to walk slowly in the heat; like learning not to look, whilst not actually looking away.

He tries to stay in bed later than eight o'clock, but it's impossible. He showers in a trickle of water that has left a brown stain running down the bath. The bath plug has disappeared, so a soak in deeper water is out of the question and impossibly slow. He takes his Malarone and picks flaking skin from the backs of his fingers. The skin beneath is pale and pink.

At breakfast the Brits are nowhere to be seen but a red-haired woman has joined the big American. They're talking quietly and earnestly. Miles folds a banana skin onto his plate and drains his coffee. Maybe it was too easy to judge people, after all. Freddie arrives with more coffee and flashes a delightful smile. On previous visits, Miles had stayed on the Makerere University campus, where he'd met a constant stream of professionals: teachers, agronomists, surgeons, nurses, educational researchers. They all seemed to be focused on what mattered, on what was worthwhile. Cutting-edge developments. Sustainable projects. Even the creation of understanding itself. It was hard to feel a part of that. A teacher from Iowa had once said to him that everyone had to find their own reason for being in Africa. But finding is one thing, believing another.

Miles finishes his toast and coffee, says *thank you* quietly to Freddie and then walks out of the compound and down the hill to buy a newspaper. The Sheraton is surrounded by a steel fence and every paling ends in a spear point. Today, soldiers in camouflage gear with automatic rifles guard the fence. Troop carriers are parked opposite the entrance, one with a heavy machine-gun mounted. Policemen with walkie-talkies are spaced all the way down the hill to Nakasero. He asks a European in khaki fatigues carrying a video camera and tripod what's going on.

'Coup-prevention. The president's giving a speech. They don't take chances.'

The journalist sounded as if he was from Australia or New Zealand.

'Where, at the Sheraton?'

'Where else? The president of Burundi's with him.'

South-African, after all. That made more sense once he'd placed the accent.

'Ok. Thanks.'

Miles had thought of going in to the hotel to use the broadband link at the business centre, but it's too much hassle. The troops wave him on. The policemen eye him cynically. He walks inside the carapace of his whiteness. His birthright of superiority. It would be so easy to believe that.

Miles shakes his head at the boda-bodas. He puts up his hand self-deprecatingly towards the taxi drivers: *Suh! Boss! Taxi Boss! Suh!* He puts two hundred shillings into the hand of the woman with the baby, though he notices the scabs on the baby's mouth and its suppurating eyes. The city is the quietest he's ever seen it. Apart from Easter Sunday that time. The time when he'd shaken his head at someone approaching his elbow, someone in the corner of his eye. Only to find it was a small boy carrying his baby brother and begging. By then they'd already turned away and were swallowed up in a crowd of impeccably dressed Ugandans emerging from a church on Kampala road. He'd left his drink at the café table. How could you survive when you were your brother's keeper, when you were only nine years old? Miles had found them eventually and put some coins into the older boy's hand. He'd looked proud and distant. Miles knew then that he'd always be there, in the corner of his eye.

Miles walks to Bomba Road and buys a *New Vision* for two

hundred shillings, an Independence Day issue. He turns into the Bancafé and orders a fresh lemon juice and a medium latte. The tables are made to look like rough-hewn tree trunks, glass-topped, the cavity beneath filled with coffee beans. The juice is sharp and sweet, the coffee mild and smooth. He reads the paper idly, then leaves the café and turns left past the shops selling suits and shoes and shirts, towards Nile Avenue. He feels for a coin when he sees a beggar on the corner: a dark shape sprawled on the pavement, crooked limbs bent under him. He wears a stained blue shirt and ragged trousers torn off at the hem. The man's hair is tangled and dusty. He cups his fingers when Miles leans down to drop the coin into them and their hands brush together. The man is about forty, though it's hard to tell. His fingers touch Miles' and pull them, tugging them gently towards himself. So that Miles has to look. The man's face is thin, meek and lined, his sternum twisted, his body a nest of black, broken sticks in which his life is huddled. His eyes are dark, the pupils ringed with bluish cataracts. His expression is one of indelible desolation. Yet he is thanking Miles. Thanking him for the worthless coin he's put into his hand.

On the way past the Sheraton Miles pushes a five thousand shilling note at the woman's hand as she cradles her baby. He crushes the newspaper, feels a prickle of heat attack his neck, that blush of sweat at his groin, behind his knees. He sees the man's face in the dust, in the blazing void of sky. He feels as if a layer of skin has been flayed from his body. He sits on the bed in the dark hotel room, the curtains pulled against the sun. That night he'll eat a pizza in the Nile Hotel just a hundred yards from where the man is sprawled. Armed guards will keep the beggars away and he'll be safe behind the fence, surrounded by ex-pats who hunch over their laptops, over their important work. He knows that as darkness

falls the man will crawl towards shelter. That he will wake
– as the woman with the baby will wake and the small boy,
and the girls who'd surrounded him with outheld hands
– to another day of eternally passing time, of hunger, of
thirst. A thousand contingencies make up their days. Better
not to look. But he had looked and the man – a man younger
than him with his life already spent – had touched him in
gratitude.

Tomorrow he'll eat a toasted sandwich with a glass of
fresh lemon juice and a latte. And the beggars will wait outside on the pavement where they are caught in the slowly
cascading dust of time. Like the traffic bollards and the termite
mounds and the cracked pavements sinking back to desert
under his heels.

★ ★ ★

Carol imagines the lump. It's part of her, so she has to love it,
because it could easily be benign. There is a medical practice
in the village, at the old vicarage where a huge copper beech
drops its leaves on the parked cars. The GP had used that
word when he referred her to a specialist. *Benign*. It sounded
like kindness. Like a form of charity. And so she thinks of it
as a pearl. Uganda is the pearl of Africa and so maybe she
has a little bit of Africa inside her. There it is, hard beneath
the skin. It glows with a radiant and unexpected light. It offers
no sensation. It gives no clue to its real nature or why it has
mysteriously appeared. So precious, so secretively asserting
itself. It is as if it has always been there and she simply
hadn't noticed.

They'd joked about such things when she went for her
medical at fifty. She and Cathy, the nurse practitioner. Her
breasts. The need to make regular checks. Now she is an

oyster and some tiny piece of grit has become a pearl growing inside her, a rare and mysterious part of nature. Of *her* nature. Now it's got between her and the world. The way secrets do. The way they take away the everyday and remake it as something profound or precious. She has to go to that other world to exist outside the everyday. Cherishing the precious thing that had taken root in her and that can't be ignored. Her own cells are dividing, growing in some glorious saturnalia, the natural order all topsy-turvy. But for no good reason. For no reason at all, when it came down to it, except that they could. Miles would be home in three days. He sounded strangely happy in his African world, inside his own shell that was burnished by equatorial darkness, wrapped in a spangled cloth of African nights.

When she is dressing for work, fastening her bra and looking from the bedroom window, she sees that the lawn is strewn with poplar leaves. The grass would need cutting one last time.

★ ★ ★

Independence Day again. But now it is evening. It's been forty-four years since the country gained its own flag then sank into war and poverty. Terror and corruption had ruined the most fertile country in Africa where it was said that even a stick planted in the ground would grow and bear fruit. That old cliché. The traffic has increased for some reason. There is smog of diesel fumes and darkness. Miles walks quickly, the way a muzungu walks, head down, always in a hurry in case they see something they'd rather not. He's wondering about the beggar on the corner of Nile Avenue above the Bancafé, but the man is not there.

He sees headlights sweeping the dense air; a father walking

hand in hand with his small son; an open lorry loaded with long-horned Ancholi cows; a man in a three-piece suit carrying a briefcase in one hand and a live hen in the other. Two boys try to sell him some eggs from cardboard trays, but he has no use for them. He sees the moon, huge and golden, nibbled away at its lower edge by termites, rising above the royal palms in the Sheraton gardens.

A tall, slim woman approaches him along the pavement. She is carrying a bible and holding hands with two little girls. The youngest is about six and wears a pink frock. When she sees Miles she breaks away from her mother and skips towards him through the dusk, holding out her hand. He takes it and she curtsies daintily. Miles introduces himself to the mother, who is wearing a knitted pork-pie hat. She is very beautiful, her cheek bones picked out by the lights of passing cars.

'Hello, I'm Miles. How are you?'

The woman shakes hands with a smile.

'I am Beatrice. How are you?'

That odd East African greeting that he's learned is not really a question. The older girl holds out her hand.

'This is Nancy.'

Miles shakes hands and looks down to the little girl who is looking up at him with huge eyes. The woman speaks again, enquiringly.

'And where are you from?'

'From the UK.'

'Ah, from the UK! That is good! Eeh!'

Miles turns to the smallest girl.

'And what is your name?'

The little girl is too shy to speak and her mother chuckles, touching her cheek with the back of her hands, a graceful movement that sways through her whole body.

'She is called Angel!'

They bid farewell and part there on the pavement. Miles crosses the road to the Shangri-La and the woman walks slowly into the night, into the fuming city. When Miles reaches his room, he sees that he's been crying.

★ ★ ★

Carol looks up from the cursor where it blinks on the screen. The moon is enlarged, almost orange, and misshapen now. The gas pipes gleam on the hillside, bleached of colour, a hundred open mouths gulping the night. The scar in the earth is a deep shadow across the contour of the hill.

Tonight she misses Miles. She hasn't lit the fire, but the central heating is at work, quietly filling the house with heat. The fridge hums in the kitchen and when her fingers press the light switches in the girls' bedrooms the bulbs brighten at once. She runs her fingers over their old CDs. Boy bands. *Take That. Wham.* How they'd scorn them now! They've outgrown everything left behind here. Carol thumbs their school textbooks lined neatly on a shelf. She opens the wardrobes to find a single tee shirt with George Michael's picture on it swaying from a hanger.

When she looks from the window there is a fox on the lawn, crouching in the light cast from the dining-room window. When she looks again the fox is gone, if it ever existed. She imagines the dark pupil of its eye, the way it watches the moon to hunt by without any knowledge of what's to come, how it will die or why.

Carol pulls the curtains closed and runs the bath, watching the bubbles she has made there gather through the steam. She undresses, touching the faint silver stretch marks on her belly with surprise. Then she steps into the almost unbearably hot water and lets herself sink, inch by inch, until only her nipples with their dark aureoles break the surface.

* * *

It is five-thirty in the evening. Shadows have lengthened, termite mounds on the open land have taken on a deep ochre hue and the sun is mild, like autumnal light back home. The woman with the baby is sprawled asleep on the pavement in her black wrap and soiled red blouse. The baby is asleep too, not cradled in her arms in the shelter of the spiked fence, not tied to her with a cloth, but lying on the bare tarmac between its mother and the road where cars poison the air. Saliva glues its face to the tarmac. Pedestrians step over them. They neither pause nor look down.

* * *

Surgical biopsy involves removal of all or part of a breast lump for microscopic examination to determine whether cancer is present. When an excisional biopsy is performed, the entire mass is removed, along with a surrounding margin of normal-appearing breast tissue. This procedure is usually done with local anesthesia. Sometimes the surgical biopsy is preceded by a procedure to mark the area in the breast that needs to be excised. Using breast X-rays or ultrasound, a radiologist places a sterile, thin wire into the lump so that the surgeon can excise the correct tissue. When an incisional biopsy is done, the same procedure is used, but only part of the lump is removed. After the biopsy specimen is obtained, a pathologist will analyse it and prepare a report documenting the findings.

* * *

The last consignment of computers has been loaded and Miles is in the office with Agnes, checking through the final paperwork. The lights blink, fail, re-ignite as the generator cuts in from the basement. A puff of smoke drifts past the window. There is load-shedding on the national grid so they have electricity one day – if they're lucky – and none the next. He notices a dark scar on Agnes' arm and wants to ask her how she got it, but a personal question is unthinkable. He asks her to re-confirm his flight for tomorrow. He sends Carol a quick email to say he'll be home soon. He's using web mail and sometimes he forgets to save a copy of his own messages. He wonders how many have gone astray. What happens to lost emails? He imagines them shrivelling like salted slugs.

He thinks about his garden, the rows of bean canes, the line of beetroot he needs to pull, the half dozen pumpkins, the mess in the shed he promised to sort out. When he goes out for lunch the boda-boda drivers wave as usual and he dismisses them as usual. He thinks about Carol back there in the cold. Here, the sun is almost overhead. Its heat is brutal on his thinning scalp. He's left his bush hat in the hotel and walks in shadow as much as possible. When he nears the café, a small boy approaches him with his hand held out. Miles has no change. He stoops down to the boy.

'Wait for me and I will bring change.'

The boy looks at him blankly. Maybe he doesn't know what change is. Maybe he doesn't understand Miles' northern English accent. Maybe he doesn't speak English. Miles tries again.

'Wait here. I will bring money.'

The boy holds his hand out pleadingly. As he steps into the gloom, Miles hears him say in perfect English.

'But I am hungry *now*.'

He is greeted by the waitress like an old friend. *Hello, how are you?* The girls leaning against the tall glass dispensers of coffee beans smile welcomingly. He orders coffee and a sandwich, thumbing through the *New Vision*. When he emerges to find the boy, he has gone. *But I am hungry now.* The logic of this is cruel. It is a whip. A sjambok of impeccable consequence. *Hungry now.* Of course. Why should he wait when the muzungu is so rich? But was it safe to give the boy a thousand-shilling note? Wouldn't he have been set on by older boys, by the desperate men that lurked on the waste-land, drunk on waragi? And where was God in all this? Where was his light?

Only the sun cauterising his scalp tells Miles how long he's been standing in the road with sun cream stinging his eyes. A marabou stork lands a few yards away. Between its shoulder blades is a knob of red flesh, like an exposed organ. Its wedged beak is huge and efficient. He watches it step away with the gait of a bird born to marshes and reed beds, delicately lifting its feet from the water and replacing them on the burning pavement.

★ ★ ★

Carol has told Miles nothing. She has an appointment at the hospital. Oncology. Such a cold sound in that word, like water congealing to ice. Maddy had given her a funny look when she asked for the morning off, but she'd said nothing. Carol's fingers stray to her breast as she watches the bowed heads of the children in her class. A first-form group. They're watching her warily, wondering what has happened to their teacher. Yesterday she let herself go and yelled at them when they were noisy. It was as shocking as if she'd smashed a window.

That night she sits looking into the garden. The moon is hidden beyond slow clouds. They drift clear to show its decayed remnant above the rooftops. The orange bellies of pumpkins lie distended in their beds.

Carol wonders what Miles will be like when he gets home this time. He's distant after a trip, incommunicative for days after the first kiss and the little presents. The coffee beans and packets of tea, the copper or bone bracelets and earrings he brings her. She remembers Zanzibar, still there as she imagines it, washed in sultry, clove-scented heat. At least Miles has his work, in which he believes. She wonders what he sees out there, but she is gifted with imagination. She doesn't need to know. Once she'd looked into his sketchbooks and seen the things he'd sometimes tried to tell her about after a glass of wine, but couldn't. Sometimes she finds him staring through the French windows at dusk gathering in the garden. Once she found him sobbing at his desk. For no reason, he said. And not to worry, these things just come over you when you're tired.

One day, she thinks, he won't make it home to ordinary things: to autumn, to jobs in the garden, their village decorated with Christmas lights. Or home to the kitchen table where they sit and share breakfast and talk and drink coffee. Sometimes she reaches out to touch him in bed and he turns away. Then they are like those marble statues that lie side by side on medieval tombs, pretending to sleep through death.

★ ★ ★

At Entebbe, the toilet floor is swimming in piss. The attendant is pushing a yellow wave from side to side with his mop, but the drains are blocked. Miles tiptoes through the flood and stands before the urinal, his bag slung over his shoulder. He has learned not to be squeamish. Such things are all in a day's work. A cloudy tide gurgles, rising and falling in the porcelain. It rises again, higher this time, threatening to spill over. Miles imagines an aquifer of rancid piss welling from below the airport to engulf him. He zips up and retreats.

Miles sleeps on the flight from Entebbe to Schiphol. He wakes with a stiff neck, then dozes again. Each hour is unbearably slow. He thinks of the desert slipping away beneath the belly of the plane, of Libya, Sicily, Italy, the Alps, then France. The aircrew pad about the cabin, smiling ghosts of the air-conditioned atmosphere. They offer water in foil tubs, headphones, an extra blanket, formula milk to the woman with the crying baby.

It's a direct flight, shaving a couple of hours off the journey. Once he spent seven hours at Nairobi waiting for a connection. Now even the hour-and-a-half at Schiphol is unbearable when home is so close. It's seven o'clock Dutch time, six am at home. He'll get in to Manchester at seven-thirty, local time, and Carol will be waiting for him, since it's a Saturday. She'll ask him if it was a good trip and he'll say yes, fine. It was fine. A good trip. He'll remember how much he loves her and ask if she's ok and enquire about the girls. They'll argue about who should drive, because he's had a long flight and she's tired after a week of teaching and preparing lessons and being alone. He'll drive, as he always does, because he feels wide awake by the time the plane touches down.

On the last leg of the flight he dozes most of the way, refusing the stodgy cheese roll and coffee served for breakfast. At last the Fokker jet is banking through clouds, its wing light dipping towards the moors, dark green fields, the motorway's necklace of amber beads. Miles feels the undercarriage bump as it falls open. Then the city appears, lit below them, still distant. Soon, a reservoir and stone villages as the plane arcs out again. Then suburbs, brick houses, a factory, a church and school. The plane circles, the land rises to meet them. The wheels touch with a thud, lift, thud again. They decelerate and the force of it shunts Miles forward in his seat. There is a collective sigh in the cabin, the click of seat belts as they taxi.

★ ★ ★

Carol watches her face in the mirror. Her eyes look tired and are ringed below with mauve like a pigeon's plumage. She's touched up her hair and put on a smart skirt. She remembers how much she's missed Miles and how familiar love is. She's made the bed up with clean sheets and planned a nice meal and a good bottle of wine because they need to talk now. She's even brought in logs from the store to fill the basket beside the fire, though she never usually bothers when he's away.

She rang the girls last night and has all the latest news: Emily's new job, Sarah's MA. She finds the car keys hanging just where they should be on the kitchen hooks and closes the front door behind her. The steering wheel is cold in her hands, but the car starts first time and she reverses into the road, which she knows she shouldn't do. She sees the village street dipping down ahead, its rows of grey stone houses still asleep apart from one grey feather of smoke. A boy is pushing newspapers into letterboxes. Leaves fall into the road from the copper beech in the doctor's garden. Dawn light rises behind the hill, showing the stack of yellow pipes, the scar that diggers have gouged into the earth. Stone walls spider across the fells, weighing down the fields. She sees the sky that holds Miles safe, incandescent above the morning sun. She changes gear, feeling cogs grind then mesh, turgid with cold. The house shrinks in her mirrors, its windows on fire under the faint ruin of the moon.

The Lesson

The old man sits on the steps of the white-painted church smoking his first cigarette of the day. His wife has been sick. She can't stand the smell of tobacco smoke in the house any more. Slow light flickers over the surface of the harbour. The blue-and-yellow-painted fishing boats are motionless, hardly moving because the sea is hardly moving. There is still a faint image of last night's moon settling beyond hills of ochre rock with their stubble of pines. The sky is pale, the air thickening under the rising sun. The old man smokes, occasionally tugging at the peak of his faded denim cap. The sun heats the town, soaking into the terracotta roofs, raising a stink of rotting fish.

A boy comes along the narrow street carrying a long loaf of bread under his arm. He wears a blue-and-white-striped tee shirt, khaki shorts and sandals. The old man watches the boy's smooth brown legs go by, noticing the dimple of paler skin behind his knees. It could have been himself sixty-odd years ago.

A large dog comes out from the butcher's yard, pulling its chain, and the boy stops to stroke its mangy coat. The dog is old and useless. Joaquim should have put it down years ago. But he's soft, for a butcher. The boy skips on and the old man lets his eyes rest on the sea again, narrowing them against its glare. His father and brothers had all been fishermen, but he'd never trusted the sea. And he'd made sure he never had to, working in the quarry, blasting back the hillside to make new roads. He'd kept his feet on the land, never even learned to swim. He dips his head then spits in the direction of the dog that still tugs at its chain.

The last apartments to be built in the town are perched on the hillside behind the church, set on platforms cut out from the rock. The new road leads the way and the apartments follow. Now families from Barcelona come out for weekends in Japanese four-by-fours that are too big for the old streets. They live life to a different rhythm, staying up all night to party in the new night clubs and discos along the bay, then lying in bed all morning, squandering the first cool of the day. They're rich and they know nothing of struggle – not as he has known it.

The old man takes a last drag of the cigarette and pinches it out between his thumb and finger. A lifetime working with stone has calloused them so that he doesn't even feel the heat. He stands up slowly, stiff from sitting so long on cold stone. He pushes back the denim cap to scratch his temple. When he lifts the lid of the waste bin to throw in the spent cigarette there's a stink of mackerel heads and sardines. Everything decays quickly here; everything is consumed by the sun.

The next day, the old man takes up the same position, easing himself onto the church steps. He thinks of the statue of Christ they've erected inside, that sly smile playing across his bronze face. In his day, they'd smashed the faces of plaster saints with their rifle butts. But no one talks about that time now, even though there'd been fighting all the way from here to Figuères. No one would talk about it, and maybe that was for the best. Even the street signs are in Catalan since Franco died. When the Republic had been crushed and the foreign volunteers gone home, he and his comrades had got out, running over the border into France. Only when things had eased had they drifted back, one by one to their villages. Or they never returned. Those that did, like him, found work and kept their heads down. They kept silence like a vow. His brothers had stayed with the sea, always, but he'd been different, felt and seen something else in the life he wanted. He'd always hankered for land – a piece of his own land. But that had never been.

The roofs of the town are made of ridged clay tiles and from his vantage point at the church they fall away in rows to the quayside. The old man lights up his one cigarette of the day, watching swifts flicker out from under the eaves on scimitar wings. They're feeding on invisible insect swarms and he hears their young chittering with hunger. He found one dead in the street once, its feathers iridescent, its legs stumpy and wasted. That was the only time the swifts touched down. When they fell, too exhausted to fly on, and died where they lay. He'd heard that they even made love in the air. Their whole lives were spent on the wing between Spain and Africa.

He thought of Lisa, that first time, before the fighting. The little stone barn in the valley that led down to vineyards above the next bay. Her eyes wide, the black dress almost hiding her in the gloom. And the heat, the sudden blush of sweat as he touched her. Touched her breasts and buried his face in her hair. The way she'd pushed him away then pulled him into her fiercely, biting his shoulder and tearing at his shirt. Now their daughters were married and had moved away to the city. Lisa has grown old, troubled by angina, hobbling down to the shops on her arthritic hip. But she won't let him help her prepare meals or clean the house, even though he wants to. It isn't his place. It hurts him to think that the girl he loved has grown old. He'd wanted to die first, for her to live forever. Forever young. Maybe she would. Maybe that's what the priests – those liars – meant by heaven.

The boy comes along the street, wearing the same clothes, carrying a bottle of Vichy water and a loaf of bread. The dog paddles out on its short length of chain and the boy holds out his hand to be licked. He pats the dog's head and the dog nuzzles him. Strange. Nobody had made much of that dog for years, and now here's this boy stroking it. Making a fuss. Pablo, Joaquim the butcher's dog: grown fat and decrepit on scraps. Not a bad life for a dog. The old man watches the boy walk away with jerky, impulsive steps, the way a young lamb or calf walks. The boy is distracted for a moment by a swallow, looking up and shading his eyes at its steel-blue flash from under the eaves. The old man catches his eye and smiles. For a moment the boy seems confused, then he too smiles and walks on.

The next day, the same. But the old man calls across to the boy in Catalan as he goes by.

'Good morning dog-boy!'

The boy looks startled, raising a hand to scratch his nose, almost dropping the loaf. He replies in Castilian. A city boy. His parents are probably loaded.

'*Buenos dias!*'

The old man grins and points to the dog that still gazes after the boy in the street. He speaks in the boy's own language.

'You've made a friend for life there boy! Old Pedro's never had so much fuss made of him.'

The boy shrugs, drawing up his shoulders, a fluid gesture of defiance.

'He's just an old dog. It's ok.'

He says it in a matter of fact manner, looks directly into his eyes, and the old man rocks back uneasily under his gaze. It's as if the boy lives in a world where all things are equal. An old dog, an old man, what's the difference? The boy walks on, holding his shoulders just a little higher.

The next day the old man waits but the boy doesn't come. He smokes two cigarettes for once, tugs at his cap, watches the dog wander out on its leash and sniff at passers by. But the boy is nowhere to be seen. The sea glitters. The town heats up like iron in a forge. Swifts scream over the rooftops and a hawk appears briefly, hovering over the scrubland above the town. The boy doesn't come and the old man sits in the reek of fish, watching the sea, thinking of Christ's mocking smile in the cool darkness of the church behind him.

He goes back home and sits in the shady kitchen of their house, watching Lisa prepare the lunch. She's making tomato bread and there's a strong scent of basil and raw garlic. Lisa puts the dish down on the table and watches him slyly.

'You're quiet today. Have the seagulls taken out your soul in the night?'

'Not the seagulls.'

She turns away, rubbing garlic over the flat loaf.

'It was you, my sweet.'

The old man speaks hoarsely, his voice thickened by the garlic, by his wife's sudden alertness to him.

'You tore my mind away and threw it to the sea!'

He rises and kisses her behind the ear where her grey hair is pinned into a bun. Lisa grins, her laughter rusty as an old key turning.

'That'll be the day old man. The day I stop your dreams!'

But he's already half absent, examining his fingers spread out on the tabletop. All that banter! It's just words. He throws them out like ashes from a volcano. And they don't amount to much in the end. Just ashes, where there'd once been fire.

They eat lunch slowly, sipping the weak red wine he's brought from the bodega. The sea seethes beyond slatted shutters, closed against the sun. A breeze billows in the net curtains, as if an invisible intruder is at the window. Then he takes a siesta, sleeping beside his wife as sun bakes the town.

The next day the boy is there, as usual, trotting along the street to where the dog hangs out its tongue. The old man greets him with narrowed eyes. Bright shears of sun flicker over the bay.

'*Hola!*'

The boy looks up from patting the dog. A string of saliva hangs from its muzzle, swaying and gleaming in the sun.

'*Hola.*'

The boy is already almost past him.

'Hey, what's the big hurry?'

The old man pinches out the cigarette stub and the boy comes to a halt, watching wide-eyed.

'Doesn't that hurt?'

'Hurt?'

The old man laughs, rubbing at his stubble.

'I've got hands like iron, boy. Feel them!'

He holds out his hands and the boy touches his fingertips.

'What happened to them?'

'What happened to my hands? Why work, boy, work!'

He scuffles his feet in the rope espadrilles and fixes the boy with a hard stare.

'I wasn't much older than you when I started work at the quarry. See those villas up there?'

He gestures behind the church and the boy shades his eyes to where the white apartments glare.

'I helped cut those out of the hillside. My God, in my time I must have lifted a mountain and put it down again!'

The boy clutches the loaf, anxious to leave. But he's an inquisitive boy.

'How did you get it out?'

'How? Dynamite and sweat! Phoof!'

The old man blows out his breath and explodes his palms together.

'Dynamite, then picks and shovels and bare hands.'

The boy nods and walks on, no longer curious.

'*Adios!*'

'*Adios*, dog-boy!'

The old man watches him go. Heat shimmers on the hills and blue shadows bloom under juniper bushes and clumps of prickly pear.

Dynamite. First they drilled a line of holes at the cliff edge and then dropped in the charges, packing them so that the explosion would force the rock outward. Then the fuses were laid and the red flags raised. When the switch was thrown a line of dust jumped at the sky and then a whole slab of the limestone would shear away, hanging for a moment as if it had abandoned God's time to fall into human time. Into its fever of change. Then the report of the explosion would bound over the bay, echoing back from the mountains and the walls of the ruined monastery opposite.

The old man feels in his pocket for a match. They should have dealt with the fascists in the same way. Those bastards. They should have dynamited them off the land. But his brothers had been fishermen, not interested in politics. They understood only the sea, the way it tugged at their nets. The way the sun rose from it, then fell back into it each day. The way it drew its shoals towards their boat each night to feed them or half-feed them. The way it kept them in poverty. The old man strolls down to the harbour, smoking and greeting people as he goes. He's smoking too much these days.

Joaquim's daughter goes by on her moped waving at him with her bare arm, her bathing costume rolled up in a towel between her legs. There are at least three fascists he knows of in the town. Not just people who'd believed, but paid-up fascists who'd carried a gun. They'd kicked over the traces pretty quickly when Franco died. Then Juan Carlos had come back. What a joke! It'd taken a socialist government to give them a king! But he's too old to heat up those grudges now.

He goes into a bar and orders pastis, knocking it back in one jerk of his arm. The peasants had always been unreliable. Treacherous. Never trust a peasant. A communist school-teacher from Montpellier had told him that when they'd gone on the run. He could still speak good French after those years over the border. He'd sent Lisa money from his job there, labouring on the roads. Somehow she'd made ends meet, raised their first daughter and waited for his return. And she's still waiting. Waiting for him to come back to her. An exile can come home, but he can never return. The old man has a child by a woman in France that Lisa knows nothing about. *Françoise*. Another daughter. A baby girl with creamy skin, chubby hands and dimpled knees. He remembers coils of blonde hair. But he hasn't seen her in over fifty years. These things happen. In wartime anything can happen. He wonders if she has kids of her own by now. Grandchildren. Unlike Lisa, she has never aged. And he knows that's a lie, too.

The pastis has cleared the old man's head. He walks out of the village to the headland where the tourists are crowded onto the pebble beach. He walks slowly now, careful of the youngsters on mopeds who race up the street. When they'd played here as kids there had been hardly any visitors. Then the villagers had grown wine, hewn stone, harvested the sea. And no one in the outside world had really cared. Now the new roads he'd helped to build had opened up the whole coastline. There was a new marina, yachts, a sailing club for the smart set from Barcelona. People in the town made money, whereas in the old days they'd just got by, or starved.

Here on a promontory of rock there's a diving board set up so that swimmers can launch themselves into the sea. The beach is full of tourists: mothers with pale, stretch-marked flesh, fathers barking at their kids, beautiful suntanned girls who preen in the water, calling to young men who swim around them, vying for their attention. Further out, there are snorkellers, their masked faces pressed in the water, staring down into the depths of the sea. He notices the boy climbing the iron ladder. Six steps. He stands for a moment, water streaming from his brown skin. Then he dives in, clean as a harpoon.

For a few seconds the sea gulps him. Then his head emerges, metres away, black as basalt in the blue-green water. The old man watches without being seen. The boy's body is fluid, like water itself, responding to whatever catches his interest as he sculls around. Then he dives back under. Soon he's lost amongst the heads of other swimmers. The old man walks home for lunch. By now half the town is frying sardines and the scent of hot fish comes down from open windows. As he passes the dog it pads out to sniff him, but he waves it away.

The next day is Sunday and the old man keeps away from the church. Instead, he takes his cigarette down to the quay-side and chats to Ramón, his last remaining brother. They stand, gazing out to sea, to the ruined monastery on the mountain across the bay. The foothills opposite are covered in collapsing terraces that peter out as the hillsides steepen. All that land had been under vines or olives when they'd been boys. The war had put paid to that. The French had made their wine too cheap. It was hard to get decent local wine now. Hard to get decent anything – chorizo, cheese, game. It was all going to the bad.

'It's this government fleecing the poor, those whores!'

Ramón smiles and sighs.

'No matter, there's enough good wine to see us out!'

'See us out? And they will, those bastards!'

Ramón had always been the same. Passive, easy-going, simple in all these matters. He'd never even asked his brother about his years in exile, but greeted him on his return as if he'd just returned from a night out in the next village. The old man says nothing more. What's the point? He gazes out to where the vines are growing wild on the hillsides, to where the boy is trailing a stick at the water's edge, electrifying a fringe of silver light, as if a shoal of sardines is leaping at his heels.

That night the old man sits in silence, watching some nonsense on the television, hardly answering his wife's questions as she sits fanning herself in the heat.

On Monday morning he's back in his usual position at the church. The boy is late, hurrying along, hardly finding time to pat the dog. He returns the old man's greeting politely, and seems to suppress a smile. Later in the morning he's there in the little bay, flipping from the diving board and breaking the surface of the sea which mirrors a blank, hot sky. The old man watches from the shade of the taverna with an iced lemonade in his hand. When he gets home for lunch he sits down to the anchovies his wife has prepared, eating without a word. She leans over him, trying to get a clue to his mood, but there's no smell of drink on him. Just the faint impression of sweat, sunlight, and tobacco, as always. She touches his neck where the white hairs grow, white and unruly. But he says nothing, staring from the dark centres of his eyes that have turned the colour of plums.

The day passes slowly, as all days do now. That night the old man dreams of the olive grove near Cadaqués where he'd shot a man in the fighting. It had all happened so quickly. He'd hardly meant to do it. The enemy had appeared suddenly, a grey uniform between the trees. He raised the rifle then felt it kick at his shoulder. The man's blood left a damson stain on the soil when they dragged him away by the heels. And he hadn't died at once. He'd woken to call for his mother, begging them to hold his hand, then gurgling and drowning in his own blood. It'd taken a whole day. They sat him in the shade of a rock and he'd died at sunset. A boy just like they were. A dark-skinned kid from the south. Whispering things they couldn't make out. They'd waited until he died, then buried him: covering his face with stones, dust filming his eyes where they stared towards home.

The old man wakes up shuddering and goes to the window, pushing the shutters open a crack. The dawn is coming up behind the town, staining the hillside opposite with apricot light. The bay lies calmed, like a turquoise stone sawn in half. The air is restless, as if there might be a storm. Leaves rustle on the fig tree beside the house. To his own amazement the old man crosses himself. He hasn't done that since he was a child. Maybe the dream had brought that on. The war wasn't something you could talk about. How could you tell your wife such things? Perhaps Lisa had guessed, though she hadn't asked what her husband had done. Not a word when he'd come home and fallen into his long silence. It was the history of their land: blood and silence in each handful of earth.

That day the old man goes to the church early and smokes two cigarettes, pulling at his cap, watching gangs of swifts scream across the rooftops. The boy is also early and has time for the dog, which barks excitedly at his approach. The boy crouches with the new loaf under his arm, pats the dog's head, speaks a few words of affection, then rises to find his path blocked. The old man has made up his mind. He speaks first.

'*Hola!*'

'*Hola.*'

The boy scuffles his feet.

'It's a fine day. Going to be hot!'

'Yes.'

The old man speaks awkwardly, gruffer than he wants to be. There's a silence and the boy scuffs his heel.

'Could I ask you a favour, boy?'

The boy considers carefully.

'A favour?'

The old man sits down on the steps and the boy sits next to him as if invited.

'See that out there?'

The boy shades his eyes and scans the sea, imagining something in particular will catch his eye.

'What?'

'The sea! You know, my father and brothers were all fisherman, my grandfather too and his father. The sea goes back in my family like blood goes back.'

He touched the boy's arm.

'Like blood. You get it? They said we had salt blood!'

'Yes...'

The boy is doubtful, clutching the loaf of bread, picking at the crust.

'But like I told you, boy, I broke with the sea. I worked the land, dug out all this damned rock. To tell you the truth – and, God knows, why should I? – I was afraid of it.'

He pauses. The boy's sandals draw little circles in the dust.

'And worse, I never learned to swim.'

'You can't swim?'

The boy is incredulous. Surely everyone could swim? He'd been able to swim almost at the same time that he could walk.

'Never learned to. Always had an excuse to get out of the damned water.'

He pauses for a second to laugh.

'And never missed it until now. Not until I saw you jump-ing off that diving board.'

Again the hoarse laugh, like a motor trying to start.

'I'm too old for diving, boy, but I have a favour to ask. Just one.'

The boy listens and nods, then hurries off clutching the loaf with a new kind of step. He seems taller, or heavier. There is more gravity in his step, yet he is a small boy in a striped tee shirt taking a loaf home to his parents.

In the Mediterranean summer all things decay. The dead are buried quickly, though without haste. Refuse rots overnight. Here, on the Costa Brava, the town council has it collected each morning. The bins are emptied and even the imported sand on the beach is swept clean to please the tourists. The refuse workers wear white overalls, tipping the green bins into their wagon. Two slim young men in peaked caps and blue uniforms empty the smaller waste bins along the waterfront with a kind of elegant ease, one tipping the bin, the other holding a refuse sack beneath it. The old man smoking on the church steps is a familiar sight. The fact that he holds a plastic carrier bag excites no curiosity. An old dog stares after him with mournful eyes, absent-mindedly wandering to the length of its chain. The sea lurches in dull shades of grey. The mountains smoulder under cloud, the monastery appearing and disappearing in mist. Dark-skinned men in yellow waterproofs and red bandanas unload crates of fish from a trawler in the harbour. This is a new day, no different from yesterday or tomorrow. The sun is rising, strengthening to a glare, burnishing the sky to a blinding pane of light.

In a few weeks it will be autumn. The bars will shutter up and only the hardiest tourists – stray Frenchmen, German hikers, hippies from Barcelona – will brave the gusts that shriek off the sea to jostle the yachts in the new marina, rattling steel cables against their masts. A wind for each season and each wind had a name. Autumn brings the Tramuntana. A harsh, dry wind that hurls over the mountains and onto the bay, shaking the almond trees. Then winter, the season of storms. After that? Well, who knows? It didn't do to look too far ahead these days.

A boy comes along the street with his shoulder bag and stops in front of the old man. They exchange a few words, the boy trailing one foot in the dust. Then they set off together, walking down to the main street that runs parallel with the sea, following its curve to the small cove where a few early swimmers are gathered. The old man's walk is stiff and stately, the boy manages to restrain his eagerness and keep in step with him. The sun is still hazy and the sea is still grey, like the hull of a naval ship. A few yachts make their way out to sea, tilting white sails. The red hills beyond are splashed with dark green pine trees.

The old man and the boy reach the beach and then walk to its furthest point where shingle slopes easily into the water,

where there are rocks to hold onto and the open sea seems
far away. When they have changed into their shorts, the boy
goes first, beckoning to the old man who has not entered the
sea since he was a child. His muscles are slack; the flesh on his
chest and upper arms is loose and covered in white hair. But
there is still some wiriness in his body, there is still strength in
the limbs that have carried a rifle and dug out the earth and
smashed and lifted rock for most of his life. The boy's skin is
smooth and brown, perfected by the sun.

They enter the water slowly, feeling warm air on their
naked shoulders, the sea cool on their legs. The boy watches
the old man, expecting him to be afraid. But the old man is
remembering the darkness of a barn in the next valley, the
scented heat, the way Lisa's body had shuddered under him,
her hair stuck to his face with sweat. Now he enters the sea.
He splashes water onto his face and it is salty like the taste of
anchovies or a soldier's sweat. He feels the water begin to
buoy him up, remembers the shocked eyes of a dying boy
under the olive trees near Cadaqués. The way the soldier
had appeared in his sights then stumbled as if he'd tripped
over a stone. He'd looked down into that drained face and felt
only relief. Relief that it was not his own life pouring away
like dregs. Briefly, he thinks of the little girl he left in France.
Françoise. A woman now. But that secret pain is long dulled.
He looks at the boy.

'Now?'

'Yes, now! Come on!'

The boy is already afloat, kicking like a little frog with his
brown legs. The old man dips his face into the sea and takes
his first stroke, kicking off from the shingle where the boy has
led him. Mist is lifting from the hills. The white buildings of
Llançà across the bay seem to be falling into and rising from
the sea. He can see the hairpin bends of the road with their

steel barriers. At home Lisa is fanning herself with a newspaper in the shuttered kitchen, the old dog is waiting, the fish van is threading its way through the streets, honking as the women gather. After this, he'll take the boy for lemonade, have a small cognac for himself, and they'll talk about how things are and about how things used to be.

The old man feels the boy's hand slip away from his. He takes a second stroke, embracing the sea and everything in it: the fish and the rocks and the sunken salt-encrusted hulks that lie where the light cannot reach. He spits out seawater and is not afraid. No, what he feels in his belly is not fear, not exactly. And if he becomes afraid as the water deepens, then it will pass, as everything passes here under the white stare of the sun.

The Prince

All summer the boy from the big house next door was dying. We saw his bandaged head flitting through the raspberry canes, saw him drifting like a sleepwalker across lawns where his father and mother watched him. Something was growing inside him, shouldering aside his life. He played slowly, prematurely aged, as if learning to be a child when it was already too late. We didn't know that he was dying then, but we sensed that we were near a great event. It was like standing at the edge of the sea that time at Scarborough, waves bigger than we'd ever imagined, their chill pulling at our legs, the shingle dragging out its mantra of elsewhere.

All summer the village whispered. Undertones in the village stores, the post office, amongst the crowd outside church on Sundays. That sudden pitying inflection tingeing voices avid with curiosity. That frisson of greed for news that runs through all villages in the world. Here was tragedy in our own midst. We felt the tremors of it underfoot as we marked out the flagstones for hopscotch or tied skipping ropes to the lamp post outside the Miner's Arms. We sensed it in the air as days turned into dusk, woke to it as light stole across the roofs of the village each dawn.

On warm days the boy would sometimes come to the garden fence to watch me play with my sister. He'd stand awkwardly, one leg tilted against the palings that separated us, his eyes expressionless. Once, when I was pulling rhubarb for my mother, carrying it in the hem of my dress, I looked up to find the boy watching me. He stared with pursed lips from under the swathe of his bandage. Then he turned away to limp down the garden into the shade of their veranda. I never once heard the boy speak.

'Poor soul.'

Was all my mother said, taking the rhubarb, scolding me for the stained frock. My mother was Italian, one of a group of girls who had come over after the war and married local men.

'I don' think he's long for here.'

As she said it her mouth went into a tight white line. She spoke English with an accent half Taranto, half Yorkshire.

'You mean he's going to die?'

She sighed, rubbing fat into a bowl of flour to make pastry for a pie.

'I don' know. He's pretty sick, I know that much.'

'What with?'

She ignored me, staring into the pastry mix. I needed to know, felt apprehension tighten in my stomach.

'What's making him ill?'

'He's got a… *tumore*… a *tumour*. In his head. The doctors can' take it out.' She shrugged. '*È triste.*'

She hardly ever spoke Italian. The words were like the stray hairs that she pushed back behind her ear as she worked.

'What's a tumour?'

'It's a kind of a lump.'

'Does it hurt him?'

'Eh, I don' know. I expect it does. Poor little lad. Now, no more questions!'

She greased the dish with the lard wrapper. Would it hurt,

that thing inside him? The lump pressing on his brain? What would it feel like to become the ghost of yourself, to be swallowed up by darkness and die? To be remembered in church on Sunday, like Mrs Delaney? She'd called every few weeks to collect the Christian Aid envelopes for Africa, labouring up the street on her horn-handled stick. Now she was just a name. The gold lettering was still bright on her headstone.

My mother rapped the bowl down, dusting flour from her hands onto her apron. I watched her roll the pastry, press it into place, ladle in the fruit, sprinkle sugar then slice pastry from the lip of the dish until everything was neatened for the oven.

That spring was the best for hawthorn blossom we'd ever had. It bloomed late in Yorkshire, appearing after the blackthorn then flowering well into June. When it came, it gushed against dandelions and cow parsley, already rife under the hedgerows. Lapwing returned to the meadows, curlews to the moor and oystercatchers to their ritual of picking over stones in the beck. A family of house martins came back from their African winter. They renovated their old nests in the corners of the upstairs windows of our cottage. Later in the summer we'd hear the young birds screaming with hunger, their parents flying in and out, frantic to feed them.

Then spring weather waned into the first overcast weeks of June. It rained so much that we hardly played out at all after school. Rain beat the blossom from the trees and we trod it underfoot. The lanes filled with the damp musk of elder-flower. On the fine days, tractors criss-crossed the village, leaving trails of slurry or silage from farm gates to fields that lay drenched in green.

The boy next door didn't go to school, though we learned

not to envy him for that. Sometimes we saw the pale oval of his face pressed against the windows of the big house. Whether he was wistful or not we couldn't tell; his face showed no emotion. With his white bandage he reminded me of the picture of an Indian prince in the encyclopaedia at school. It was an unlikely setting for a prince, though. He should have been reclining in a jewelled sedan chair or swaying along on the back of an elephant under a fierce sun. Instead, rain trickled against the windows and ran down the roads, reflecting the grey light of a northern summer. And I knew that his turban was only there to hide the wound in his head. It gave him a mystical quality, a connection with another realm. As if he lived half in this world and half in the world of shadows that lay beyond; half in this life and half in the life everlasting.

The boy's house had a classical frontage and pillars like a Greek temple. It had once belonged to the local doctor who'd also owned the first motor car in our village. My grandfather had worked as his driver and we had a picture of him with his flat cap, moustache and leather puttees, standing with a hand on the bonnet of an Austin Seven. He'd learned to drive in the Royal Engineers during the Great War, fought the Turks in Mesopotamia, and died on a motorcycle when my father was still a boy. The rest was all forgotten, sunk into the past. Our house was a rented cottage, built next to the big house where the boy lived. Square set, with four windows and a door it was just like a child's drawing of a house. It had an outside toilet and no bathroom and the lime-washed walls were yellow with damp. When plaster fell from the walls we could see the horsehair beneath. The road went on past our front door. It ran over the fells to the next village and the next. It held the pull of distance, of everything beyond our valley, of the faraway country where my mother was born. Once, when a letter arrived from Italy, she cried in the kitchen and we squabbled over the stamps.

The wet weather set in for weeks. The road gleamed with water, slate roofs shone with reflections of the sky and the kitchen garden became completely overgrown. My father would stand at the kitchen window, shaking his head and pulling at his ear. After which he'd pick up the newspaper and lose himself in the sports pages. He'd once been a keen cricketer. On Saturday afternoons he'd wander down to the local ground to watch our village team play, shaking his head at the softness of youth. Now he was a quarryman, drilling holes for charges and blasting out the limestone cliff that ate into the hillside at Horton. The hollow curve of rock resembled the inside of a skull picked clean. The stone was broken by hand and hauled onto conveyer belts for machines to crush.

It was a record year for slugs and snails. They fed unhurriedly on our vegetable patch, turning cabbages and lettuces into a fine lace of greenery and then into slime. My father caught hundreds of them in jam jars filled with beer that he cadged from the pub. He sank them level with the ground, then slugs and snails, avid for the stale beer, were drawn in. They drowned there and stank until he emptied them onto the compost heap. We hated the slugs, but pitied the snails with their beautifully turned shells. Their intelligent heads searched ahead of their armoured bodies, pilgrims of the vegetable world, carrying their houses wherever desire took them. Or until a thrush's beak thrashed them against the stones of the path. Or until they slid, unsuspecting, into the beer traps.

Wet days dried up, but the inclement weather dragged on into the strangest summer. Days were overcast, pregnant and menacing, threatening us with storms that hovered but never came. There was a heaviness in the afternoon air. Lapwings questioned the dusk with broken cries. Electricity seemed coiled in the atmosphere, which thickened as we drew on it with an almost tangible effort to breathe. Each evening my father came home late from the quarry, exhausted, his work clothes dark with sweat. We would already have eaten with our mother, so he'd collapse into a chair, bolting his tea from a plate balanced on his knees before falling asleep to the voices on the radio or the television news. His white hair drifted over his forehead, his overalls hung at the back door of the flagged kitchen, reeking of the dust that would choke his lungs and kill him in the end.

Now each day passed in charged suspense. Tension sparked between children, arced between husbands and wives. There were quarrels in the street, raised voices behind drawn curtains at night. The whole village sweltered in expectation. Still the boy's face came and went at the window of the big house, seeming to float under its swaddling bandage. Then one night a storm broke and my sister Maddy and I huddled together at the foot of our bed watching lightning ripen and flicker beyond the line of hills. We pretended to be terrified, hysterical in the sudden frisson of electricity. But it was pure release.

The sky flashed over with brilliant blue light and rain slammed the window sashes. We dozed off to sleep as the storm subsided and were woken by a huge thunder-crack that brought our mother to the bedroom door to soothe us. A tree was hit three fields from the house and in the morning we rose to its white-splintered wound. A blackbird was singing into a new day. Sun had already begun to warm the freshened air. Summer began all over again: days of warmth and light in which the gardens were gradually brought back under control. Grass was mown, weeds pulled, and what had survived of the vegetables lined up in neat rows. A robin came to our garden and fed on a glut of caterpillars, flicking its beak like a rapier, much to my father's approval. There was a sense of return. A sense that whatever had brought us close to the edge of ourselves had retreated.

That year we couldn't afford a holiday at Bridlington or Scarborough and so spent hours in the garden skipping with a length of washing line or gathering elder blossom to make our witches' brews. We went on expeditions as far as the ford and the clapper bridge beyond the village, taking picnics of jam sandwiches and pretend lemonade, which was really water with a spoonful of sugar dissolved in it. Sometimes we heard the hooter from the quarry, then the dull crumpling of rock under the explosion.

My grandmother – my father's mother who lived in Skipton – came to stay in July and for two weeks there was a smell of boiled sweets and the whisky she sipped from a flat brown bottle. My grandmother insisted on lighting the fire and sat in front of it knitting up balls of fusty wool that she'd rescued from other garments, shaking her head at the ways of her foreign daughter-in-law. She flattened her name – *Maria* – taking all the music out of it with her heavy vowels. She wanted waiting on night and day, calling from the parlour for someone to help her hank the wool or bring her a cup of tea. She'd gone bitter with age, my father said: adding mysteriously that it was one of two ways. Nan slept in our bed and Maddy and I shared an old iron put-up bed downstairs where we could hear my father coughing and grumbling at my mother in the room above.

Then Nan went home, pressing her cold face to ours as the train drew into Settle station. We were alone again. But the boy from the big house was gone, too. When I asked my mother where he was, she said that he'd been taken back into hospital to see if anything more could be done. I was almost twelve and my body had begun to surprise me. I'd grown two inches in a year. After the summer I'd be going up to the high school, but where would the boy be? The thought of those long shadows pulling at him made me shudder. And that other thing, growing inside him, taking him over, bullying him out of this life into whatever lay beyond.

When the boy was brought home in an ambulance the neighbours gathered in doorways, peered from behind net curtains, pretending not to watch. There was a shaking of heads that seemed half pitying, half vengeful. The boy's father was a solicitor in Bradford, travelling each day to work in his black Rover. The boy's mother had once been a singer, or so we were told, though I'd never heard her sing. She had a long, graceful throat just like a bird. Like the spotted flycatcher that came to our garden, flitting in intricate figures of eight from the electricity cables, elegant and alert to every insect that moved. It was the same alertness I'd seen in our cat when it heard the young martins crying from their nests and sat expectantly, trying to figure out a route that would take it from drainpipe to rooftop to window ledge. But the boy was home and the village held its breath.

One day, about a fortnight after the boy arrived back, my mother announced that we were to go to his birthday party. His mother had sent an embossed card to invite us, along with half a dozen other children from the village. We were buttoned into our best frocks; our hair braided into pigtails and tied up with little scraps of satin ribbon. I wore the blue leather shoes that we'd bought in Skipton the previous summer and that were getting too small for me now. My job was to carry the boy's present, wrapped in special paper with a pattern of blue-winged swallows.

'What is it, Mum? What're we giving him?'

'It's a book.'

She paused to remember the title.

'It's called *Wind in the Willows*. Very nice, with pictures.'

My mother pressed my hair into place.

'No use giving the poor lad toy, so I though a book would be best. Now, *velocemente!*'

A book would be best. I liked the phrase. I was thinking about it when Maddy snatched it from my hands and held it up.

'A book!'

Maddy was scornful but I told her to shut up, knowing that we couldn't really have afforded anything more. Not the way money was in the house right now. It was a mean gesture to her, but not to me. I loved reading and revelled in the library van, the torch-lit smell of books smuggled under sheets at night. I wondered if the boy read like that too, his bandaged head tottering above the page as he lay propped up against his pillows, following Ratty and Mole into the Wild Wood.

Our mother took us round to the big house, through the iron gate to the front door with its brass knocker in the shape of a wolf's head. Our knock was answered by a maid in a neat black skirt and a pinafore with lace at the hem. She said, 'Well, come in Maria, they're about ready.' I thought it was odd that the woman knew my mother's name. I didn't want to go into the house, but a jab in the small of the back sent me over the threshold. Maddy followed, holding tightly to mother's hand. The entrance-hall of the house wasn't covered in linoleum like ours, but had a thick beige carpet, soft and tricky under-foot. The maid led us to a large room with striped wallpaper and Indian rugs and complicated plaster mouldings at the corners of the ceiling. She took the wrapped-up book and placed it on a little pile that the boy would struggle to open later and regard with no interest.

The boy's mother wore a blue silk dress with a Chinese collar. Her brown hair was coiled and glossy, held in place with a silver feather pin. She met us in front of a table piled with dainties. Sausage rolls and pastries, tarts and buns, and a large cake set on a silver platter in the middle. On the cake were twelve candles and the words *Happy Birthday Terence* written in blue icing sugar. It was the first time I'd heard or seen the boy's name. It was an odd feeling, a sinking feeling. His name had somehow brought him far too close.

There were a few of the more respectable kids from the village in the room, some of them already stuffing their faces and dropping crumbs onto the floor. The Holliday twins, the Edmondson girls and the Strongs from Israel Farm were there. Terence sat in a padded armchair near the window, a plaid rug over his knees, the bandage swathing his head. He looked towards us as we entered, then his dark eyes turned away. He seemed to recognise us, nodding slightly, as if satisfied that we'd come. But he didn't speak and for most of that excruciating afternoon he just sat and gazed ahead. His mother fed him a piece of cake from a china plate and his head came forward for the morsels like a tortoise. He was begging us to ignore him, and so we did.

When, after games of hide and seek and pin the tail on the donkey, we were rounded up to sing 'Happy Birthday' I was the only one who knew his name. His eyes moved in my direction as I sang it out, loud and clear. They seemed to flicker with sudden hatred: a look I'll never forgot. For the rest of the time the boy stared into a corner of the ceiling, his face pale, that arrogant or sensitive mouth tilted against the light. His mother talked to us children in a brittle, animated voice, glancing towards her son from every point in the room, letting odd tinkles of laughter spill out from her long throat. Then my own mother was at the door to collect us and it was raining again as we stepped onto the path that led to our house.

The weather cleared again and a flawlessly hot summer began. The boy must have been made stronger by his visit to the hospital, because he appeared in the garden again, wandering at the edges of the flower beds, watching the gardener at work as he cut grass and tipped cuttings in the field beyond. Once I saw him with a brass spray gun, squirting soapy water onto the roses to keep down the green-fly. In that moment of normality I realised that he couldn't always have been ill, that he must once have had another life, a child's existence.

I turned that thought over and over in my head. Then I tackled my mother again as she was clearing the table after tea.

'Where was he before he was ill?'

'Who?'

'Terence?'

'The lad next door?'

I followed her from the room. She was washing up at the stone sink, sliding plates into the hot water so that they wouldn't crack.

'Yes, where?'

'Oh, away. He was at school.'

I couldn't remember ever seeing the boy in our village school where we were taught in two big classes.

'Why away?'

'His parents are quite... well off... rich, you know? They had him at a private school. He was a boarder.'

'Did he stay there all the time?'

'Yes – apart from his holidays. It was at Richmond, I think.' She said *Richer Mond*, making it drip on her tongue.

'You mean he slept there?'

'Well, it be too far to come home at night!'

'Why?'

'Why what?'

She was getting impatient at my questions, throwing me the tea towel, indicating that I should help her.

'Why send him away when he's ill?'

'He wasn't ill then, he *got* ill. That thing inside him, it just start to grow. It's just their way, sending their kids away to school. Getting up over on people like us who jus' have to make to do.'

She slotted a plate into the rack on the dresser.

'They sorry now.'

They would be. Sorry for getting one over on us. Sorry for all the days and nights that their son had been away from them. And now he might slip away for ever. They'd left him alone. Left him where the shadows at the edge of the world could reach out and take him.

By mid-August the Yorkshire countryside was parched, burnt golden brown where the hay and silage had been taken off. It looked like the Australian outback. The newsmen on the radio and television kept talking about the water shortage and we were asked to be careful when we cleaned our teeth and flushed the toilet. *Waste not want not*. It was as if the climate was conspiring with my father's often-repeated advice to *Just make do*. What it really meant was that we'd do without, make the best of what we'd got. He'd grown up in hard times and was used to drawing his belt in. It reassured him to know we were up against it, fighting the drought. Hardly a drop of water was wasted in our house.

Parched leaves began to turn autumnal red and brown. The water in the beck fell steadily and when we leaned from the crooked bridge there were no trout or sticklebacks. The water trickled in stagnant scum. Terence was confined to a wheelchair now, and every day his mother pushed him through the village, his head lolling under the huge bandage, his eyes exhausted and vacant. The boy's father had stopped going to work and his black Rover stood in the gravel driveway of their house. On fine evenings they brought the wheelchair into the garden and sat with their son, talking to him in voices so low that we never heard the words. I guessed that they were saying all that they had never said when he was away from them. Making up for lost love. Making do in their own way.

August was the hottest for years and the drought went on, searing the land. Even the vicar prayed for rain, but God turned a deaf ear and sent the sun to bake us in biblical heat. At night, a hollow yellow moon hung low over the village, rising in the east and then drifting to the west. The young martins flew the nest, leaving our cottage walls and windows spattered with their droppings. The spring lambs were sturdy now with short, tight fleeces and thickened legs. Foals had grown into young colts, calves into skew-eyed bullocks that dipped their heads and pawed the ground and snorted at our approach. The plague of slugs and snails had dried up. Every evening the blackbird returned to the garden to sing a descending minor scale; the same cadence over and over, like a lament. At dusk moths blundered against the cottage windows, drawn by the blue light of our television set where it shone out from the village, connecting us to a world beyond this world.

My own birthday was on August the eighth and for a treat my mother made a lemon sponge cake, which she covered with whipped cream. My father came home from work early and changed out of his overalls. His face wore a secret smile of triumph. After the singing and cake-cutting I was led into the hallway where a brand new girl's bicycle lay propped against the panelling. My first bicycle. A Raleigh. Royal blue, with three derailleur gears operated by a lever on the handlebars. It was the most perfect surprise after months of feeling that the family were almost too hard up to eat. I remembered my father stumbling home after working overtime, my mother putting her own food onto our plates, scraping back her hair as she sat down to the table.

My parents' happiness was the saddest thing. I stood in front of them and to my sister's amazement, I began to cry. Maddy hadn't been let into the secret. She was only seven, not old enough to know what that bicycle had cost. I loved the cold feeling of the brake levers against my hands, the smell of gear oil and brake blocks and the sprung leather saddle. My father showed me how to pump up the tyres and then press them with my thumb to check the pressure. But for me that bicycle would always be tainted with his sweat, with my mother's burden of care.

That night I woke to a bright light shining through the gap in our bedroom curtains, throwing shadows on the lime-washed walls. The casement window was half open and a faint draft came into the room. Maddy lay fast asleep, her face turned aside on the pillow. I got out of bed to sit at the window. I pushed the curtains aside to look at the night, to read its faint glitter of stars that the moon had pressed back. My bicycle stood downstairs in the hallway, the tyres hardly scuffed by its one ride through the village when I'd shown it off like a scar. The bloated moon was the colour of old urine. It hung low over the gardens. It looked down onto my father's bean canes, his rows of cabbages, the bent-over stems of onions that were